Empowering Labor

Empowering Labor uses a comparative study of Chile, Portugal, and Uruguay to analyze the underlying political dynamics that shape the use of wage policy as a pre-distributive instrument of leftist parties in power in unequal democracies. The book theorizes that the unity of the Left and labor's political legitimacy are two main drivers for the usage of wage policy as a pre-distributive instrument for promoting inclusion. These factors are shaped by elite long-term strategies toward labor. Such strategies, when dominant for long enough periods, create path dependency, shaping differential opportunities for further options down the road. The book integrates large-scale historical processes with frequently analyzed short-term and agency-based factors to elucidate variation in the crafting of wage policies and reshapes the debate on the politics of pre-distribution in unequal democracies by situating the cases in a longer historical arc.

Juan A. Bogliaccini is Professor of Political Science and Dean of the Graduate School at the Catholic University of Uruguay. He has published in academic journals and edited volumes on comparative politics and political economy. He is author of *Twittarquía: la política de las redes en Uruguay* (2019).

T0384953

Empowering Labor

*Leftist Approaches to Wage Policy
in Unequal Democracies*

JUAN A. BOGLIACCINI
Catholic University of Uruguay

CAMBRIDGE
UNIVERSITY PRESS

CAMBRIDGE
UNIVERSITY PRESS

Shaftesbury Road, Cambridge CB2 8EA, United Kingdom

One Liberty Plaza, 20th Floor, New York, NY 10006, USA

477 Williamstown Road, Port Melbourne, VIC 3207, Australia

314–321, 3rd Floor, Plot 3, Splendor Forum, Jasola District Centre,
New Delhi – 110025, India

103 Penang Road, #05–06/07, Visioncrest Commercial, Singapore 238467

Cambridge University Press is part of Cambridge University Press & Assessment,
a department of the University of Cambridge.

We share the University's mission to contribute to society through the pursuit of
education, learning and research at the highest international levels of excellence.

www.cambridge.org
Information on this title: www.cambridge.org/9781009433525

DOI: 10.1017/9781009433549

First published 2024

A catalogue record for this publication is available from the British Library

*A Cataloging-in-Publication data record for this book is available from the Library
of Congress*

ISBN 978-1-009-43352-5 Hardback
ISBN 978-1-009-43350-1 Paperback

To my beloved Clara, Felipe & Lucía

Hoy el aire te lleva en el aire,
hoy el viento te hace volar.
Hoy en el suelo sentirás las caricias
de todos aquellos que lejos están.
(Gladys Hebe De Lodrón
[Mayadis], 1923–2022)

Contents

Figures

Tables

Acknowledgments

This book is the result of more than a decade of research into the eternal struggle over distribution that every society confronts. The work focuses on the conditions under which leftist governments decide to use wage policy as a pre-distributive instrument. Two premises form the base of the analysis. First, the distributive process is primarily a slow-moving political and historical process that unfolds through repeated interactions. Second, our comparative analysis efforts are enhanced whenever we engage in cross-regional comparisons, which enable us to transcend regional specificities.

Many bright and generous people helped improve this book. The list is long, but my indebtedness is deep. First and foremost, I thank Evelyne Huber, my doctoral advisor, and Juan Pablo Luna for their continued insistence that I should finish the book and for reading the entire book several times. Alongside them, Andrew Schrank was very generous in reading the entire book and participating in a book workshop during December 2020 together with Evelyne and Juan Pablo. While the original plan was for an in-person workshop, the COVID-19 pandemic forced us to an online format. This circumstance deepens my indebtedness to the three colleagues for their commitment to the task in the face of the hardships imposed by the pandemic.

This book is the product of a decade-long research project. Funds for field research in Chile, Portugal, and Uruguay, and for writing the book, were provided by the Clemente Estable Fund (FCE_2017_1_135444) granted by the Uruguayan National Agency for Research and Innovation (ANII) for the period 2018–2020. I am thankful to ANII for their support. Much of the primary source material upon which this book is based, particularly interviews and archival documents for the period 2008–2011 in Chile and Uruguay, is derived from material previously collected for my doctoral dissertation. The fieldwork for this earlier period was funded by the Graduate School at the University of North Carolina at Chapel Hill (UNC-CH). I am also thankful to UNC-CH for their support.

Several colleagues and friends have helped me advance the project over the years, reading parts of the book or my previous work on this topic. Santiago Anria, Rui Branco, Matthew Carnes, Andreas Feldman, Fernando Filgueira, Robert Fishman, Candelaria Garay, Cecilia Giambruno, Jonathan Hartlyn, Aldo Madariaga, Andrés Malamud, Felipe Monestier, Sara Niedzwiecki, Martin Opertti, Ken Roberts, John Stephens, and Sara Watson each read one or more chapters along the way. I also benefited from ideas and advice generously offered by Rodrigo Barrenechea, Christopher Chambers Ju, David Collier, Antonio Costa Pinto, Kent Eaton, Sebastián Etchemendy, Gustavo Flores-Macías, Diego Gianelli, Santiago López-Cariboni, Pablo Pérez Ahumada, Rafael Piñeiro, Rosario Queirolo, Cecilia Rossel, Andrés Schipani, Jimena Valdez, and Ignacio Zubillaga. I am also thankful to the participants in several seminars, conferences, and workshops who provided comments on various chapter drafts.

I am indebted to Mr. Manuel José Guzmán, the Chilean Senate's Archive Director, and Mrs. Ana Margarida Rodrigues and her team at the Information and Culture Direction at the Congress Historical Archive (Direção de Informação e Cultura from the Arquivo Histórico Parlamentar) in Lisbon for their helpful assistance with my search of parliamentary documents. In Uruguay, a wonderful online parliamentary archive made it possible to retrieve remotely almost every document I needed. Andrés Malamud, Darius Ornston, Jimena Valdez, and Sara Watson were extremely generous in sharing their fieldwork knowledge, contacts, and materials for my research in Portugal. The General Confederation of Portuguese Workers (Confederação Geral dos Trabalhadores Portugueses) was also extremely generous and helpful in opening their archives for my research. I am thankful to the Political Science Institute at the Catholic University in Chile, the Center for Social and Economic Policies at the Major University in Chile, the former Institute for the Study of Poverty and Social Inclusion at the Catholic University of Uruguay, and the Institute of Social Sciences at the University of Lisbon for hosting me during the different stages of my fieldwork. Finally, I have had in Cecilia Giambruno and Martin Opertti two excellent and dedicated research assistants. Their contributions to the final product exceed the expectations for any research assistant. Santiago Carrere, as a research assistant, masterfully helped with the preparation of the final text. I thank David Schwartz for editing the book. I also wish to express my thanks to Rachel Blaifeder, Political Science and Sociology Editor at Cambridge University Press, New York, who has been generous and extremely helpful along the way.

My family and friends have generously tolerated my occasional moods and frustrations. Writing a book can be a very gratifying process as well as a frustrating one. However, I have not shared my gratification as readily as I have shared my frustration. I am thankful for their patience and understanding. Clara and Felipe were born during this project and have been too patient with their father during this decade-long endeavor. I love them both.

Lucia, my partner in this and many other journeys, has been supportive and patient since my graduate years at UNC-CH and particularly so during the different fieldwork and writing stages for this project. Moving back to Latin America to pursue an academic career has proved more challenging than expected. Her support, however, included continually exhorting me to balance my obstinate preference for work with the other good things in life. Although I have not always appreciated this exhortation, I am lovingly thankful to her, with whom I am as fortunate as one can wish to be.

Abbreviations

AD	Democratic Alliance (*Alianza Democratica*)
AES	Economic and Social Agreement (*Acordo Económico e Social*)
ARU	Uruguayan Rural Association (*Asociación Rural del Uruguay*)
BE	Left Block (*Bloço de Ezquerda*)
CAP	Agrarian Confederation (*Confederaçao dos Agricultores de Portugal*)
CAT	Autonomous Workers Central (*Central Autónoma de Trabajadores*)
CCP	Commerce and Services Confederation (*Confederaçao do Comércio e Serviços de Portugal*)
CCU	Construction Chamber of Uruguay (*Cámara de Construcción del Uruguay*)
CDS	Center Social Democratic Party (*Partido de Centro Democratico Social*)
CGTP	General Confederation of Portuguese Workers (*Confederaçao Geral dos Trabalhadores Portugueses*)
CIP	Industrial Confederation (*Confederaçao da Indústria Portuguesa*)
CNT	National Workers' Convention (*Convención Nacional de Trabajadores*)
COSUPEM	Business Superior Council (*Consejo Superior Empresarial*)
CPC	Production and Commerce Confederation (*Confederación de la Producción y del Comercio*)
CPCS	Permanent Commission for Social Concertation (*Comissão Permanente de Concertação Social*)

CSL	Superior Labor Council (*Consejo Superior Laboral*)
CTP	Tourism Confederation (*Confederaçao do Turismo Portugês*)
CUT	Workers' Unitary Central (*Central Unitaria de Trabajadores*)
EC	European Commission
ECB	European Central Bank
ECLAC	United Nations Economic Commission for Latin America and the Caribbean (*Comisión Económica para América Latina y el Caribe*)
EFTA	European Free Trade Association
EMU	European Monetary Union (*Unión Monetaria Europea*)
EPL	Employment Protection Legislation Index
ETN	National Labor Statute (*Estatuto Nacional do Trabalho*)
FA	Broad Front (*Frente Amplio*)
FP	Popular Front (*Frente Popular*)
GATT	General Agreement on Tariffs and Trade
IFI	International financial institution
ILO	International Labor Organization
IMF	International Monetary Fund (*Fondo Monetario Internacional*)
ISI	Import substitution industrialization model
MFA	Armed Forces Movement (*Movimento das Forças Armadas*)
MLN	National Liberation Movement – Tupamaros (*Movimiento de Liberación Nacional*)
MPP	Popular Participation Movement (*Movimiento de Participación Popular*)
OECD	Organization for Economic Cooperation and Development
PC	Colorado Party (*Partido Colorado*, Uruguay)
PCP	Portuguese Communist Party (*Partido Comunista Portugués*)
PDC	Christian Democracy Party (*Partido Demócrata Cristiano*, Chile)
PDP	Portuguese Democratic Party (*Partido Democrático Portugues*)
PIT-CNT	Workers Inter-union Plenary – National Convention of Workers (*Plenario Intersindical de Trabajadores – Convención Nacional de Trabajadores*)
PN	National Party (*Partido Nacional*)

PPD	Party for Democracy (*Partido para la Democracia*)
PPP	Purchasing power parity
PSD	Portuguese Social Democratic Party (*Partido Social Demócrata Portugués*)
PSP	Portuguese Socialist Party (*Partido Socialista Portugués*)
RN	National Renovation (*Renovación Nacional*)
SUNCA	Construction Sector Union (*Sindicato Único Nacional de la Construcción y Anexos*)
UDI	Independent Democratic Union (*Unión Democrática Independiente*)
UGT	General Union of Workers (in Uruguay, *Unión General de Trabajadores*; in Portugal, *União Geral dos Trabalhadores*)
UP	Popular Unity (*Unidad Popular*)
WB	World Bank (*Banco Mundial*)

Introduction

> The justice of a society is not exclusively a function of its legislative structure, of its legally imperative rules, but is also a function of the choices people make within those rules.
>
> (Cohen 2000)

Distributive conflicts are remarkably common in modern democracies. From Uruguay to Bolivia, from the United States to Sweden, as conflicts increase, they help to shape the policies that govern markets, the extent of workers' and unions' rights, and even wage differentials between low-skilled workers and top executives. Why?

This question has attracted increasing scholarly attention since the period of welfare state retrenchment beginning in the 1970s, and the growth of austerity plans throughout the Western world. As market reforms advanced, many leftist parties around the world became convinced of the ungovernability of market forces, leading to dramatic shifts in their goals and programmatic orientation. These shifts included a preference for abandoning wage policy as part of their distributive strategies, heavily investing instead in redistribution through tax and transfers. A distributive strategy, as used in this book, is a policy blueprint for ameliorating poverty and inequalities consisting of two main components: pre-distributive policies are those that try to prevent inequalities occurring in the first place, while redistributive policies are those that try to ameliorate them via taxes and benefits once they have occurred. Instruments in parties' distributive strategies are choices made by party cadres within the rules of democratic capitalism and the opportunities and challenges given by their parties' societal linkages and electoral alliances. However, the debate over pre-distributive policies and, in particular, wage policy ramped up in developed nations as inequality widened, especially after 2008, when the global economic crisis made it abundantly clear that the burden of the crisis would be borne inequitably. The crisis was revelatory for leftist parties and leaders worldwide.

Previous scholars have recognized the importance of what happens before redistribution as a key factor shaping social and economic outcomes (Hacker and Pierson 2010; Piketty 2017). This conceptual distinction between pre-distribution – a term coined by Hacker (2011) – and redistribution as two components of distributive strategies allows us to focus on the importance of pre-distributive instruments, such as wage policy, for advancing equality.

While authors in the pre-distributive camp have identified how governments might seek to create more equal outcomes even before redistribution, they largely overlook the long-term historical forces that shape the opportunities governments have for doing so. These forces include the political economy of pre-distributive policies, such as wage policy, and the opportunities and challenges parties confront in advancing such instruments, such as electoral politics and party-linkages. Through a comparative study of three small countries – two in the Southern Cone of Latin America (Chile and Uruguay) and one in Southern Europe (Portugal) – this book theorizes about the underlying political dynamics that shape the use of wage policy as a pre-distributive instrument of leftist parties in power. The key insight is that the unity of the Left and labor's political legitimacy are the two main drivers of wage policy as a pre-distributive instrument for promoting inclusion. These factors are shaped by elite long-term strategies towards labor. Such strategies, when dominant for long-enough periods, created not only path dependency but shaped differential opportunities for further options down the road. This book, then, is an effort to (1) integrate large-scale historical processes with frequently analyzed short-term and agency-based factors to elucidate variation in the crafting of wage policies, and (2) reshape the debate on the politics of pre-distribution in democracies outside the developed world by situating the cases in a longer historical arc.

WHY STUDY WAGE POLICY AS A PRE-DISTRIBUTIVE INSTRUMENT?

Pre-tax inequalities have usually been treated as a given by the welfare state literature, which concentrated on analyzing the various redistributive policy options for social inclusion. Pre-distributive policies, such as wage setting instruments other than minimum wage policies, fell from grace with the end of Keynesian economics at the dawn of the economic liberalization period. Leftist parties had to confront the emerging idea that, in the globalized era, market forces lie beyond the reach of governments. The rise of "third wayers" within the leftist camp reinforced this strategic trend. Economics trumped politics. Reality, however, trumped economics as inequality continued its upward trend throughout the West. In this context, several literatures have recently begun to focus on pre-tax inequalities to understand this upward trend.

Recent scholarly work has postulated that the evolution of pre-tax income inequality is a significant factor underlying contemporary trends in inequality in various countries (Beramendi and Cusack 2009; Bozio et al. 2020; Hacker 2011; Hacker and Pierson 2010; Piketty 2017). For example, Bozio et al. (2020) compared pre-tax income distribution trends in France and the United States and found that the magnitude of pre-tax inequality in the historical reduction of inequality is about three times greater than the magnitude of post-tax inequality. Beramendi and Cusack (2009), in turn, find that the policy of increasing wages via wage coordination is a prime instrument for reducing disposable income inequality. This policy raises the wage floor indirectly by increasing the reservation wage.

Wage policy, a potentially helpful instrument from long-ago Keynesian times, remains a tool in leftist governments repertoire for achieving predistribution. Wage policy that involves more than simply setting minimum wages implies strengthening organized labor when moving from completely decentralized settings to more centralized ones or the mandatory character of bargaining rounds. Policies involving any combination of mandatory and centralized wage-setting empower subordinate groups, which moves the policy discussion from a purely economic realm to political terrain.

Empowering subordinate groups such as organized labor has effects beyond social inclusion; it promotes a much richer and deeper understanding of inclusion that combines social inclusion and political inclusion. However, it also involves party-society linkages that give subordinate groups a voice and veto in policymaking and legislation: empowered inclusion.[1] Adding chairs to the decision table potentially can help reduce

---

[1] According to Warren (2017, 44), empowered inclusion requires that "those who have claims for inclusion by virtue of being affected by collective decisions possess the powers of speaking, voting, representing, and dissenting." This idea goes beyond consultation; people who are affected, or potentially affected by collective decisions, must have a voice and veto power in policymaking.

structural inequality. Perhaps, then, political considerations should again play a role in our analyses of pre-distribution.

There is a rich scholarship on the use of wage policy by leftist governments of advanced capitalist democracies during the Keynesian and post-Keynesian periods. However, we know much less about the use of wage policies in less developed, more inegalitarian regions such as the Southern Cone of South America – Uruguay, Argentina, Brazil and Chile – and Southern Europe.

Leftist governments in these two regions are deeply linked by cultural roots and historical developments. They also have embraced quite different pre-distributive instruments in their distributive strategies in the aftermath of the simultaneous transition to democracy and the market economy – that is, the "dual transition." Social policy expansion is a trademark of leftist governments. However, the use of wage policy as a pre-distributive instrument –by setting a minimum wage, centralizing wage-setting mechanisms above the firm level, or moving from voluntary to mandatory bargaining – exhibits significant variation across the two regions. What are these different strategies, and where do they come from? Why do we find different uses of wage policy among leftist governments, with some relying almost exclusively on redistribution while others incorporate, to varying extents, wage policy mechanisms as pre-distributive instruments?

Understanding this divergence in the use of wage policy as a pre-distributive instrument is important for two reasons. First, it is important because we observe substantive variation in wage policy across countries. Small nations, such as Chile, Portugal, or Uruguay, were expected to converge on a decentralized wage-bargaining system after the dual transition because of their small size and common exposure to pressures from the global economy (Katzenstein 1985). They did so for a period following the transition. The three countries are, like many peripheral economies, ultimately price takers and concentrate their exports on primary-sector goods and low-tech manufactures, with tourism as a labor-intensive activity. However, the countries once again began to exhibit heterogeneous responses to the potential use of wage policy as a pre-distributive instrument during the 1990s and 2000s along the lines of the level of centralization of wage coordination and the mandatory character of such bargaining rounds.

Second, the use of wage policy as a pre-distributive instrument after the dual transition has received little scholarly attention beyond the commonly studied advanced capitalist democracies. No one studying Europe posits that region as a homogeneous entity, yet the literature on comparative capitalism has overlooked variation in wage policy when studying Latin America. Authors have debated how many different models there are. The literature on Latin America suggests that the countries that compose it are similar with respect to wage policy and that Latin America is different from other regions.[2] Comparative analysis within the Southern Cone is therefore valuable for breaking down regionalism and focusing more on institutional characteristics and on their similarities and differences. The analysis of variation in wage policy, especially when this variation entails heterogeneous use of such policy, is central for advancing our understanding of the long-run evolution of inequality.

THE USE OF WAGE POLICY
AS A PRE-DISTRIBUTIVE INSTRUMENT

The book unpacks the use of wage policy for pre-distribution within the Left. Why is the use of wage policy a defining element for distributive strategies? Because of the unique consequences that moving toward centralized or mandatory wage coordination has on the political empowerment of subordinate groups, particularly organized labor. This potential empowerment, in turn, has consequences for future electoral opportunities of leftist parties in government similar to those long-ago proposed by Przeworski and Sprague (1988) for European socialism. The emergence of a variety of wage policy uses within the Left necessitates incorporating two crucial factors regarding relations between the Left and labor, factors that the literature has overlooked outside of advanced industrial democracies: the unity of the Left and labor's political legitimacy as drivers for advancing wage-based predistribution that promotes inclusion. These two factors are central in defining distributive strategies.

This book identifies linkages and connections between the empowered inclusion of organized labor and the unity of the Left with the use of wage policy as a pre-distributive instrument. Empowered inclusion entails both political inclusion – the empowerment of subordinate groups, or other groups with claims of inclusion, as makers and shapers of policy – and

[2] It is important to mention a few – predominantly descriptive – exceptions in the scholarly debate on models of capitalism in Latin America, such as Huber (2003) or Bogliaccini and Filgueira (2011). Regarding wage policy, the work of Etchemendy (2019) on wage coordination and neocorporatism in Argentina and Uruguay is another late reaction to this dominant assessment of a unique model of capitalism in Latin America advanced by the seminal work of Schneider (2013).

social inclusion, that is, the degree to which social policy includes "outsiders."[3] Different paths of empowered inclusion are shaped by the repetition of certain political practices – social actions commonly organized or enabled by institutions that serve labor-legitimizing functions – form elite strategies toward labor. These political practices affect subordinate groups' recognition, representation, resistance, ability to join associations freely, and vote enfranchisement. Integrating large-scale historical processes with short-term and agency-based factors aids to elucidate variation in the crafting of pre-distribution.

This crucial diversity in the usage of wage policy shapes three different distributive strategies – that is, strategies entailing pre-distributive instruments alongside redistribution: *left-liberalism, state-led concertation* and *neocorporatist policymaking*. What are these strategies and how do they vary regarding the inclusion of wage policy as an instrument for pre-distribution? In Chile, a *left-liberal* strategy developed based almost solely on the administrative setting of minimum wages. This strategy is oriented to alter market outcomes only via redistributive policies (Iversen and Wren 1998). Cooperation between employers and labor, as social partners, which, in the European experience has historically been nurtured by the state over the long run, has been absent. Leftist governments of the Concertación coalition between 1990 and 2010 invested in efforts to alter market outcomes using social policy as the main instrument for (re)distribution. The Concertación avoided the use of wage policy other than to increase the minimum wage.

In Portugal, socialist governments have relied on redistribution and the frequent use of administrative increases in minimum wages and extensions of collective wage accords (*portarias de extensão*) in a context of Left disunity, mainly between the Communist and Socialist parties. This divide has also marked party-labor relations, precluding the Socialist party from pursuing coalition politics. Instead, the Socialist party in Portugal consolidated a strategy based on *state-led concertation*, which relies on social concertation. Avdagic (2010, 637) defines social concertation as "publicly announced formal policy contracts between the government and social partners" over a series of policies, including pre-distributive (e.g., income, labor market) or redistributive (e.g., welfare) policies. These contracts, usually made in Portugal in the context of binding institutions such as the tripartite Permanent Commission for Social Concertation (Comissão Permanente de Concertação Social – CPCS), "explicitly identify policy

---

[3] See Warren (2017, 44) or in footnote 1 in this chapter.

issues and targets, means to achieve them, and tasks and responsibilities of the signatories." Concerning wages, social pacts born out of the CPCS merely set guidelines for the average wage increase at the national level. As conceptualized in this book, state-led concertation implies the establishment of labor's political influence via institutionalized consultation settings where government is the only actor that retains the capacity to initiate policy. Consistently, wage coordination is semi-centralized, occurring mostly but not only at the industry level (Campos Lima 2019).

Uruguay reinstituted wage policy based on mandatory and centralized wage coordination mechanisms during the Frente Amplio (FA) governments. This pre-distributional approach was at the forefront of the FA's distributive strategy alongside social policy. While mandatory and centralized wage coordination had existed before, a solid party-labor alliance between the Frente Amplio and organized labor promoted this policy after the dual transition with a key innovation: it ceased to be a prerogative of the Executive to call for bargaining rounds. From 2005 on, bargaining rounds would be held periodically for all formal workers, consolidating a neocorporatist policymaking strategy. Neocorporatist policymaking consists of a tripartite, consensual approach to income policy under the umbrella of a well-defined macroeconomic plan (Marks 1986a, 253). In this approach, cooperation, despite possible class animosity in a context of empowered inclusion where subordinate groups can set a collective agenda and engage in collective decision-making, is essential. Differently from state-led concertation, neocorporatist policymaking is only possible through coalitional politics.

The distinctive use of wage policy that molded the three distributive strategies has developed through – and has been reinforced by – several labor reforms and the establishment of institutions serving the labor relations arena in the post-dual transition period. These reforms and the political and parliamentarian debates around them are the fingerprint of how the Left perceives opportunities and challenges associated with the empowered inclusion of subordinated groups. The political economy of wage policy is analyzed next.

THE POLITICAL ECONOMY OF WAGE POLICY: LABOR LEGITIMACY AND THE UNITY OF THE LEFT

Why do we find different uses of wage policy as a pre-distributive instrument among leftist governments? What are their proximate and long-run historical-structural causes? In the long-term, different strategies toward the empowered inclusion of labor during the first part of the 20th century provided different settings for establishing labor's political legitimacy.

The notion of political legitimacy is crucial for understanding the prevalence of pre-distributive instruments that either privilege the elite's political domination or promote more cooperative scenarios in which political and social actors bargain for distribution, that is, scenarios that include subordinate groups in the political process. Political legitimacy refers to the degree to which labor organizations are valued for themselves and considered right and proper as political actors (Lipset 1959, 71). The gradual accrual of political legitimacy, over the long run, is the result of large-scale historical processes of labor political activism and political responses to it.

Southern Europe and the Southern Cone of Latin America share the characteristic of having developed intransigent business classes and class-based combative labor movements during the 20th century. These labor movements became more or less combative depending on the dominant elite strategies toward the empowered inclusion of labor during the first part of the 20th century – strategies that developed in diverse institutional contexts, from authoritarian to democratic.

The argument of this book is that, in the short-run, the use of wage policy as an instrument for pre-distribution is closely related to the unity of the Left or, more precisely, to the relationship between leftist parties or factions with a zeal for macroeconomic stability and labor-mobilizing parties or factions. This is because leftist governments that cannot moderate labor's wage demands tend not to risk using wage-setting mechanisms – such as centralized or mandatory wage coordination – to increase labor's political power. Leftist governments may use the instrument of minimum wages, but they otherwise rely almost exclusively on social policy as a redistributive instrument (Table I.1).

An ideational factor, the perceived tradeoff between job creation and wage egalitarianism, relates elite strategies toward labor and leftist unity to the outcome. This factor, primarily dependent on power constellations, is linked to the rise of economic liberalization and the demise of Keynesian economics. The idea that market forces are beyond the reach of domestic politics grew in strength and traveled from International Financial Institutions (IFIs) and leading nations to developing nations willing to emulate the practices of the global leaders. The question of whether there is, in fact, a tradeoff between job creation and wage egalitarianism lies in the domain of economics, as explained in Chapter 1. The perceived tradeoff lies in the realm of politics and concerns how domestic

TABLE I.I *Explaining variation in the use of wage policy: Labor political legitimacy and the unity of the Left.*

		Is labor considered a legitimate political actor?	
		No	**Yes**
Is the Left divided?	Yes	*Left liberalism* (Chile) Voluntary, decentralized wage coordination	*State-led concertation* (Portugal) Voluntary, semi-centralized wage coordination
	No		*Neocorporatist policymaking* (Uruguay) Mandatory, semi-centralized wage coordination

elites legitimize alternative models and policies. The book shows how leftist governments in the three countries interpreted the political challenges born out of this perceived tradeoff in different ways. The varying perceptions depended, primarily, on the countries' legacies of elite strategies toward labor and the unit of the Left and gave rise to differences in the use of wage policies to achieve distributive goals.

How did leftist governments interpret the alleged tradeoff between employment creation and wage egalitarianism as articulated for the service economy? In the two regions, the new globalized, deindustrialized, and democratic context of the aftermath of the dual transition brought about great uncertainty about sustainable distributive strategies and their compatibility with office-seeking strategies.[4] The nature of fiscal and monetary constraints changed significantly under the open market economy, though Left-Right partisan differences have remained relevant during the past three decades. As in the developed world, leftist governments have been more inclined than right-wing governments to increase social expenditure during the period in the two regions, as Huber and Stephens show for Latin America and Iberia (2012). However, in both regions, Left-labor relations became a defining factor in shaping leftist governments' electoral and distributive strategies, as was the case in advanced industrial democracies (Kitschelt 1994; Przeworski and Sprague 1988). Central to these governments' decisions was their assessment of the potential governability risks associated with advancing wage policies oriented

[4] For a detailed account of social democratic party strategies in developed countries during the period, see Kitschelt (1994).

toward greater wage equality. Wage-policy centralization or turning it mandatory may imply the political strengthening of a combative, wage-militant, organized labor.

THEORETICAL AND EMPIRICAL CONTRIBUTIONS

The book addresses a classic puzzle that lies at the intersection of political sociology and political economy, linking together strands of scholarship that remain unconnected, introducing a novel argument regarding the politics of pre-distribution. It analyzes the linkage between long-term elite strategies toward the empowered inclusion of labor and short-term factors related to power constellations, mainly the unity of the Left, as a primary driver of variation in leftist governments' use of wage policy after the dual transition. It thus examines a previously unexplored aspect of the political economy of distribution that is particularly important for understanding persistent inequality and the overall health of democratic institutions in these two regions.

The argument connects the classic dilemma of electoral support that characterizes democratic socialism–what happens to social democratic parties as they build alliances between the working and middle classes (Przeworski and Sprague 1988)–with more recent scholarship on the potential tradeoff between the goals of employment creation and wage egalitarianism in the post-industrial economy (see Iversen and Wren 1998). The analysis unpacks social-democratic leftist (or center-left) types, showing significant variation that is not apparent from analyses solely of redistribution.[5] This variation is directly related to the problem of empowered inclusion, a central problem for democracy (Warren 2017), and to how empowering subordinate groups may provoke a crisis of social domination if established elites perceive threats to their interest (O'Donnell 1988, 26–27).[6]

While there is a large literature on redistribution or pre-distribution from the welfare state, scholars have not problematized wage coordination structure as a pre-distributive instrument outside the pool of advanced

---

[5] Europe-centered scholars have shown how wage coordination mechanisms outperform social pacts as vehicles for welfare expenditure within left-wing governments (see Brandl and Traxler 2005). However, the literature on Latin American political economy has understudied the redistributive effects of wage policy.

[6] Collier and Collier (1991) and Rueschemeyer, Stephens, and Stephens (1992) have referred to the dilemma elite groups face regarding the inclusion of subordinate groups, further analyzed in Chapter 2.

capitalist democracies (Beramendi and Rueda 2014; Wallerstein 1990, 1999). Previous works have advanced our knowledge of labor politics or the different types of leftist governments.[7] Flores-Macías (2012, 188) finds that the process through which economic policy reforms are conducted matters for the future stability of such changes. Flores-Macías argues that in both Chile and Uruguay prevailed a process of accommodation and consensus-building that characterizes highly institutionalized party systems. This prevailing process improved the perceived legitimacy of economic transformations and consequently the odds of their survival. This book takes a step back and elucidates the political economy of the distributive conflict in modern developing capitalist societies and how it has directly affected the prevalence of cross-class cooperative or domination-based arrangements. Cooperation and reciprocity, as Moore (1978) argued, do not flow from an innate tendency in human nature. Rather, cooperation and reciprocity result from rules born out of large-scale interactions, often following painfully constricting situations. I will argue that the process of accommodation and consensus building was highly different in the three countries. In Chile, it was processed at the level of political and economic elites, without the participation of subordinated groups, while in Portugal and Uruguay it was processed across class-lines, albeit in very different ways. These differences, I argue, are crucial for understanding the long-term survival of growth models and their distributive outcomes.

A first implication is that wage-bargaining settings should not be considered exclusively as an economic issue but also a political one as they importantly affect political participation, which, in turn, may affect political decisions. The main problem associated with the use of wage coordination as a pre-distributive instrument is that it empowers labor and, as such, leftist parties and governments need to trust labor. From this perspective, wage-bargaining arrangements have a proper political role in democratic consolidation, being valuable in a democracy as instruments for inclusion, empowerment, and collective decision making.

An innovative aspect of the book's argument, then, consists of relating long-standing elite strategies toward the empowered inclusion of labor

---

[7] The work of Etchemendy (Etchemendy 2008, 2019; Etchemendy and Collier 2007) on wage coordination in Uruguay and Argentina, unions in Argentina, and a proposed neo-corporatist model of interest representation in the two countries is a welcome exception to this gap in the literature and is consistent with the idea of the importance of coalition politics for the existence of neocorporatist policymaking. The two approaches to neocorporatism, as a form of interest representation (Schmitter 1974) and as a form of policy (Marks 1986a), are closely related, as explained in the next chapter.

to the political arena. The bulk of the literature on distributive conflict has mainly studied the post-dual transition period. This book shows that the variation in Left-labor relations explained by relatively short-term developments partly depend on long-term, slow-moving elite-labor relations that have developed since the turn of the 20th century. Therefore, it is essential to understand causal processes as historical, path-dependent phenomena wherein proximate causes derive from long-term elite strategies toward labor that, viewed from a distance, experienced little disruption during the dual transition.

A second implication of the book's argument concerns historical continuity and long-term causes related to the opportunities and challenges distributive efforts face in the present, vis-à-vis political sustainability and, eventually, even democratic stability. Elites develop and sustain stable strategies toward the empowered inclusion of labor, balancing the goals of political stability vis-à-vis the political inclusion of subordinate groups. The book shows how, against the backdrop of massive disruptions in the political and economic life of each country – regime change, military intervention in politics, economic crises, entering the European Union (in the case of Portugal), and globalization – these elite strategies adapted to the new democratic and open market contexts while maintaining important continuities after the dual transition. As the countries navigated the question of whether elites would allow subordinated groups a voice in public decision-making or perpetuate their exclusion, they exhibited impressive stability, with change occurring slowly and gradually over time. This question is important in the context of the post-dual transition new inclusionary turn (Cameron 2021; Kapiszewski, Levitsky, and Yashar 2021), as exclusion remains the crucial problem in Latin American democracies.

A third implication of the book's argument is related to the findings of recent scholarship concerning the politics of institutional weakness (e.g., Brinks, Levitsky, and Murillo 2020). While Latin American and Iberian institutions are weak in the sense of being unstable, volatile, and lacking enforcement power; research has shown that – in accord with the epigraph by Cohen that begins this chapter – these institutions nevertheless bind people in consequential ways, even in the face of this weak institutionalism. This apparent contradiction calls for a deeper understanding of how institutions in these two regions shape subordinate actors' access to the political arena, assign roles to individuals over time, and how, in the face of institutional weakness, these roles are sustained.

The book also contributes to the stream of scholarship that focuses on comparative capitalisms in developing countries. The book suggests that current models of capitalism in contemporary Latin America, which conceptualize the region as compromising a set of homogenous instances of Hierarchical capitalism, need to be revisited in light of the striking differences among countries in the region with respect to the prevalence of cooperation versus domination dynamics.[8] The book proposes a model of capitalism that is rooted in the common heritage Latin American political economies share and in the role hierarchies have played in organizing the region's productive systems. Moreover, the book's historical perspective makes it possible to view differences between countries in their distributive strategies in terms of the tension between cooperation and domination in the labor relations arena. Finally, the book's argument suggests that we can reasonably expect more mature democratic and productive systems to develop meaningful differences in distributive policies alongside their domestic characteristics.

PLAN OF THE BOOK

The organization of the book is as follows. Chapter 1 describes the dependent variable and its variation. It also discusses the political implications of the way in which the (perceived) tradeoff between employment creation and wage egalitarianism binds the use of wage policy for pre-distribution to elite approaches toward the empowered inclusion of labor and the unity of the Left. Chapter 2 provides the theoretical framework for analyzing the use of wage policy in unequal societies under open market capitalism and presents the book's theoretical contributions. This chapter theorizes that elite strategies toward labor and the unity of the Left are important factors for understanding leftist governments' use of wage policy as a pre-distributive instrument. Chapter 3 offers a large-scale historical review of elite strategies toward the empowered inclusion of labor before the dual transition. This macro-historical process of elite response to labor political activism shapes dominant elite strategies and, over the long term, affects labor's ability to build political legitimacy. Chapter 4 analyzes the decline of previously dominant elite strategies toward labor in each of the three countries and the electoral strengthening of leftist parties at the onset of the dual transition during a period

---

[8] While the leading proponent of the hierarchical model is Schneider (2013), other works have pointed out meaningful intra-regional differences in diverse aspects of the productive system. See for example Bogliaccini and Filgueira (2011), Bogliaccini and Madariaga (2020), Huber (2003), and Schrank (2009).

of political radicalization. In doing so, the chapter analyzes through a comparative lens leftist unity and Left-labor relations during and after the dual transition within the scope of power constellations in each country. Chapter 5 analyzes how the short- and long-term factors analyzed in the previous chapters combine in shaping leftist governments' decisions regarding stable distributive strategies. The analysis focuses on the use of wage policy as a pre-distributive instrument by reviewing labor reforms and the evolution of wage-related institutions and their use by these governments. Conclusions concludes by discussing the theoretical merits of analyzing how distributive strategies are based on the outcomes of wage policy reforms. This final chapter also draws theoretical lessons and identifies possible challenges that may lie ahead for leftist governments in their quest to reduce inequality.

Use of Wage Policy for Pre-distribution

Although it was not one of the so-called "structural reforms" of the government program, the changes to the Labor Code gained great prominence in 2015 and became a new focus for business mistrust after the tax reform. The logic of the original project was simple: give unions more power to negotiate, incentivize unionization and eliminate mechanisms attacking workers' rights. It assumed that stronger unions would result in better income distribution and, possibly, more social peace. (…) It is important to recognize that labor regulation is a public policy in which efficiency and productivity objectives easily collide with those of equity.

(Valdéz 2018, 265–266)[1]

1.1 THE OUTCOME: USING WAGE POLICY AS A PRE-DISTRIBUTIVE INSTRUMENT

Distributive strategies are combinations of pre- and redistributive instruments. The term "distributive" is used instead of "redistributive" as it entails strategies for social expenditure after-tax transfers as well as pre-distributive instruments, as explained in the previous chapter. Among the latter, I analyze the use of wage policy, which regulates the distribution of benefits between labor and employers to produce goods and services. Specifically, while the literature on welfare states has convincingly

---

[1] Rodrigo Valdéz was Finance Secretary during the debate concerning the 2016 labor reform under the second Bachelet administration. He held office for 842 days. We had the opportunity to talk extensively about these issues of growth and distribution in a personal interview held in Santiago de Chile in September 2019, when neither Valdéz nor myself could possibly foresee the social protests that would unfold in Santiago only a few days later.

demonstrated there is considerable variation in the use of redistributive instruments in advanced democracies (Esping-Andersen 1990; Huber and Stephens 2001) and even in Latin America (Castiglioni 2005; Filgueira and Filgueira 2002; Garay 2016), the analytical framework advanced here focuses on the variation in wage policy as an instrument for pre-distribution. Even Pribble's seminal work that compares Chile and Uruguay in terms of party politics in the building of welfare states in the post-dual-transition period does not analyze in depth the use of wage policy as a pre-distributive instrument, though it notes in passing such a reform in Uruguay by the Frente Amplio and refers to increases in the minimum wage in the two countries (2013, 80, 83, 88).

Over the past three decades, Latin America and Southern Europe have experienced a "new inclusionary turn." While there has been an expansion of recognition, access, and resources for popular sectors (Anria and Bogliaccini 2022; Kapiszewski et al. 2021), the exclusion of the lower classes remains the Achilles heel of the two regions' democracies (Benza and Kessler 2020; Ferrera 2005; Filgueira et al. 2012; Katrougalos and Lazaridis 2003). After the dual transition in both regions, leftist governments crafted distributive strategies that combined the use of instruments in the areas of pre-distribution and redistribution. The use of wage policy as a pre-distributive instrument is a particularly salient political issue as it may imply the empowerment of the labor movement.

Why is the use of wage policy as a pre-distributive instrument important? Wage policy refers to the legislation of government action undertaken to regulate the level or structure of wages. Prominent policies in this area in our three cases have varied on two important dimensions: the level of centralization of wage coordination, either within firms, groups of firms, industries or economic sectors, and whether wage coordination is mandatory or voluntary. There is a reasonable consensus in the economic literature that minimum-wage policies modestly alleviate poverty and improve family incomes at the bottom of the distribution while having little to no effect on employment levels.[2] However, there is much debate regarding the effects of mandatory wage-bargaining centralization on employment in the period since the turn away from

---

[2] See Dube (2019a) for a detailed account of the international evidence on how minimum wages affect employment, and Dube (2019b) for the effect of minimum wages on family incomes. See Rueda (2008) for an analysis of how minimum wage regulations affect the distribution of earnings indirectly by raising the wage floor indirectly.

Keynesian economics.[3] This debate affects politics and the political economy of distribution because, unlike other policy areas, wage policy tends to affect workers' and employers' political interests. Under certain circumstances, wage policy may even activate a class-oriented cleavage that reinforces class conflict. These two dimensions, wage-setting centralization and its mandatory character, are essential for understanding wage policy's potential effect on wage egalitarianism. The latter, however, only becomes relevant with the former's presence, as no wage regime imposes mandatory coordination rounds at the individual level.

This initial chapter characterizes the distributive strategies adopted in each of our three cases and emphasizes the diversity in the way wage-egalitarian-oriented policies have evolved. It discusses the political factors that shape the choice of wage policies, namely whether labor will overreach in pursuit of higher wages, which would jeopardize any leftist party's long-term office-seeking strategy. This question arises from the perceived economic tradeoff between job creation and wage egalitarianism and concerns regarding the macroeconomic perils of wage-led inflation and its effects on unemployment. The book reformulates this perceived tradeoff into a political dilemma about the political risks of empowering the labor movement to achieve acceptable levels of cooperation between employers and labor while maintaining macroeconomic stability at a time when Keynesianism was growing unpopular among leftist parties. The use of wage policy as a pre-distributive instrument is also influenced, then, by how the Left manages to overcome the ideational foundations of post-transitional austerity,[4] that is, on how the Left manages to perceive alternative legitimate economic and labor-related models and policies. This new element in the theory as proposed in the book's argument, termed an *anchoring bias*, is explained in the following section.

1.2 POLITICALLY CONSTRUCTED SEVERITIES AROUND THE EMPLOYMENT–WAGES TRADEOFF

In its original formulation, the employment–wages tradeoff is rooted in the new constraints that deindustrialization placed on governments in advanced political economies beginning in the 1970s. During the

---

[3] See Calmfors and Drifill (1988), Iversen (1999), and Rueda and Pontusson (2000) for a political economy-oriented debate on the topic in the advanced capitalist democracies.

[4] See Bremer and McDaniel (2019) and Bremer (2018) for a related argument focusing on social democratic parties in Europe.

industrial expansion period, encompassing the 1950s and 1960s, governments that pushed for wage egalitarianism did not confront major dilemmas in employment creation, as proposed by the Rehn–Meidner model (see Erixon 2010; Meidner 1974; Rehn 1985).[5]

The perceived tradeoff between employment and wages arose from the problem of stagflation. First noted during the late 1960s, stagflation denotes the concomitant increase in inflation and stagnation of economic output, causing both unemployment and prices to increase.[6] Thus, the proposed tradeoff is based on a postulated negative relation between wage egalitarianism and employment creation. This postulated negative relation, combined with external pressures for austerity, became part of the dominant political rhetoric in Latin America and Southern Europe, usually voiced by those influenced by the fiscal orthodoxy promoted by international financial institutions (IFIs) involved with the politics of structural adjustment. It later also became relevant for governments in Southern Europe during preparations for joining the Euro and again during the Sovereign Debt crisis beginning in 2008.[7]

What role does wage coordination centralization play in this employment–wage tradeoff? Calmfors and Driffill (1988) analyzed the relation between the structure of labor markets and the macroeconomic performance of advanced capitalist democracies and found that the worst employment outcomes occur in systems with an intermediate degree of wage centralization. The main factor behind this finding is, partly, political: the relationship between employment and wages depends on two forces: the market power of unions and the effect of wages on prices.[8] The authors observe that, on the one hand, "large and encompassing unions tend to recognize their market power and take into account both the inflationary and employment effects of wage increases" (Calmfors and Driffill 1988, 14). These unions are found primarily in highly centralized wage-setting systems because it is under such conditions that

---

[5] See Erixon (2010) for a complete and detailed account of the Rehn–Meidner model and its evolution in Sweden.

[6] See Mudge (2018) for an excellent account of the origin of the debate concerning stagflation in the United Kingdom in the 1970s.

[7] See Malamud and Schmitter (2011), Scharpf (1996), and Streeck (2012) for comprehensive perspectives on the effects of the integration into the European Community of the Southern European countries, and Baer and Leite (1992) and Royo (2010) for an analysis of the Portuguese case. See Bogliaccini (2013), Huber (2003), and Schneider (2013) for different perspectives on the effects of Washington Consensus policies on Latin America.

[8] See Calmfors and Driffill (1988) for a detailed explanation of the economic foundations of the proposed tradeoff.

workers find unionization most attractive. On the other hand, in entirely decentralized (voluntary) systems, unions have no market power and, therefore, wage-militancy and wage-led inflation are not an issue. Calmfors and Driffill argue that the tension between wages and employment occurs at intermediate levels of union centralization –such as sector or industry levels– because while unions can exert some market power, they can also ignore the macroeconomic implications of their actions. This argument suggests that union centralization, and not the relative bargaining strength of employers and unions, is what matters for understanding the potential tradeoff between wages and employment. As Calmfors (1987) explains, the critical aspect of centralization is that as unions centralize their interests and cooperate, they internalize conflict and set wages with the welfare implications of other unions in mind. By contrast, when unions bargain for wages independently, each union tends to maximize its own welfare, ignoring the potentially adverse (or positive) effects on other unions.[9]

While Calmfors and Driffill (1988) treat the relationship between job creation and wage egalitarianism as an actual tradeoff, I refer to it in this book as a "perceived" one. The proposition of a perceived tradeoff between employment creation and wage egalitarianism does not deny that an actual tradeoff might exist. At the extremes, if wages grow too much or wages remain persistently low, unemployment will go up.

Empowering labor may generate electoral opportunities and challenges for governments. While it can enhance the mobilization capacity of certain actors, it can also entail the risk that including subordinate groups will undercut the influence of constituted powers (Cameron 2021, 453). Even leftist parties in government should consider the risk that labor may radicalize or come to be seen as untrustworthy by the median voter, in which case an alliance with labor may obstruct a party's preferred office-seeking strategy. The idiosyncratic character of unions also influences leftist governments' wage policy decisions. This character is, in part, a consequence of past elite strategies in which labor inclusion was either empowered or subject to continuous repression. As Mares (2005) points out for the case of advanced capitalist democracies, among unions there are those that care about social policies and those that care only about salaries. While the former type may be willing to exercise wage restraint in exchange for welfare state expansion, the latter may exacerbate wage

---

[9] With Rosario Queirolo, we provide an analysis based on these premises of the evolution of wage bargaining rounds in Uruguay after 2005 (Bogliaccini and Queirolo 2017).

militancy, producing either profound internal conflicts inside a coalition or damaging an allied party's electoral opportunities.

Ultimately, the perceived tradeoff is a binding constraint for leftist parties and governments, a politically constructed challenge they confront. However, this binding constraint has multiple solutions, depending on how much leeway political leaders and technocrats in left-wing governments think they have available to them.[10] I show in this book how leftist parties and governments in Portugal, Chile, and Uruguay differ in how they construe their historical and present contexts.

The use of wage policy as a pre-distributive instrument in this context, aside, simply, from setting minimum wages, would depend on whether leftist parties in government attempt to consolidate their economic credibility with middle-class voters or, instead, respond by advocating post-Keynesian economics (PKE) (Baccaro and Pontusson 2016; Stockhammer 2022) in order to accommodate employment and wage egalitarianism.[11] Specifically, the PKE model highlights the instability of the growth process and underlines the importance of understanding income distribution and power relations to foster sustainable growth. As stated above, the amount of leeway political leaders and technocrats in left-wing governments believe they have is related, in part, to an ideational construct (Bremer 2018; Bremer and McDaniel 2019). When Keynesian economics fell out of favor, the managerial, discretionary character of Keynesian professional ethics was replaced by a rule-centered, anti-discretionary ethic advocated by neoliberal thinking, which elevates the market over politics (Mudge 2018, 367).[12] This change was significant in both Latin America and Southern Europe given the rapid collapse of previous economic models and the strong influence of neoliberalism as advocated by IFIs at the time. It conspired against the capacity for political intermediation, party–union relationships, and the relationship between center- and far-left parties.

---

[10] Centeno (1993, 313–314) provides a widely accepted definition of a technocrat in the study of Latin America: a public official who seeks to impose a policy paradigm based on the application of instrumental rationality and the scientific method. Dargent's (2014) study of technocracies in Peru and Colombia argues that the imperative to maintain macroeconomic stability during the post-democratization decades motivates politicians to cede control of economic policy to technocrats. Joignant (2011) defines technocrats by their skills as applied economists, following Williamson (1994).

[11] See Bremer (2018) and Bremer and McDaniel (2019) for a detailed overview of this dilemma, focusing on Western European social democratic parties' response to the austerity dogma.

[12] See a similar argument for the analysis of social democracies in Europe by Bremer and McDaniels (2019)

The perceived tradeoff between job creation and wage egalitarianism anchors government decisions regarding the use of wage policy to achieve distributive goals in long-term elite strategies concerning the empowerment of labor and the (dis)unity of the Left. The concept of an anchoring bias refers to the fact that different initial positions – for example, different country contexts – yield outcomes biased toward the initial values in a given situation.[13] The anchoring bias applied to the problem of the empowerment of labor suggests that how the tradeoff is perceived is shaped by beliefs about the policy space available given the constraints and opportunities associated with historically constructed relationships between labor, parties, employers, long-term elite strategies toward labor, and labor political legitimacy. In Uruguay, for example, labor's status as a legitimate political actor, the tradition of dialogue between elites and subordinate groups, and a united Left enabled the Frente Amplio – especially its moderate factions – to perceive a wide policy space available for centralizing wage coordination and empowering labor. The tradeoff is an anchor because it brings together long-term elite strategies toward labor and post-transitional power constellations. It is the lens through which leftist elites perceive the opportunities and constraints associated with including different wage policy instruments in their distributive strategies.

Employers' interests are a vital input for governments when setting employment-related policies. The tradeoff, then, is more or less politically salient based on employers' relative capacity to build political support and the capacity of the Left to counterbalance employers' political objectives. Following Thelen (2001), employers' support for economic coordination is assumed in the analysis to be strategic and contingent on labor's countervailing power. This assumption is important for the argument that the distributive conflict is political in nature, as opposed to the dominant idea in the Varieties of Capitalism (VoC) approach that employers' preference for coordination in a market economy is pre-strategic (Soskice 1999).

[13] For a detailed account of the original idea of an anchor, as developed in the field of prospect theory, see Tversky and Kahneman (1982). Anchoring is a source of bias in judgement under uncertainty, which makes decision-makers boundedly rational (Kahneman 2003; Simon 1979). In the field of political science, Weyland's work on how decision-makers are captivated by available models in the context of policy diffusion, drawing potentially biased conclusions from limited data, constitutes a seminal example of the use of the idea of bounded rationality and the potential biases that influence policymakers' decisions (Weyland 2009a).

The perceived tradeoff is also related to case selection, because the relation between wages and employment is significant for economies like Chile, Portugal, and Uruguay. In small, export-oriented economies that have confronted rapid changes imposed by economic liberalization, it would be reasonable to expect policy convergence on completely decentralized wage-setting mechanisms, a phenomenon the literature has coined the "liberal convergence hypothesis." This hypothesis predicts institutional convergence along a neoliberal trajectory among advanced capitalist societies (Baccaro and Howell 2017, 9). The specific form of this hypothesis in the context of the argument advanced in the book is discussed in length in the following chapter. This expectation for Chile, Portugal, and Uruguay is based on these countries' susceptibility to the so-called "middle-income trap." Their economies are disadvantaged relative to low-wage economies in the competition to produce manufactured exports and disadvantaged relative to advanced capitalist economies in the competition to produce innovations and highly skilled workforce.[14]

1.3 EMPLOYMENT STRUCTURE AND WAGE EVOLUTION AFTER THE DUAL TRANSITION

Before analyzing the policies toward wage egalitarianism in the three countries, I briefly characterize their employment structures and recent trends regarding employment protection. The employment structure in the two regions relies on low wages at the bottom of the earnings distribution to facilitate the expansion of employment in the service sector. It is also characterized by rapid and premature deindustrialization and low skill levels. It is important to note that, in contrast to advanced democracies, productivity levels were already distorted during the inward-looking industrialization period due to rent-seeking incentives found in most countries in the two regions. The loss of productivity increases due to the transition to the service economy was not the primary problem driving the Southern Cone and Southern European experiences. Productivity levels were already low, which directly impacted the disappearance

---

[14] For detailed accounts of the middle-income trap, see Kharas and Kohli (2011) and Doner and Schneider (2016). For accounts of skill distributions and its relationship with inequality in our two regions and the advanced industrial democracies, see Bogliaccini and Madariaga (2020), Busemeyer (2014), Busemeyer and Trampusch (2012), and Busemeyer and Iversen (2012).

of entire sectors in the wake of trade liberalization. In this transition process, deindustrialization in the context of already low productivity contributed to an increase in unemployment, inequality, and informal employment in all three countries.[15]

Before the dual transition, each of the three countries had moved away from "labor protective strategies" toward economic liberalization. This included the strong flexibilization – or deregulation – of the labor market. The transition in Chile from a political economy with large, nationalized sectors and public employment differed from the transition in Portugal. In the latter country, the transition was managed by prioritizing employment – job security and low unemployment – with an eye toward integration into the European Community (see Bermeo 1993). In Chile, the transition occurred in the context of neoliberal concerns to control inflation and promote labor-market flexibilization (see Muñoz Gomá 2007). In both cases, however, large privatization programs took place (Clifton et al. 2005; Muñoz Gomá 2007). In Uruguay, the transition also privileged concerns over inflation and the promotion of employment flexibilization during the 1990s, but privatization attempts failed. Uruguay thus did not experience a large nationalization program associated with the dual transition as Chile did during Allende's administration and Portugal after the 1976 Constitution.

In terms of employment protection, Portugal historically has had greater levels of protection for labor contracts and temporary contracts and greater protection against individual or collective dismissals than have Chile and Uruguay. Portugal's level of protection is also well above the average among OECD countries, based on the Employment Protection Legislation Index (EPL).[16] On a scale from 0 and 6, with 6 denoting maximum protection, the OECD average was 2.08 in 2014, while Portugal's score was 2.81. Chile, with a score of 2.86, also ranked above the OECD average, while Uruguay ranked below average with a score of 1.72. EPL data for Uruguay and Chile are scarce, but Portugal's score on the index has moved steadily downwards over the past 20 years from a score of 4.10 in 1998.

High levels of employment protection have both positive and negative effects. On the one hand, some argue that protection against arbitrary

---

[15] See Emmenegger et al. (2012) and Rodrik (2016) for different approaches to the problem of deindustrialization in our two regions.

[16] The OECD constructs this index. See the following URL: www.oecd.org/employment/emp/oecdindicatorsofemploymentprotection.htm

dismissals makes firms bear some of the social consequences of such dismissals (Cahuc and Malherbet 2004; Cahuc and Postel-Vinay 2002). On the other, some have argued that high levels of employment protection also contribute to labor-market dualization (Cahuc et al. 2008; Emmenegger et al. 2012; Valadas 2017). There is no consensus in the literature about the effects of high levels of EPL on unemployment rates. Blanchard and Portugal (2001), for example, comparing Portugal and the United States as extreme cases in terms of employment protection, find no evidence to support the hypothesis of differential effects on unemployment.

There is a consensus in the literature that higher employment protection is associated with lower overall wage levels. The causal mechanism proposed is that employers tend to shift firing costs onto wages (see Brancaccio et al. 2018; Leonardi and Pica 2007, 2013). The evolution of average wages in Portugal during the post-dual transition period, as explained below, is consistent with these expectations. As Branco (2017) notes, the Portuguese emphasis on employment protection and on maintaining low unemployment rates produced weak unemployment protection, lower wages, and unpaid wages during economic downturns.

While the three countries differed in their use of wage policy after the dual transition, leftist governments in the three countries made use of minimum-wage policies in the decades following the dual transition. Figure 1.1 shows the evolution of purchasing power parity (PPP)-adjusted minimum wages and linear trends for 1992–2017. The literature suggests a general positive effect of minimum-wage increases on low-end inequality. However, the magnitude of the effect varies by country, usually depending on several factors such as enforcement, informality, or actual increases vis-à-vis average wages.[17]

Linear trends of PPP-adjusted minimum wages in the three countries are parallel during the period, albeit Uruguay shows two markedly different periods (Figure 1.1). Before 2005, minimum wages remained unchanged in PPP terms. After 2005, with the reinstallation of mandatory collective wage bargaining, the adjusted minimum wage began a steep upward trend that persisted during the Frente Amplio's tenure in office.

---

[17] See, for example, Martins (2020) for the case of Portugal; Álvez et al. (2012) for Uruguay; Grau and Landerretche (2011) for Chile. Collateral negative effects have been reported, such as a negative impact on employment or firm closures for Chile and Portugal.

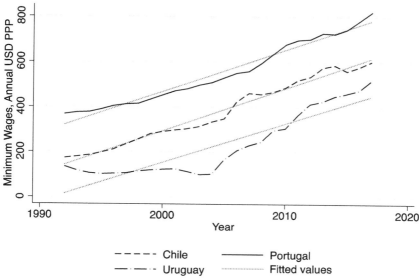

FIGURE 1.1 Evolution of PPP-adjusted minimum wages (1992–2017).
Note: Annual USD value of minimum wages.
Source: Official data, consulted online at the national statistics institutes in Chile, Portugal, and Uruguay.

In Chile, the Concertación governments increased minimum wages during the period. The law established these increases under government initiative and after parliamentary sanction. It is important to note that, like the case in Portugal, the overall evolution of the minimum wage was not altered during periods in which center-right parties were in office. Overall, leftist governments have included increasing minimum wages in their distributive strategies during the three decades under analysis. In the case of Uruguay, furthermore, the change in policy in 2005 is evident. Unlike in Portugal or even Chile, Uruguayan governments from the Right and the Left have made very different use of the minimum-wage policy.

The evolution of PPP-adjusted average wages looks quite different (Figure 1.2). Chilean average wages have followed a constant upward trend during the last three decades, except for the period between 2004 and 2008 – the second part of Lagos's administration (2000–2006) and the beginning of Bachelet's first administration (2006–2010). While in both Chile and Uruguay, the period between 1997 and 2002 was marked by a series of international financial crises – from those in Asia to the

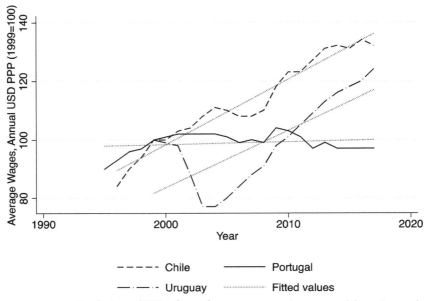

FIGURE 1.2 Evolution of PPP-adjusted average wages (1999=100) (1996–2017).
Note: Annual USD value of average wages.
Sources: OCDE & CINVE.

Argentinean crisis – the effect of these crises on wages (and unemployment, see Figure 1.4) was more marked in Uruguay.

Chile and Uruguay both had completely decentralized wage bargaining until Uruguay recentralized it to the sector level in 2005. Average
wages in Uruguay trended upward after 2005 following this change,
yielding the steepest slope of the three countries. Chilean wages, which
remained under a decentralized bargaining scheme, were much less elas-
tic to the upper and lower parts of the economic cycle, as described
above. In Portugal, average wages have remained stable during the last
two decades. While minimum wages are set by administrative decree,
average wages depend on collective bargaining, which in Portugal has
been voluntary since the 1980s (see Traxler et al. 2001). This evolution
is consistent with the overall high EPL levels in Portugal over the two
decades, in comparative terms.

Finally, the ratio between minimum and average wages best reflects
wage egalitarianism policies. This measure allows one to grasp how
wage policy is used differently in the three cases, producing different pre-
distributive effects. Figure 1.3 shows these ratios. The resulting picture is

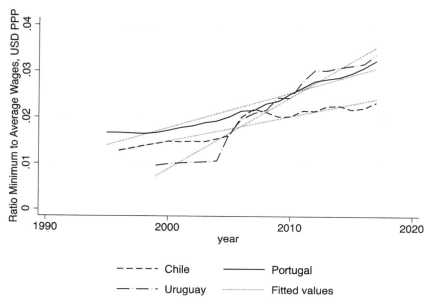

FIGURE 1.3 The ratio of minimum to average wages (1996–2017).
Sources: Income Distribution Database (OECD 2020), Data on salaries and prices, Uruguay (INE 2020).

consistent with theoretical expectations. Chile exhibits lower wage egalitarianism, consistent with its completely decentralized bargaining system (Beramendi and Cusack 2009; Iversen 1999). Portugal shows a more egalitarian trend, though during the last decade the evolution of wages has been marked by an overall freezing of salaries, following the 2008 Sovereign Debt crisis (see Hijzen et al. 2017). The gap between minimum and average wages closed by 5.9 percent in the decade between 1997 and 2007, at an average yearly rate of half a percentage point. Between 2008 and 2017, the gap closed by 13 percent at an average yearly rate of 1.3 percentage points.

Uruguay, a country in which labor relations changed drastically with the reintroduction of mandatory collective wage bargaining at a sectoral level in 2005, is illustrative in two senses. First, the ratio between minimum and average wages has a clear inflection point precisely in 2005. Before that, in a context of completely decentralized wage bargaining, the trend is parallel to the Chilean one at a lower level, while the upward slope in the evolution of the gap between 2005 and 2017 is the steepest of the three countries. In 2012, the rate at which the Uruguayan gap closed moderated, paralleling the Portuguese rate at a higher level. At the same time, it is not possible to make precise comparisons between the Uruguayan and Portuguese trends because of, among other things, the entirely different growth and employment expansion contexts in the two countries between 2008 and 2012. The change in Uruguay's wage coordination mechanisms in 2005 moved the country toward wage egalitarianism. It is also clear that in Uruguay and Chile, which had comparable growth and employment expansion contexts, the trends diverge.

Overall, Figure 1.3 is consistent with the idea that the level of wage coordination has implications for the capacity of the Left to effectively promote distribution. As Cusack and Beramendi (2009) find, while left-wing governments in any wage coordination situation retain their capacity to reduce inequality through redistribution, their leverage to affect inequality of disposable income varies with the form of wage coordination. This leverage is more limited in cases of decentralized wage coordination, as shown in the figure for the case of Chile. Also consistent with Chile's experience under the Lagos and Bachelet administrations, minimum wages become the tool to compress the wage distribution (Rueda 2008).

Finally, a comparison of the relationship between unemployment and wage egalitarianism presents a mixed picture (Figure 1.4). In Chile and Uruguay, wage egalitarianism improved in the context of high employment expansion. Unemployment rates fell during the commodity boom. In Portugal, the upward trend in wage egalitarianism coincided with a gradual but steady increase in unemployment that peaked in response to the Sovereign Debt crisis. These schematic pictures suggest that, while unemployment is linked to economic cycles, wage egalitarianism – not real wages but the structure of wages – is a long-term political construction.

The preceding analysis maps divergence in the use of wage policy and, most importantly, in using wage policy as an instrument for predistribution. This divergence occurred under the dominance of neoliberal rhetoric that strongly advocated subordinating equality-enhancing policies to the goal of preserving incentives for market competition. As explained above, this view derives from a conception of unemployment as a supply-side problem demanding active labor policies and changes in labor-market arrangements.[18] This divergence is conceptualized in the following section, which describes three meaningfully different distributive strategies.

---

[18] See Hall (2002) for a detailed analysis of changes such as unemployment problems and third wayism. See Mudge (2018) for a comprehensive analysis of neoliberal rhetoric toward wage egalitarianism.

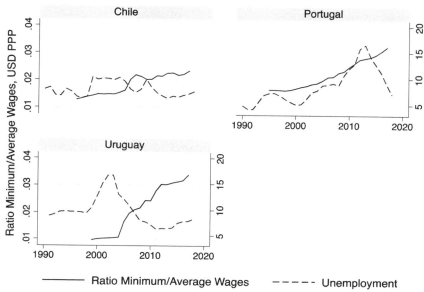

FIGURE 1.4 Unemployment and ratios of minimum-to-average wages (1990–2017).
Sources: World Development Indicators (World Bank 2020); Income Distribution Database (OECD 2020); Data on salaries and prices, Uruguay (INE 2020).

1.4 THE USE OF WAGE POLICY
IN DISTRIBUTIVE STRATEGIES

Governments with a distributive zeal can combine redistributive policies and wage policies in at least three different types of strategies. As analyzed in this work, these strategies do not consider the level of expenditure in social and wage policy as it is considered endogenous to the kind of strategy a leftist government has chosen to pursue. In the long run, I assume that leftist governments spend as much as possible on redistributive policies. They do so within the constraints of their macroeconomic plans and their interpretation of how the perceived tradeoff between job creation and wage egalitarianism constrains those plans. The divergence among the three strategies is a consequence, as shown schematically in Table 1.1, of the elements of wage policy incorporated into each strategy: minimum wages, decentralized or centralized wage settings, and the mandatory character of wage coordination.

In the context of the two regions studied here, *centralized wage settings* denote centralization to the sector or industry level. There are no cases of peak-level bargaining. Industry- or sector-level centralization is sometimes referred to in the literature as a *semi-centralized* or *semi-decentralized* system. Such systems are also positioned around the middle of Calmfor's and Driffill's (1988, 15) proposed hump-shaped distribution that relates wage-setting centralization and wage levels (Calmfors and Driffill 1988, 15; Iversen 1999, 26–28).

Similarly, in the context of the two regions, the mandatory character of wage coordination refers to the extent to which, in a context in which social partners are legally mandated to periodically coordinate wages, there is compulsory *ad hoc* arbitration when the social partners are unable to reach an agreement. This conceptualization of mandatory wage coordination draws from Traxler et al.'s (2001) important conceptualization of voluntary and non-voluntary modes of coordination.[19] The evolution in wage coordination that has occurred during the last 25 years requires a new conceptualization of the categories in the important distinction regarding the role of the state in wage coordination. However, under compulsory arbitration, unlike any other form of state intervention, "the state acts as a sovereign power" (Traxler et al. 2001, 162). Therefore, the presence of compulsory arbitration in a context of legally-mandated periodic bargaining rounds makes wage coordination mandatory. This is the case in Uruguay, where ad hoc compulsory arbitration occurs as a supplementary measure when a deadlock is reached between the social partners during bargaining rounds.

The category of voluntary (or non-mandatory) wage coordination I adopt follows Traxler et al. (2001). The authors propose that voluntary coordination, in contrast to non-voluntary, may take a wide range of forms ranging from tripartite modes in which the state sponsors coordination but does not force arbitration of any kind, to bipartite arrangements in which the state may have a conciliatory role, to simple non-coordination (as is the case in Chile).[20]

---

[19] Traxler et al. (2001) distinguish between non-voluntary and voluntary modes of wage coordination. Non-voluntary coordination occurs under state-imposed regulation, which is present when one of the following three conditions is met in wage coordination in the private sector: unilateral state regulation, regular arbitration by the state, or ad-hoc arbitration. Most countries had abandoned these provisions by the mid-1980s (most notably in New Zealand, the Netherlands and Canada) and 1990s (Belgium), or 2000 (Norway, Australia, or Denmark). However, arbitration in Denmark or Norway includes provisions for ad hoc arbitration by the Minister of Labor (Norway) or legislation (Denmark) that the literature classifies as compulsory supplementary measures to make non-complying firms comply with the accords.

[20] Traxler et al. (2001) consider the following as categories of voluntary coordination or bargaining modes: inter-associational coordination, intra-associational coordination,

In this book, the conceptualization of the mandatory character of wage coordination is kept binary, distinguishing between mandatory and voluntary coordination. Following Traxler et al., this conceptual distinction applies only to the macro coordination of wages and does not consider the following instances of non-voluntary imposition of wage policy explicitly cited by the authors (2001, 167): (1) minimum wage legislation, because it lacks coordinating effects on bargaining; because of this, the book refers to the use of wage policy other than setting minimum wages; (2) provisions supporting collective bargaining, such as one finds in Portugal with statutory extensions of agreements (*portarias de extensão*). The latter had important implications for the development of distributive strategies for Portuguese leftist governments.

Overall, the mandatory or voluntary character of wage coordination would have important implications for the political empowerment of labor. A such, it would be an important issue for the analysis of wage policy and, for our case studies, an important issue for the wage policy debate in Portugal and Uruguay, as analyzed in Chapter 5.

Left Liberalism

A *Left-liberal* strategy oriented to alter market outcomes via redistributive policies – also sometimes labeled as *third wayism* (Mudge 2018, xiv) – is consistent with a decentralized wage policy. It privileges competition over coordination. Distribution occurs mainly based on market competition and governments only use social policy to alter market allocations of wealth and risks. While governments may still use minimum-wage policy, labor union density in these contexts tends to fall as unions fail to be effective vehicles for political influence (Beramendi and Cusack 2009; Rueda 2008). Such has been the case of the Chilean Concertación governments.

Left-liberalism benefits from labor movements that lack market power and are politically delegitimized, because it faces less pressure to incorporate wage policy as a pre-distributive instrument. The sole use of redistributive policies minimizes the intra-Left conflict between the amalgamation of demands from subordinate groups and macroeconomic

---

state-sponsored coordination, pattern bargaining and non-coordination. While this categorization exceeds the scope of this book and its argument, it is important to note that the authors concede the categories are not exclusive. For this reason, among others, the authors mostly worked with the bivariate distinction between voluntary and non-voluntary, and mostly for descriptive purposes (2001, 166).

policy. It also grants governments more latitude to quickly adjust budgetary expenditure to growth expectations at the cost of expenditure levels or more efficient budget allocation. That is not to say Left-liberalism does not confront budgetary pressures from insiders, but decentralized firm-level wage coordination allows for greater control over those pressures, at least in the private sector, and precludes the empowerment of subordinate groups.

Left-liberal distributive strategies appear, in this context, when corporatist policies give way to pluralist labor markets – as in Chile – where labor unions are legally free to organize, bargain collectively, and agitate politically but enjoy minimal legitimacy. Left-liberalism usually arises from a broken relationship between leftist parties and labor, wherein the former usually exclude labor from the political arena. Perhaps an iconic example is the British Labor Party, which reconstructed itself during the mid-1990s by seeking, for electoral and representational purposes, to build a coalition centered on the middle class, distancing itself from its long-term ally, the *Trades Union Congress* (TUC) (McIlroy 1998; Mudge 2018). Mudge even argues that there has been an Anglo-American transnationalization of third-wayism (2018, 330). This broken relationship is usually a consequence of deep economic crisis, such as that experienced in New Zealand, in the above-mentioned British case, or even in Chile.

As in the British and Chilean examples, the break-up between the political Left (or part of it) and organized labor occurred after strong labor repression during processes of deep reformism under the auspices of neoliberalism during the dual transition (Edwards 2022; Etchemendy 2008; Pierson 1994). Labor political participation after the dual transition may even be constrained by law, as it is the UK, many US states, New Zealand, and Chile (Carnes 2015; Crouch 1993; Huber and Stephens 2001). In Chile, for example, the right to strike and protection of strikers are legally limited, while employers do not face significant legal constraints (Bogliaccini 2020; Cook 2007).

State-Led Concertationism

Concertationist and *neocorporatist policymaking* (see below) strategies are plausible only when labor is considered a legitimate political actor – a necessary but insufficient condition. These two distributive strategies are oriented to alter market outcomes by using wage and social policies. However, they differ in their use of wage policy, depending on how governments believe organized labor will respond to the potential problem of wage militancy in the context of economic restrictions. This is so because any coordination-based equilibrium requires the cultivation of minimum levels of cooperation. The perceived tradeoff, in these cases, is understood as a political severity to be resolved. In other words, the possibility of coalitional politics, which is absent under *state-led concertationism*, is a necessary condition for the development of *neocorporatist policymaking*.

The concept of social concertation is widely used in Europe as a counterpoint to coalitional politics. Afonso (2013) states that party considerations on the part of governments drive concertation. Cooperation can be a long-term arrangement or ad hoc but requires minimum linkages between labor and party leaders. While these linkages do not constitute coalitions per se, they facilitate informal bargaining and improve communication channels. Amable (2016), for example, finds the relationship between governments and their social partners to be the most important factor for understanding the different labor reform strategies used by leftist and right-wing governments in France. French leftist governments opted not to pursue a decentralizing labor reform because their political base would not have accepted legal reforms that made it easier for employers to fire workers. Fishman (2011, 2019) illustrates the importance of cooperation for democratic practice over the long run by analyzing the Portuguese and Spanish democratic transitions. Overall, concertationism and neocorporatist policymaking provide the moderate Left with the necessary confidence, by different means, to use wage policy – beyond minimum wage policy – as a pre-distributive instrument. This confidence is based on the expectation that the leftist government in a given country could use wage policy instruments (other than setting a minimum wage) without imposing significant risks to its macroeconomic management of the employment-salary tradeoff.

Under *State-led Concertation*, leftist governments address the perceived tradeoff between job creation and wage egalitarianism by binding labor's political power within institutions and rules. Institutions are the boundaries that define the available space for the political game. A system of industrial relations is a system of rules, and collective wage bargaining has significant effects on production costs (Hayman 1975).

Social concertation specifically implies that governments formally share power with non-elected actors in institutionalized settings. Therefore, the political empowerment of organized labor is institutionally bounded. As an alternative to coalitional politics, social concertation may become preferable in conflictive contexts or to advance reforms concerning contested issues. Chile and Portugal (see below) illustrate this point. Democratic governments with the power to decide institutional settings act by combining long-term policy goals and short-term goals related to the satisfaction of their electoral constituencies (Garrett and Lange 1995; Iversen 1999; Przeworski and Wallerstein 1982).

Governments share their policymaking prerogatives with unions and employers by formally institutionalizing a bargaining table (Baccaro and Simoni 2008, 1325). In Portugal, corporatist institutions – such as the CPCS – and the government's ability to administratively extend collective bargaining accords over entire sectors – extension ordinance or *portarias de extensão* in Portuguese – became mechanisms for channeling labor or employers' demands while controlling the relevant policy agenda. Institutions like these have proved beneficial for sustained cooperation between organized employers and labor.

In the Portuguese case, decisions over wage policy have been debated and agreed upon within the CPCS since the mid-1980s (Avdagic et al. 2011). Under such conditions, leftist governments have used wage policy alongside redistributive policies. During the last three decades, the Portuguese Socialist Party, ruling through a majority or minority government, has set minimum wages, usually backed by a social concertation agreement, and has used the extension ordinance (Baer and Leite 1992; Hijzen and Martins 2016). This use of wage policy protects competition by binding coordination.

Neocorporatist Policymaking

A *neocorporatist policymaking* distributive strategy uses mandatory and centralized wage bargaining policy alongside redistributive policies.[21]

---

[21] Neocorporatist policymaking is a form of wage policy, an institutionalized practice. Neocorporatism as a form of interest representation (Schmitter 1974) refers to the structural aspect of neocorporatism (Streek and Kenworthy 2005). There have been important contributions to understanding this aspect of the proposed new surge of neocorporatism in the Southern Cone (Etchemendy 2001, 2008; Etchemendy and Collier 2007; Schipani 2019) and the resurgence of party-union relationships in Argentina and Uruguay. Neocorporatist policymaking, which entails the political coordination between interest associations and the state, refers to the functional aspect of the notion of neocorporatism (Fligstein et al. 1982; Streek and Kenworthy 2005). Only a few recent works have focused on this second dimension of the concept in the Latin American context

It requires collective interests to be centralized and broadly based instead of specialized and fragmented (see Streek and Kenworthy 2005). In neo-corporatist policymaking, the role of governments in negotiating cooperation among employers and workers is critical as varying degrees of class animosity may surface during bargaining rounds in which wage restraint is necessary (Marks 1986a, 253). This is particularly important in the Southern Cone and Southern Europe, where cooperation between labor and employers has not been the rule.

Under this strategy, governments share decisional authority, and labor agrees to take on part of the burden of responsibility for public policy performance, risking membership dissatisfaction and dealing with potential wage militancy. This power-sharing is only feasible when no relevant divisions exist within the Left and labor is a legitimate actor in the political arena. This sharing of decision authority in neocorporatist policymaking is a distinctive feature of this strategy in relation to state-led concertationism, where government retains the exclusive initiative for policymaking and the institutions within which concertation occurs are solely consultative.

In addition to the political legitimacy requirement, there should be no divisions within the labor movement. This is particularly important when wage restraint is necessary and dissident unions have the opportunity to be free riders (Marks 1986a, 264). The degree of labor unity also signals to governments with a distributive zeal whether to engage in neocorporatist policymaking, institutionalized concertation, or to simply follow a Left-liberal strategy. Neocorporatist policymaking requires the practice of coalition politics and usually relies on solid party-labor coalitions, as was the case in Uruguay under the Frente Amplio governments. A coalition between the FA governments and labor (*Plenario Intersindical de Trabajadores – Central Nacional de Trabajadores*; PIT-CNT) made it possible to craft a distributive strategy grounded in semi-centralized and mandatory collective wage coordination and the use of minimum-wage policy alongside redistributive policies.

(Bogliaccini 2012; Etchemendy 2008, 2019; Etchemendy and Collier 2007; Schipani 2019). The present work contributes to this line of research, as a first effort to compare neocorporatism with other distributive strategies.

2

Elite Strategies toward Labor,
Left Unity, and Wage Policy

The Left Bloc and the Communist Party do not sit together. We negotiate with the Communist Party, and then we go and negotiate with the Left Bloc. It is because when we formed the government, it was a separate negotiation. The other part, I think it is because the Communist Party and the Left Bloc are not the best friends. Furthermore, the Communist Party preserves this kind of relationship with the Socialist Party. (...) The Communist Party is like every Communist Party, without much linkage to other parties. I think we never had a socialist delegation in their headquarters as we had three years ago. (...) However, I do not think it is possible to have a very strong sense of "we will be together until the end." It will not be good for the Left. I think that is the consensus among us [Socialists]. So that is fine, because everyone is keeping their promises. They vote against us many times. We know that, too.

(Senior official at the Prime Minister's Office,
personal interview held in Lisbon, January 2019).

This chapter presents the book's central argument about how long-term elite strategies toward the empowered inclusion of labor and the short-term (dis)unity of the Left shape leftist governments' use of wage policy, shaping their distributive strategies. We know little about the conditions under which different uses of wage policy are plausible for leftist governments outside advanced capitalist democracies. The overall framework of the present work connects the classic electoral trade-off that democratic socialism faces, masterfully depicted by Przeworski and Sprague (1988), with two other relevant literatures to analyze the political economy of the distributive conflict. The first of these literatures is the scholarship on the political hardships in advanced industrial democracies arising from the relationship between wages and macroeconomic equilibria.[1] As a consequence of the transition away from Keynesian economics, leftist governments in Latin America and Southern Europe also confronted a potential tradeoff between wage-egalitarianism and employment. The second literature encompasses the scholarship on power resources theory, which long ago pointed to the importance of understanding power constellations for developing welfare states and models of capitalism.[2]

At the dawn of the 21st century, numerous scholars proposed that the most crucial distributional cleavage for post-industrial democracies was that which separated those countries supporting market allocations of wealth and risk from those favoring government efforts to alter market allocations.[3] European-centered scholars have focused on issues such as social pacts and corporatism.[4] Compared to scholarship focused on Latin America, this literature has explored more fully the issue of intra-Left differences or conflicts related to welfare capitalism.[5]

My argument is twofold. First, I propose that present constellations of power are deeply rooted in long-term historical struggles by subordinate groups, mainly organized labor, to gain political participation and, ultimately, to be recognized as legitimate political actors. Against the backdrop of weak institutionalization and regime instability in the two regions under study here, the evidence I will present strongly suggests that long-term elite strategies toward the empowered inclusion of labor are resilient and vigorously shape present power constellations. In a recently published book, Ondetti (2021) advances a related

---

[1] Some seminal works in this literature exploring different aspects of the relationship between wages and macroeconomics are Calmfors and Driffill (1988), Iversen (1999), Iversen and Soskice (2006), Iversen and Wren (1998), Pontusson (2018), Pontusson and Swenson (1996), Rueda and Pontusson (2000), Soskice (2008), and Soskice and Iversen (2000).

[2] Some seminal works on this literature exploring the role power constellations have played in shaping distributive outcomes are Bradley et al. (2003), Esping-Andersen (1990), Esping-Andersen and Korpi (1986), Huber and Stephens (2001), Korpi (1978), Korpi and Palme (2003), and Stephens (1979).

[3] See, among this literature, Garret (1998), Iversen and Wren (1998), and Hall and Soskice (2001).

[4] For example, see Afonso (2013), Avdagic (2010), Avdagic et al. (2011), Baccaro and Simoni (2008), and Pochet and Fajertag (2000).

[5] See Fleckenstein and Lee (2017), Korpi and Palme (2003), Rueda (2007), and Watson (2015). Although this discussion has not been central to the debate in Latin America, Pribble (2013) raises the issue for the analysis of social policy advancement, while Luna (2014) puts forward a related discussion of the idea of segmented representation that acknowledges the possibility for intra-party disputes over policy issues.

argument in analyzing the long-term causes of variation in taxation levels among Latin American countries, finding that historical large-scale redistributive processes – in particular those that threaten property – produced a long-lasting political effect on future opportunities for widening tax bases.

Second, I argue that intra-Left relations shaped post-dual transition leftist governments' efforts to include wage policy – beyond setting minimum wages – as a pre-distributive instrument in the service of implementing their distributive strategies. Intra-Left relations are essential because of the consequences of strengthening labor's political power, which comes with mandatory centralized wage-setting mechanisms. Intra-Left relations – particularly intra-bloc levels of unity and coherence – consolidated in the context of the dual transition. As Watson (2015, 32) proposed, the Left in Latin America and Southern Europe is not a unitary actor in many instances, which differs from the experience in northern European social democracies. Unions and leftist parties, in such instances, do not necessarily share common goals, strategies, and may not be inclined to coordinate strategies.

Leftist governments' preferences regarding wage policy have become stable. An ideational struggle between the neoliberal and PKE rhetoric anchors such preferences. This ideational conflict, which is associated with how leftist parties perceive the range of political alternatives available to address the proposed wage-employment tradeoff, anchors long-term elite strategies toward labor and the unity of the Left to the use of the wage policy as a pre-distributive instrument. In other words, the range of options leftist governments perceive to be available to them to manage the tradeoff is strongly affected by both long- and short-term factors. The three countries I focus on offer the opportunity to trace the development of three different leftist government distributive strategies based on the differential use of wage policy as a pre-distributive instrument. Recent influential works have pointed to this ideational factor as an important issue for understanding the evolution of the Left in Western countries. Mudge (2018), in analyzing the ideological evolution of social democratic parties in Sweden and Germany, the British Labor party and the Democratic party in the United States, suggests a convergence of the four cases toward an economistic leftism, which she terms the "neoliberalization" of the Left. Scholars have vigorously debated the robustness of the "neoliberal" convergence hypothesis in Europe before the Great Recession and the role of globalization in diminishing policy preferences within

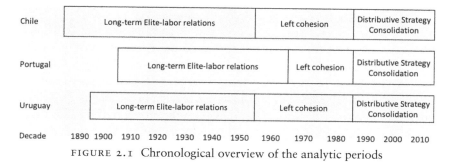

FIGURE 2.1 Chronological overview of the analytic periods

the Left. Bremer (2018, 2023) finds that, while social democratic parties in Europe shifted to the left with regards to redistribution but reinforced their commitment for budgetary rigor and austerity, there is also evidence for the argument that European social democratic parties reacted to the Great Recession by reversing the neoliberal convergence scholars had previously observed.

The periods relevant for analyzing the different building blocks of the argument in the different cases may overlap. For the sake of rigorously determining the relevant periods in each case and to build the comparative story, Figure 2.1 offers a schematic organization of periods by country. Dominant elite strategies toward the empowered inclusion of labor in Chile and Uruguay began to form at the turn of the 20th century with the end of each country's civil war. In Chile, the civil war ended in 1891 and in Uruguay it ended in 1904. In Portugal, this period begins with the birth of the First Republic in 1911. However, given the turbulent decades that followed and the increasing hostility toward labor during the transition from the First Republic to the Estado Novo, dominant elite strategies consolidated only after 1933.

The decline in the dominance of these elite strategies become evident during the second part of the 20th century. In Chile, the analysis identifies a turning point at the first of several important vote franchise extensions in 1958. In Uruguay, 1958 witnessed the electoral victory of the conservative National Party for the first time in 93 years, signaling the beginning of the demise of a pro-labor coalition that dominated national politics between 1904 and 1958. In Portugal, the replacement of long-term Estado Novo corporatist dictator Salazar by his successor, Caetano, as Prime Minister in 1968 triggered a set of reforms that allowed for higher levels of political mobilization. The Carnation Revolution in 1974 put an abrupt end to the Estado Novo.

Concomitantly with the decline in the dominance of the abovementioned elite strategies, leftist parties became electorally stronger. In Chile, this occurred after the Socialist and Communist parties moved away from collaboration with centrist parties, forming the Unidad Popular alliance that won an electoral victory in 1970. In Uruguay, a gradual process of political interest centralization occurred in parallel in the labor movement and the political Left, ending with the creation of the National Workers Convention (CNT – *Convención Nacional de Trabajadores*) in 1966 and the Frente Amplio in 1971. In Portugal, the Communist and the newly created Socialist parties became central political actors in the post-revolutionary years, while labor gained autonomy during the period. In the years after the revolution, two competing labor centrals consolidated: the General Confederation of Portuguese Workers (*Confederação Geral dos Trabalhadores Portugueses* – CGTP) and the General Union of Workers (*União Geral dos Trabalhadores* – UGT).

In Chile, the dual transition period began with the abrupt turn toward liberalizing the economy during the military regime and ended with the transition to democracy in 1990. In Uruguay, it began with the economic liberalization plan of 1974 and ended with the transition to democracy of 1985. In Portugal, the period began with the Carnation Revolution of 1974 and ended with the country's 1986 accession to the European Community and the reform of the Constitution. The 1989 Constitution opened the door to re-privatization.

2.1 LONG-TERM ELITE STRATEGIES AND THE EMPOWERED INCLUSION OF LABOR

The first building block entails analyzing long-term elite strategies toward labor. Considering the large-scale relations between elites and organized labor is essential precisely because each society builds its own inclusionary patterns over the long run, which, I argue, may inform present-day power-sharing dynamics. Power is a structural phenomenon that determines the form and substance of systems or ecologies of interaction (Stinchcombe 1968, 149–55). Power relations evolve in time. Theoretically, the structuring of political, social, and economic orders is done, over the long haul, by institutionalizing values and concentrating power in the hands of those groups that believe in those values (Stinchcombe 1968, 107–9). These institutionalized values, through large-scale historical elite strategies toward the empowered inclusion of subordinate groups – in particular, for our purposes, the inclusion of labor – tend to generate cultural legacies (Fishman 2019, 1) and systems of domination (O'Donnell 1988, 24–28; Rueschemeyer et al. 1992, 57–62).

This path-dependent process whereby long-lasting elite strategies strengthen cultural legacies by institutionalizing values is put in tension by the processes of legitimizing new groups, such as labor.[6] O'Donnell (1988, 24–27) proposed that expanding inclusion to previously subordinate groups can erode those values and generate tensions between newly empowered actors and established elites, provoking a crisis of social domination. In such circumstances, as proposed by Rueschemeyer, Stephens, and Stephens (1992), expanding political inclusion and, thus, risking the destabilization of the underlying pact of domination may trigger opposition from those actors who stand to lose privileges and influence. In other words, political stability tends to be at stake during processes of empowered inclusion, producing political tension as the dominant values sustaining the political order of the day are challenged.

Accounting for this large-scale process is important for two reasons: first, because political legitimacy, a complex social system character intimately related to long-lasting elite strategies, is a prerequisite for empowered inclusion; and second, because the fact that elite strategies toward labor, which became dominant in the three countries under study here during the mid-20th century, showed impressive continuity via adaptation to the new democratic and market-oriented context.

Political Practices as Building Blocks of Elite Strategies

To properly dissect these long-term elite strategies and their long-lasting effect on labor's political legitimacy, this book draws on Warren's (2017) theoretical contributions to the field of democratic theory. Although my analysis of long-term elite strategies toward labor does not directly engage with the issue of democratization, or of political legitimacy, these strategies are directly related to the issue of empowered inclusion discussed above. Empowered inclusion, in turn, is defined by Warren as one of the main problems a political system needs to solve if it is to function democratically.[7] Empowered inclusion requires the legitimation of subordinate groups.

---

[6] This framework is also helpful for other societies or other periods, for example, for accounting for incorporation processes of ethnic minority groups, women, or the LGBT community.

[7] Warren (2017, 39) proposes three main problems: how a political system empowers inclusion, forms collective agendas, and wills, and organizes collective decision capacity.

Warren (2017, 45–49) defines several political practices that address empowered inclusion[8], three of which are directly related to the problem of legitimacy, or the degree to which labor organizations are valued for themselves and considered right and proper as political actors (Lipset 1959, 71). These are *recognition, representation,* and *joining.* A fourth political practice, *voting,* becomes relevant in contexts where elections of some sort are allowed. It signals an indirect recognition of the political legitimacy of workers, not as a collective actor but as a political equal to dominant elites. Tolerating *resistance* is still another political practice that serves as an indirect indicator of legitimacy recognition.

Warren (2017, 49) states in accord with Lipset that *recognizing* is the most basic act of inclusion, the first inclusionary moment, as it provides legitimacy to collective bargains and compromises. Recognition, in Warren's work, entails moral inclusion and support for rights and duties of citizenship, in this case, for subordinate groups.

Representing allows constituencies to have a "seat at the table" (Warren 2017, 48). By so doing, in accord with Lipset's definition of legitimacy, representing expands inclusion over space and time. It provides instruments for managing complexity by allowing large groups to bargain through their organizations and representatives.

Joining practices also contribute directly to empowered inclusion and legitimacy by forming constituencies, empowering resistance, or even inducing organizational responsiveness. These political practices allow subordinate groups to decide about representation (Hirschman 1970; Putnam 1994). Associations created by subordinate groups themselves, such as unions, empower these groups to achieve collective purposes. These political practices strengthen the empowering functions of representing and recognizing.

Voting contributes directly to the empowered inclusion of subordinated groups and indirectly to the political legitimacy of labor as a collective actor, allowing citizens and constituencies to elect their representatives from their constituencies and to veto disfavored policies. An example of voting's indirect effect on political recognition is that the practice of representing needs the practice of voting to make representatives accountable.

---

[8] Warren's proposed practices are *recognition,* fostering *deliberation,* tolerating *resistance,* allowing subordinate groups to *vote,* allowing *representation* of subordinate groups, allowing *joining* organizations, and allowing *exiting* organizations.

TABLE 2.1 *Political practices related to the political legitimation of labor.*

Political Practices directly or indirectly related to political legitimation[1]	Strengths of empowered inclusion[1]	Elite dominant response regarding each political practice before the dual transition[2]		
		Chile	Portugal	Uruguay
Recognition	Moral inclusion and support for rights and duties of citizenship	Limited	Unlimited	Unlimited
Representation	Expands inclusion over time and space	Limited	Limited	Unlimited
Joining	Constituency formation and the empowerment of resistance	Unlimited	Limited	Unlimited
Voting	Distributes empowerment	Limited	Limited	Unlimited
Resistance	Incentivizes inclusion	Repressed	Repressed	Tolerated
Elite dominant strategy		Biased Contention	Controlled coordination	Consociationalism

[1] Based on Warren (2017).

[2] Based on the analysis of each case, which is expanded later in the chapter and in Chapters 3 and 4.

Resistance is not a practice carried out by elites but by subordinate groups. As such, it limits or at least undermines the power of elites. As Warren states (2017, 47), "acts of resistance so often lead to eventual inclusions that they stand as a class of practices on their own." Consequently, resistance can be tolerated by elites or repressed. Resistance may or may not lead to the recognition by elites of the political legitimacy of subordinated groups, even in a scenario of toleration.[9] While not inherently related to a principle of legitimacy, in the case of labor and early contexts of democratization, resistance is a practice that is oriented to undermine domination.

Table 2.1 lists these five important political practices that are related, directly or indirectly, to the problem of legitimacy (see above). Thus, for each country, the table provides a qualitative score for each practice which, as shown in the last line of the table, leads to a long-term elite strategy. In the methods section below I explain the scoring and how the analysis of this long-term factor is pursued in the book. The three dominant elite strategies in the three countries are briefly introduced as follows and analyzed in depth in Chapter 3 in light of the five explained political practices.

Dominant Elite Strategies

The notion of *elite-biased contention* builds on Huntington's (1968) idea that, to maintain social and political order in societies with high levels of inequality, powerful elites seek to dominate subordinate groups, effectively inducing them to acquiesce to their rule. Elites either deny subordinate groups inclusion or offer them minimum levels of empowered inclusion in exchange for their acquiescence. The core of such a strategy is to deny or minimize political legitimacy to subordinate groups. This elite strategy may include anti-democratic practices in a democratic context, as was the case in Chile, such as labor repression,

---

[9] Deliberating is defined as "practices that generate influence through the offering and receiving of cognitively compelling reasons about matters of common concern" (Warren 2017, 47). Deliberation implies bargaining and negotiation between collective actors that formed and revealed preferences (Warren et al. 2016). Elites who open the door to deliberation allow the strengthening of subordinate groups' collective agenda and will formation without directly contributing to inclusion or legitimizing collective decisions. The Portuguese case under the Estado Novo corporatism illustrates this distinction. Exiting induces organizational responsiveness. However, whenever the practice of joining is present in our cases, exiting is also present. Therefore, for reasons of parsimony, exiting is not included in the analysis.

disenfranchisement of subordinate group voters, or even handicapping the collective decision capacity of subordinate groups by outlawing their encompassing organizations.

The notion of *controlled coordination* builds on Luebbert's (1987) account of how authoritarian corporatism used state-controlled associations as vehicles to provide benefits and coercion. A critical difference between traditional authoritarian regimes and fascist corporatism – that is, the case of Portugal – concerns the attitude toward political participation. Authoritarian corporatism organizes political participation hierarchically from the top in state-created corporations. This type of political participation did not legitimize labor organizations at the time, which were primarily state-managed puppets. Over the long term, however, political recognition born out of continuous political participation in conditions like those of employers – even under contention – was instrumental in legitimizing labor as a political actor. There is a crucial difference between the legitimation of labor as a political actor and that of labor organizations. Labor legitimacy comes from the fact that labor shared a seat alongside employers in corporatist bodies despite the reduced political freedoms labor enjoyed. This differentiation is key to the argument of this book. The process of continuous bargaining alongside governments and employers, albeit within authoritarian corporatism in Portugal, enhanced the perceived legitimacy of labor as an actor after the dual transition. This is an essential difference with the Chilean case, where labor has been sidelined from the political arena.

The concept of consociationalism builds on Lijphart's (1969) definition of consociational democracies. Such democracies achieve stability, albeit with high levels of social segmentation, by consultation among labor, parties, and employers. This strategy needs political parties to play a central role in taking employers' and labor interests into the political arena. It is also a necessary condition for political elites to recognize labor as a legitimate political actor. Consociational strategies are sustained by informal linkages between party and labor leaders, as occurred in Uruguay, or, more commonly, are institutionalized from the top-down as in post-dual transition Portugal. Consociationalism does not eliminate conflict but provides forums and rules for deliberation and negotiated solutions. There is a large literature on consociationalism in Europe showing that this strategy does not eliminate conflict even in the seemingly peaceful societies of Scandinavia, post-war West Germany, and Austria. In all these cases, social policymaking continued to involve intense conflicts among different groups and classes (see Esping-Andersen and Korpi 1985). In our two regions, however, the strengthening of inward-looking industrialization softened class conflict through strong state subsidization of industrial development.

Elite Strategies' Adaptation after the Dual Transition

Elite strategies toward labor persisted through the dual transition despite intense political and economic turbulence. The core elements of the previous dominant elite strategies toward labor adapted to the post-transitional democratic and open market environments, showing high levels of continuity.[10] Despite the tensions that emerged during the dual transition, previous strategies were adapted to sustain the causal loop by which political elites balanced the empowered inclusion of labor and political stability.

While neither *elite-biased contention*, *controlled coordination*, or *consociationalism* survived the transition as such, post-transitional elite strategies in each of the three cases are meaningfully rooted in these pre-transitional approaches. In other words, previously existing elite strategies are reshaped by present power distributions.

The process of elite strategy adaptation implies that the concrete form specific practices took toward labor political empowerment in the previous period were no longer feasible under the new scenario consisting of economic liberalization in Western societies and democratic consolidation after the so-called Third Wave of democratization in western peripheral societies. For example, voting restrictions based on income or education may not be feasible, but a combination of voluntary voter registration and the imposition of administrative or bureaucratic barriers, as has occurred recently in some states in the United States, may provide this adaptation (Barreto et al. 2009; Keele et al. 2021). The following section describes how some practices adopted in our three cases are examples of the adaptation mechanism at work. The cases are analyzed in depth in Chapters 4 and 5.

In Chile, the passage of laws that limit labor's right to strike or that give employers the right to replace a worker during a strike or to lockout striking workers still hinder labor as a political actor (see Table 2.1). These measures all erode labor's political legitimacy because they severely limit the range within which representation, resistance and bargaining are deemed legitimate political practices.

---

[10] For a seminal work providing a detailed account of the structure of historicist explanations, see Stinchcombe (1968).

More nuanced voting-related mechanisms were also included during the democratic transition, such as a return to non-mandatory voter registration and the introduction of a binomial electoral system.[11] Both measures severely hinder the empowerment of subordinate groups. The literature is overwhelmingly consistent that increasing barriers to voter registration has regressive effects on turnout.[12] Regarding the binomial electoral system, there is also a wide consensus among scholars studying Chile that this system limits the number of parties with parliamentary representation and that it was adopted in order to benefit right-wing parties.[13] Chile switched to voluntary voting in 2012, making voter registration automatic in the same reform, during the first center-right administration (the first Piñera administration, 2010–2014) since the return to democratic rule.

In terms of the political practices presented in Table 2.1, the military and conservative elites crafted the abovementioned legal provisions affecting the practices of voting, resistance, and recognition to hinder the empowered inclusion of subordinate groups and to defend the economic model built under the dictatorship. These legal provisions are evidence of how pre-transition elite strategies have adapted to – and, thus, persist in – the new democratic environment.

In Portugal, the creation of the CPCS allowed governments to balance political stability and empowered inclusion in a context in which both the Left and labor were divided. Institutionalized concertation in post-transitional Portugal is entirely democratic, neither top-down nor deliberately repressive, and has been a prime instrument for carrying out the remarkable expansion of social protection and the country's welfare state under democratic rule. Still, Portugal's experience shows how

---

[11] The binomial voting system is a D'Hondt system that appoints two representatives per district to the Congress. The election of only two candidates in each district results in the second majority list being overrepresented. This system, invented in Poland in 1980, fosters political stability in electoral competition. In Poland and Chile, it was instituted to prevent challenging parties from obtaining large majorities.

[12] For example, Ansolabehere and Konisky (2006) offer an excellently crafted analysis of voter registration effects on voter turnout in the United States. The authors estimate that eliminating registration barriers raises voter participation rates by 10 percent.

[13] The binomial system was established by Law 18.799 of May 1989 and eliminated in April 2015. See Siavelis (1997), Navia and Sandoval (1998), and Polga-Hecimovich and Siavelis (2015) for a complete assessment of the binomial electoral system in Chile. Marambio et al. (2017) provide a detailed account of the relationship between the Concertación and the Communist Party during the period. See, for example, Polga-Hecimovich and Siavelis (2015) for a detailed overlook of the binomial electoral system and its bias.

pre-transitional elite strategies based on the institutionalization of political participation adapted to the new democratic environment.

In a post-transitional democratic context, the widespread recognition of labor as a legitimate political actor is paired with the crafting of institutional instruments by which governments can limit labor's political power. The pre-transition elite strategy of controlled labor political participation facilitated the post-transitional empowerment of labor. Institutions of the pre-transition period – corporatist ones in this case – are a critical factor in the crafting of post-transitional elite strategies.

In Uruguay, pre-transitional consociationalism based on the full recognition of labor and a general disposition for dialogue persisted throughout the transitional period. Center-right democratic administrations during the conflictive period of economic liberalization continually promoted ad hoc dialogue between government officials, employers, and labor. Elites' toleration of resistance during this period, as shown below in Chapter 5, illustrates their commitment toward not reversing the country's heritage of empowered inclusion.

The heritage of consociational politics played a vital role in the post-transitional construction of neocorporatist policymaking. Consociationalism still shapes the relationship between labor, employers, and right-of-center parties. The consolidation of this distributive strategy is also attributable to the willingness of the moderates within the FA to incorporate mandatory, centralized wage coordination as a pre-distributive instrument and to their acceptance of the challenge of maintaining fiscal and monetary orthodoxy under this scenario.

2.2 THE (DIS)UNITY OF THE LEFT AFTER THE DUAL TRANSITION

Power constellations are a vital factor for understanding the differential development of welfare states and models of capitalism. A rich scholarship on power resources has consistently pointed out the importance of leftist parties and labor unions in developing social welfare instruments in exchange for a strategic orientation toward wage restraint (Esping-Andersen and Korpi 1985; Korpi 1978; Stephens 1979). Against the backdrop of this tradition, Watson (2015) proposes that the mutually beneficial relationship between leftist parties, which has been documented primarily in scholarship that focuses on northern European social democracies, does not necessarily hold in other regions of the developing world. In comparing Portugal and Spain, Watson proposes that actors within the leftist bloc may not all have overlapping or compatible goals and may not be willing to behave strategically to achieve collective goals (2015, 32). This idea of the Left (or the Right) having coordination problems, advanced by Watson in studying Iberia, becomes relevant for the analysis of the short-term factors explaining the use of wage policy as a pre-distributive instrument. In other words, the argument regarding the importance of the unity of the Left for how leftist governments shape their wage policies builds on Watson's proposition that divisions among the Left importantly influence whether social democracy is economically and politically functional for the Left. As previously explained concerning whether to consider employers strategic actors (following Thelen) or prestrategic actors (following Soskice), a consistent assumption is made for labor and, most importantly, parties. I assume parties in government act strategically in their design of distributive strategies, the use of pre-distributive instruments and the use of wage policy.

Leftist unity, a second factor for explaining wage policy use, took shape during this period. As was the case in Chile, Portugal, and Uruguay, political regimes nurtured in a context of strong protectionism suffered greatly under these transitions. The transition toward open-market capitalism took different forms. Globalization fostered deindustrialization and an abrupt change from highly regulated schemes to deregulated industrial relations. The reshaping of taxation, industrial relations, and welfare schemes took different forms, from gradual layering to radical displacement.[14] In the three analyzed cases, however, wage coordination became voluntary during this liberalization period, and in Chile and Uruguay it became completely decentralized. Therefore, when analyzing leftist governments' decisions about whether and how to incorporate wage policy as a pre-distributive instrument, it is important to understand the policy status quo in each case and to ponder the relative importance of party-labor relations to intra-Left relations as a plausible causal mechanism. Leftist governments after the dual transition had to move policy from voluntary to mandatory or from decentralized to centralized wage policy.

Party preferences over wage policy, once formed, are usually stable. In general, while governments willing to favor firms in the exposed

---

[14] See Mahoney and Thelen (2009) for a conceptualization of institutional change. See Etchemendy (2011) for a detailed account of liberalization processes and the role the state, employers, and labor played in them in our two regions.

sectors prefer decentralized wage coordination, governments concerned with unemployment and wage equality – usually left-wing ones – prefer mandatory wage coordination centralization, as explained in Chapter 1 (see Iversen 1999, 103). The use of wage policy as an instrument for pre-distribution is closely related to the relationship between center-left parties and far-left labor-mobilizing parties or factions. In other words, the unity of the Left would affect how leftist governments approach using wage policy as a pre-distributive instrument.

The rationale for this claim is that leftist governments that cannot moderate labor activism or even far-left parties' activism – particularly wage militancy – would not risk moving away from the status quo toward mandatory or centralized wage-setting mechanisms that would increase the political power of labor. These governments may use the instrument of minimum wages but would rely almost exclusively on redistributive instruments.

The proposed relevance of intra-Left unity for understanding the use of wage policy is not equivalent to denying the importance of Left-labor or intra-labor relations for coalitional politics or labor policy in particular, as the literature analyzing Latin America has largely proposed (Cook 2007; Etchemendy 2019; Murillo 2001). In the nascent service economy scenario, Left-labor relations became an important factor influencing leftist governments' willingness to risk governability in favor of advancing labor policy or even wage policies oriented toward greater wage equality. Similarly, intra-union rivalries are also an important factor, informing leftist governments about the potential benefits and challenges of alternative distributive strategies (Watson 2015). However, the sparse literature on the use of wage coordination mechanisms in the aftermath of the liberalization period, during the "left turn," has analyzed either the cases of Argentina and Uruguay, where no significant far-left party challenged leftist governments and there is diversity in terms of intra-labor relations (Etchemendy 2019), or have focused on the case of Chile in the absence of a comparative lens (Bogliaccini 2020; Pérez Ahumada 2021).

This book, in analyzing three cases for which there is variation in terms of Left unity, labor unity or Left-labor relations, and under the assumption that parties and unions act strategically in a context of liberal wage policy status quo, proposes that relations between leftist parties supersedes the other two possible sources of conflict within the left-wing bloc, those between parties and unions and intra-union rivalries. Parties are the primary vehicle for politically representing societal demands. Labor-mobilizing parties develop strong linkages with unions.

TABLE 2.2 *The structure of Left (dis)unity.*

		Left-Bloc Organization	
		Moderately Strong Far-Left Party	Dominant Center-Left Party
Electoral Arena	United left front	(I) Chile under Unidad Popular (1969–1973)	(II) Uruguay under Frente Amplio (1969–present)
	Divided left front	(III) Portugal (1974–present)	(IV) Chile under Concertación (1990–2010)

In contrast, non-mobilizing parties tend to have weak organic relations with labor, albeit sometimes party and labor leaders still have strong coordination capacity. While parties have to accommodate broad societal interests, unions represent the narrower interests of their membership. Unions may be unwilling to subordinate their specific interests to coordinate their political action with parties.

In this sense, when conflicts between labor unions occur over political issues, these conflicts tend to be strongly related to conflicts between political parties. The Portuguese case illustrates such a situation. When conflicts between parties and unions occur in the political arena, it often reflects a conflict between labor-mobilizing and non-labor-mobilizing parties. The Chilean case after the dual transition also illustrates this situation, as explained below. Therefore, these two sources of conflict are secondary to the rivalry between leftist parties in the electoral arena. The analysis in Chapters 4 and 5 examines party-union conflicts and intra-union conflicts to understand leftist government decisions regarding the inclusion of wage policy in the government's distributive strategy.

The book analyzes the (dis)unity of the Left in terms of two dimensions, as depicted in Table 2.2: How the Left bloc organizes itself and how it participates in the electoral arena. Distinguishing these two aspects in the description of the left-wing political camp helps us to understand cooperative or competitive dynamics. To privilege conceptual consistency regarding distance from the ideological center, in analyzing the organization of the left-wing political block the analysis differentiates between far-left and center-left parties. In addition, the two categories depicted in Table 2.2 regarding left-bloc organization concern whether the center-left party is dominant or coexists with a moderately strong challenger from the far Left. The second dimension in Table 2.2 shows how actors on the Left enter the electoral arena, that is, how the Left organizes itself for electoral purposes. Meaningful variation occurs when multiple electorally relevant parties exist on the Left, as they can cooperate to present a united left-wing front or compete by presenting a divided front.

Table 2.2 provides the scoring for each case for this second factor, which is described and justified below. The three countries under study here provide enough variation to fill the four quadrants. For different reasons, leftist parties in each of these countries gained political relevance at the dawn of or during the dual transition. In Portugal, the Socialist Party was founded right before the democratic transition, while the Communist Party became a central actor during that period. In Chile, both the Socialist and Communist parties allied in the Unidad Popular coalition and with other minor parties by the 1960s. However, this coalition did not survive the dual transition. In Uruguay, the Socialist and Communist parties formed the Frente Amplio alongside other minor parties and groups in 1968. While the Portuguese and Uruguayan cases exhibit temporal continuity, the Chilean case evolved from quadrant I to quadrant IV during the periods analyzed here.

Leftist parties in the Southern Cone and Southern Europe, growing in electoral strength at the dawn of the dual transition, entered the political scene in a context of high economic and political uncertainty. As noted above, left-wing labor-mobilizing parties, mostly Communist and Socialist ones, gradually became central political actors in a context in which political instability led to regime changes in all three countries by the early 1970s.

Regime change, however, occurred in different directions. While Portugal inaugurated the third democratization wave in 1974, Chile and Uruguay experienced democratic breakdowns in 1973. Both breakdowns were followed by long periods of authoritarianism under military-led Bureaucratic Authoritarian regimes (Huntington 1991; O'Donnell 1996). Uruguay joined the third democratic wave by 1985 and Chile did so in 1990.

The harsh political conflict around the dual transition, which included radical regime changes in Chile, Portugal, and Uruguay, affected the unity of the Left in the decades to follow, particularly the relationship between Communist and Socialist parties. This unity or disunity would also affect Left-labor relations for decades. Disunity may entail a process of weakening party-societal linkages or of forming two or more camps where at least one of them continues to be labor-mobilizing. The former scenario occurred in Chile while the latter occurred in Portugal.

The unity of the Left during this period was affected by strong political divides within leftist parties over political strategy. Attitudes toward democracy and open capitalism varied greatly across the three cases and within the left-wing bloc in the Portuguese case. In Chile, the Unidad Popular government (1970–1973) attempted to move the economic model toward socialism while maintaining a democratic regime. This bold strategy, paired with the intense repression that followed from the military regime, decisively affected the unity of the leftist camp.

The divide between the Portuguese Communist Party (PCP), which sided with the radical sectors within the Armed Forces Movement (MFA – *Movimento das Forças Armadas*) and the Socialist Party (PSP), which sided with the moderate sectors in the MFA regarding the direction of the political transition also illustrates this divide (Costa Pinto 2008; Fernandes and Branco 2017). It has been argued that the 1976 Constitution was committed to constructing a socialist economy (Brito and Carreira da Silva 2010). Once again, a bold move on the part of the Communist party in the political and economic arenas ended up creating a lasting division between itself and the more centrist and electoral-oriented Socialist Party.

In Uruguay, by contrast, leftist parties and labor organizations remained within the democratic camp by not officially supporting Tupamaro's violent guerrilla action (1967–1972).[15] The cooperative mood that prevailed between Socialists and Communists and between them and the other minor parties and groups that created the Frente Amplio remained intact during the dual transition. The Frente Amplio became a major political actor after the country's return to democracy, gradually displacing the Colorado Party from the electoral arena.

Repression of leftist politicians and party activists, in turn, affected the unity of the Left differently in different countries. While in Uruguay, repression helped strengthen the Frente Amplio, it aggravated political divisions within the Left in Chile and Portugal.

Outcomes regarding the unity of the Left varied from case to case. In Uruguay, the Socialist and Communist parties remained united

---

[15] While individual politicians and labor leaders did join the Tupamaros, neither the Frente Amplio nor the PIT-CNT backed the guerrilla. After democratic restoration, ex-Tupamaros did join the Frente Amplio. A prime example, though not the only one, is ex-president José Mujica (2010–2014).

under the umbrella of the Frente Amplio (FA), which allowed the FA to become a labor-mobilizing actor in the post-transition period (Roberts 2013). In Chile, the Left changed during the dual transition from being united under the Unidad Popular and having a high labor-mobilizing capacity to being fragmented after democratic restoration. In this latter period, the Chilean Left remained divided. The Communist Party was unable to gain parliamentary representation until 2009, and a socially unrooted Concertación coalition governed for 20 straight years from 1990 to 2010 (see Luna and Altman 2011; Roberts 2007). In Portugal, the division between the Socialist and Communist parties marginalized the Communist party (see Bosco 2001; Morlino 1986).[16] The Portuguese Communist Party nevertheless remained electorally strong compared with other Communist parties in Europe and Latin America and remained closely allied with the country's main labor confederation, the CGTP. The Socialist Party also maintained a fluid relationship with the country's other labor confederation, the UGT.

2.3 LIBERAL CONVERGENCE AS AN ALTERNATIVE HYPOTHESIS

The liberal convergence hypothesis that became dominant throughout the West during and after the dual-transition rested on the idea that market forces, particularly financial markets, were beyond political control and that leftist parties should accept this premise (Hall 2002; Mudge 2018). This idea entailed assuming that traditional national policies, such as labor or tax policies, or even health or education, would gradually converge and grow more similar (Drezner 2001; Kerr 1983). At the end of the 20th century, the increased ability of ideas to permeate across borders together with the erosion of capital controls in an increasingly globalized world lent support to the idea that global market forces would diminish national policy autonomy. However, claims regarding policy homogenization have previously been made at different periods in recent history. For example, a similar convergence hypothesis (Keohane 1984) became widely accepted at first but was ultimately

---

[16] The literature on party systems has even coined the idea of inner and outer party systems when dealing with systems in which some parties are allowed to participate in elections but are considered unviable for the parties in the inner circle to access government (see Morlino 1986). In Chile and Portugal, these conflicts led to the Communist Party, the main labor mobilizing party within the left bloc in the two cases, being excluded from the inner party system for several years (Bosco 2001; Roberts 1995).

disregarded as Western European capitalisms initially evolved toward the American style of embedded liberalism after WWII.

The liberal convergence hypothesis informed important literatures that are relevant to the argument I am advancing, such as the literatures on models of capitalism and on types of leftist parties. The models of capitalism literature born out of this period in which capitalism dramatically expanded from the West to the socialist bloc and to what were then called "third world" countries. While this literature initially focused primarily on the evolution of capitalist institutions in the pool of advanced democracies, its focus later moved toward analyzing developing regions such as Latin America or Southeast Asia.[17] Consistent with the postulate of the liberal convergence hypothesis regarding the decreasing ability of political systems to cope with global market forces, the literature has primarily downplayed the role of political conflict or organized labor in the crafting of different models or types of capitalism and has instead emphasized economic coordination and the role of employers as the main factors driving the observed variation, an approach for which it has been widely criticized.[18]

Against the backdrop of the convergence hypothesis, the literature on varieties of capitalism shows the meaningful differences that exist between liberal and coordinated market economies (Hall and Soskice 2001). However, the application of its theoretical framework outside advanced industrial democracies has consistently emphasized regional similarities over differences. Consequently, regionally-based models of capitalism (Bogliaccini 2012) are consistent with the neoliberal idea of homogenizing factors being regionally strong, under the influence of international organizations with enforcement capabilities, such as the IFIs in Latin America during the post-transitional period (Drezner 2001, 60).

In the Latin American context, this hypothesis gained support from the fact that education, social security, and health reforms became the subject of regionwide reforms financed and designed by IFIs, mainly in the backward countries in the region. For example, the Chilean model of social security and health reform, strongly based on liberal principles, spread widely throughout the region. The growing literature

---

[17] For a detailed account of this literature see Hall and Sosckice (2001), Kitschelt et al. (1999), Amable (2005), and Schneider (2013).

[18] See Hancké, Rhodes and Tatcher (2007) and Pontusson (2005). See also Huber (2003) and Bogliaccini and Filgueira (2011) for particular discussions of this issue for Latin America.

on policy diffusion in the region focused on these and other policy changes, exploring their domestic and foreign legacies. However, as Keohane (1984) proposed, scholars also began to ponder the counter-balancing role of domestic institutions in the crafting of such policy reforms, mainly in Europe and in some of the most advanced Latin American countries.[19]

There are important scholarly works in the literature on Latin America disproving the convergence hypothesis in the camp of redistribution, as noted in previous sections. Prominent among them is Pribble's (2013) seminal work comparing Chile and Uruguay in terms of party politics in the building of welfare states in the post-dual transition period. However, these works do not analyze in depth the use of wage policy as a pre-distributive instrument. Pribble (2013), as an example, limits its analysis to discussing wage coordination centralization reform in Uruguay by the Frente Amplio and referring to the increases in minimum wages in the two countries (2013, 80, 83, 88). However, there is no systematic analysis in this strand of the literature to pre-distributive instruments such as wage policy.

The liberal convergence hypothesis had concrete political manifestations in politics. The "third way" or "third wayism" flourished in European leftist parties during the 1990s, following the electoral success of Blair's Labor government in the United Kingdom (Hall 2002; Iversen and Wren 1998; McIlroy 1998). Other European leftist parties, such as the French Socialists (Amable 2016), also experienced a weakening of their previously strong ties to labor. Similar developments occurred in Latin America (see Roberts 2007, 2013). Throughout the West, liberalization affected leftist parties' position on distribution.

Importantly for the argument advanced in this book, recent works on the ideological and rhetorical evolution of leftist parties in advanced democracies have pointed to a more subtle but robust convergence toward an economistic leftism as early as the 1960s (Mudge 2018, 53). This trend is based on expert management of the economy by technocrats. Mudge argues, and provides evidence – that social democratic parties in Sweden and Germany were affected by what she terms the "neoliberalization of the Left" (2018, 1). Naturally, as with the literature that analyzes policy change, this literature on party change recognizes the uneven

---

[19] See, for example, Weyland (2009a), Brooks (2009, 2001), Sugiyama (2011), or Gilardi, Jordana, and Levi-Faur (2006) for detailed policy analysis and theory building about policy diffusion during the 1990s and 2000s in Latin America and Europe.

effects of liberalization on political parties' organizational and ideological evolution (Bremer and McDaniel 2019; Mudge 2018). Bremer, particularly, finds that center-left parties in Europe retracted some of their "Third Way" policies after the Great Recession, in particular regarding redistribution and budgetary austerity (2018, 20). In other words, there is evidence in the literature about a neoliberal convergence among center-left parties in Europe and a debate on subsequent divergence around the time of the Great Recession. However, these works have not addressed wage policy specifically.

While there also have been several important contributions to the study of comparative party-labor relations in the post-dual transition period in Latin America,[20] there is a gap in the literature linking wage policy to the political economy of party-labor relations. Two notable exceptions to this are the seminal work of Murillo (2001) on the policy implications of party-labor relations in contexts of solid liberalization in Latin America during the 1990s, and the work of Etchemendy (2019) on segmented-neocorporatism. However, this literature linking policy to party-labor relations was overshadowed by a growing stream of scholarship advancing different typologies for classifying left-wing parties and governments in the region in a context of important changes in parties and party systems.

The role of intra-Left conflicts over employment and wage egalitarianism has remained largely unexplored in Latin America. There has been no scholarly work published on the use of wage policy as a pre-distributive instrument. There is no parallel to Mudge's work for Latin American or Southern European leftist parties in governments after the period of economic liberalization during the 1980s and 1990s. The literature on the types of the political Left has focused mostly on leadership styles and other top-down features related to party formation and evolution. At least in the Latin American context, this literature does not pay sufficient attention to long-term legacies. Little has been written about structural factors related to the political sociology of conflict, history, or power constellation issues about unions or employers. The literature on industrial relations in Latin America has, for the most part, not incorporated Iversen's insights on distributional

---

[20] See Levitsky (2003), Burgess (2010), Kitschelt et al. (2010), Roberts (1995, 2002), Levitsky and Roberts (2011), Cook (2007), Cook and Blazer (2013), Luna (2014), Rosenblatt (2018), Anría (2018, 2016), Etchemendy and Collier (2007), Perez et al. (2019), Anría and Cyr (2017), and Anría and Bogliaccini (2022).

outcomes. While the left turn in Latin America revitalized a literature on the study of political parties and, particularly, the relationship between parties and their political bases and societal roots, it shifted scholarly attention away from the analysis of the distributive conflict under open market capitalism.[21] Recent additions to the literature on party politics in Latin America, focusing on how parties function (or not) as channels for citizen representation (Luna, Piñeiro Rodríguez et al. 2021), building on a larger literature on the functional dimension of parties and the problem of vertical interest aggregation (Kitschelt 2000; Lipset and Rokkan 1967), represent an opportunity for bringing back the attention to the problem of distributive conflicts and how social groups align and channel their interests through parties into the political arena, politicizing this conflict in the context of democratic competition and open market capitalism.

There is an important branch of the left turn literature that focused precisely on how leftist parties in government embraced macroeconomic management. Prominent works in this literature are those of Flores-Macías (2010, 2012) or those in the edited volume by Weyland et al. (2010), focusing on how economic policy exploits the divide between orthodoxy and statism in different types of leftist governments – usually within the divide between moderate Left and the radical Left. However, there is no systematic treatment regarding wage policy and labor empowerment in these works, which focused primarily on macroeconomic management and how domestic economies related to the global market in the aftermath of the liberalization period. These works did not systematically examine important macroeconomic management divergence within the so-called moderate wing of the Left – that is, Chile, Brazil, and Uruguay among others.

What, then, would the liberal convergence hypothesis expect in terms of the evolution of leftist governments' distributive strategies? According to this hypothesis, as noted above, small and vulnerable countries such as Chile, Portugal, and Uruguay should converge on decentralized wage coordination in a context in which the Left would converge, as Mudge (2018) finds in advanced democracies, in a "neoliberalized" ideology, an economic leftism. In such a scenario, the expectation is for leftist parties

[21] See Castañeda (2006), Weyland (2009b), and Levitsky and Roberts (2011) for detailed accounts of the left-turn literature postulates and categorizations of leftist parties in government. See Beramendi and Rueda (2014) for an analysis of the role that inequality plays in the distributive conflict and its long-term relation to wage coordination.

to converge to some form of *third wayism* or left-liberalism, particularly to a distributional strategy based on redistribution without using wage policy as a pre-distributive instrument aside from the use of the minimum wage instrument.

The rationale behind this expectation is twofold. On the one hand, it is grounded in the idea that the economic pressures for convergence are based on the risk that increasingly mobile capital will exit, causing non-convergent countries to lose their competitiveness in the global economy. In this sense, a wage policy other than the setting of minimum wages would distort competitiveness. On the other hand, the liberal convergence hypothesis postulates that a set of beliefs with sufficient normative power, such as the wages-employment tradeoff postulated in Chapter 1, incentivizes domestic leaders to alter legislation and institutions. Leaders do so moved by the fear that they will appear as laggards if they do not comply with the dominant credo (Drezner 2001, 57). Wage policy, given these postulates, would be predicted to converge, fueled by the teaching of IFIs and eventual mimetic copying of policies domestic elites perceive as successful, into a completely decentralized outcome to reduce distortions and maximize competitiveness regionally or globally.

The analysis advanced in this book incorporates these two postulates of the liberal convergence hypothesis. On the one hand, the analysis recognizes the uncertainties and challenges the political system faces during the liberalization process, showing in Chapter 5 how political elites in each country processed the most critical labor and wage reforms. In such a scenario, leftist parties would follow some sort of convergence towards economic leftism, as found by Mudge (2018) or even Bremer and McDaniel (2019). On the other hand, the analysis incorporates the postulate that beliefs about the need for austerity and the erosion of belief in Keynesianism gave rise to the perceived tradeoff between wages and employment.

Against this backdrop, the analysis shows how the three countries that are the focus of this analysis developed divergent distributive strategies. The use of wage policy as a pre-distributive instrument lies at the center of this divergence, a wage policy shaped by political conflict. The book suggests how domestic structural factors associated with power-sharing, reciprocity, cooperation and domination, and, ultimately, power constellations engage with the productive system and market forces to shape different political responses to the distributive conflict. There are, then, political foundations that influence how each country shapes market coordination and distribution.

2.4 CASE SELECTION AND EMPIRICAL STRATEGIES

In comparing the crafting of distributive strategies and how they use wage policy as a pre-distributive instrument, case selection rests on identifying "diverse cases" (Mahoney 2000). In other words, the cases – Chile, Portugal, and Uruguay – represent three of the four potential outcomes of the relationship between the (dis)unity of the Left and labor political legitimacy, as depicted in Table I.1 in the Introduction (Seawright and Gerring 2008). The book does not analyze a case in which labor is not considered a legitimate political actor and the Left is united. Two of these cases, Portugal and Uruguay, are "critical case studies" that challenge existing theory in that, as explained in the discussion of the convergence hypothesis, neither behaves as expected given the status quo in terms of wage policy at the time of their incumbency by 2005.[22] The analytical framework, in turn, is based on a controlled comparison (see Slater and Ziblatt 2013).

Case Selection by Identification of Diverse Cases

The three cases, Chile, Portugal, and Uruguay, are small countries vulnerable to the pressures of the trade and financial markets after the dual transition. They have learned the hard way about the perils of protectionism. As such, it would be reasonable to expect policy convergence on completely decentralized wage-setting mechanisms. However, the analysis finds meaningful variation in the outcome, as explained above. While the relation between wages and employment is significant for economies like these, we observe divergence instead of convergence. Chile does conform to the expectations under the liberal convergence hypothesis, but Portugal and Uruguay do not: the outcome in Portugal is one of centralized but voluntary wage setting, while in Uruguay, the outcome is one of mandatory centralized wage setting (as shown in Table I.1). While elites in these countries have no choice but to let international markets force economic adjustments – as Uruguay did in 2002 or Portugal in 2009 – the three cases present meaningful variation in the use of wage policy as a pre-distributive instrument (Goertz and Mahoney 2012; Mahoney 2000).

The analysis also takes advantage of the fact that these three cases display important historical continuities grounded in their previous political

---

[22] Seawright and Gerring (2008) describe the diverse case method as bearing some resemblance to Mill's joint method of agreement and difference (Mill 1872).

history in the formation of durable, dominant elite strategies toward labor during the first half of the 20th century, common Iberian roots, and paths of conservative modernization. These divergent historical processes against a background of shared cultural and underlying institutional conditions provide the analytical power needed to elucidate why the same pressures in different settings allowed for different causal processes that, in turn, led to diverse outcomes. This variation in both the causal process and the outcome enables the analysis to claim representativeness within the universe of small-N samples.

In our "diverse cases" setting, the three cases have different causal paths for different outcomes. In other words, they have different dominant elite strategies toward the political legitimation of labor and different situations in terms of Left unity after the dual transition. These divergent paths anchor leftist governments differently at the outset of their terms in office during the post-liberalization period. Therefore, the empirical analysis is focused on the causal mechanisms linking causes and outcomes (Mahoney 2000). With this purpose in mind, the analysis provides qualitative scores for the three countries for the two factors at play – as shown in Tables 2.1 and 2.2 – and underlines the sequences that connect each factor with the potential outcome. The analysis shows, in doing this, how for each country different causal mechanisms are at play that produce different outcomes.

The country is the unit of analysis, where mechanisms connect causes to effects (see Ragin 1992; Stinchcombe 1968, 2005). Selecting the country level reflects the conflict over power and distribution, capturing complex and meaningful processes where the conflict between domination and cooperation occurs.

A Path Dependent Causal Account

What characteristics do the causal processes and the outcomes have in terms of time horizons and temporal continuity? The outcome, the use of wage policy as an instrument to achieve a government's distributive goals, shapes its distributive strategy and has a short time horizon. The effects of these outcomes, once in place, on pre-distribution and inequality are long-term ones. However, the use of the instrument in the distributive strategy is an outcome that materializes in the short term, usually after passing labor reforms.

Given the time horizons and the temporal separation of the causes and outcomes, the analytical timeframe should reflect the long-term nature of the causal process at hand (Pierson 2012). The proposed explanation for the outcome obeys a path-dependent causal account. The historical causes related to the empowered inclusion and legitimation of labor and the unity of the Left are slow-moving processes that are separated temporally from the outcome.

This historical causation generates increasing returns via feedback loops after emerging tensions are resolved (Stinchcombe 1968). In other words, path dependency occurs when historical events give rise to processes – even institutions – with certain reinforcing qualities that elevate the cost of changing paths to increase returns, even when tensions emerge and challenge the extant path (Mahoney 2000, 2004; Pierson 2012). As explained above, the dual transition represented one of these emerging tensions, but did not rupture the elite strategies that were dominant in the three countries. In other words, in this path-dependent process, the dual transition did not present itself as a critical juncture in the sense of those new enduring institutions and structures narrowing the range of potential outcomes. On the contrary, the argument postulates the historical continuity of previous elite strategies toward labor that adapt to the third wave of democratization. The book argues that, even when vital changes in the party system occurred during the dual transition, such as the emergence or strengthening of leftist parties, the mapping of Left (dis)unity and government choices regarding distribution depends on whether elites accord political legitimacy to labor. This legitimacy is built in the context of previously dominant elite strategies, as explained above.

The process of labor political empowerment is a long-term and slow-moving process occurring through the long-term repetition of dominant elite strategies in each case. These strategies, in turn, exhibited continuity through adaptation from the pre-transitional to the post-transitional period. Elite-biased contestation (in Chile), state-controlled coordination (in Portugal), and consociationalism (in Uruguay) adapted to the new democratic and liberalized environments of the post-dual transition period.

The current pattern of power distribution supports the reconstruction of these old equilibria. Employers' intransigence to any reform attempted by the Left encourages the contentious relationship in the Chilean case. In Portugal, the government's partnership with labor does not threaten employers in those consultative institutions. In Uruguay, the country's consociational history made it so that even the Right accepted labor as a legitimate actor. In the three cases, this continuity is facilitated by an adjustment of expectations, that is, a learning effect.

A long-term process involving the evolution of leftist parties during the 20th century and their relationship with organized labor unifies or divides the Left in the post-dual transition period. The dual transition presents itself, as previously noted, as an emerging tension. Democratic breakdowns and the abrupt change in economic models imposed new challenges on the extant dynamics of cooperation or competition among parties of the Left, which produced reinforcing dynamics in terms of intra-Left cooperation and, consequently, on Left-labor relations.

The anchoring factor, the ideational construction of the tradeoff between wages and employment, is a short-term factor that, in the post-dual transition period, relates the unity of the Left and the empowered inclusion of labor to the use of wage policy. The anchoring bias, as explained in the literature, causes individuals to rely too heavily on the previous piece of information they have about a topic (Kahneman 1992, 2003). The anchoring bias applied to the problem of the empowerment of labor suggests that when debating wage policy, the Left in each country interprets the conflict from the reference point of its anchor, instead of seeing it objectively.

However, this anchoring factor is also relevant for understanding the path dependency of long-term historical factors. As North's (1990, 2010) seminal works argue, ideas may be powerful in fortifying path dependency. In this case, beliefs about the policy space available given the constraints and opportunities associated with historically constructed relationships between labor, parties, employers, long-term elite strategies toward labor, and labor's political legitimacy shape how the employment-wages tradeoff is perceived. Chapter 5 analyzes these ideological anchors for each country.

For example, when analyzing the intra-Left conflict over wage policy in Chile, the experience of the Allende government is a strong anchor for the older generations within the Concertación coalition. A Chilean Socialist Congressmember put it succinctly: "We are the offspring of the Popular Union's defeat and collapse. We have two things in our genes: We reject inflation and fiscal deficits; and we are afraid of social disorder when there is a crisis" (Interview with Socialist Congressmember, 2010). In Chile, the Left's reflection on its own role alongside organized labor during the Allende and Pinochet periods became important for shaping intra-Left relations after the dual transition.

Finally, the continuity through adaptation of previously existing elite strategies to the post-dual transition period, as an underlying condition, supports the idea of the historical continuity of long-term processes even in the face of disruptive historical events. This argument cautions us against looking only for immediate, short-term causes while neglecting to examine the long-term slow-moving processes.

A Controlled Comparison Combining
Within-Case and Comparative Analysis

While the book provides stylized quantitative descriptions in several places, the analytical framework is grounded in a controlled comparison of the three cases (Slater and Ziblatt 2013). The methodology combines a within-case analysis of historical and policy trajectories and a comparative analysis. The within-case analysis is relevant for increasing the internal validity of the comparative method. It ensures that the hypothesized causal mechanisms are in place when, as is so often the case, the cases under study cannot be controlled perfectly on all relevant variables (Beach and Pedersen 2016; Blatter and Haverland 2012, 79). The comparative analysis maximizes control over the alternative proposed explanation based on the liberal convergence hypothesis. The analysis of the three countries provides representative variation with respect to both causes and outcomes, as explained above.

The empirical strategy has three main components. First, the analysis proposes a historical comparison of the processes through which labor gained political leverage and, eventually, legitimacy during the first part of the 20th century. The main goal of this part is to characterize three archetypical elite strategies toward the empowered inclusion of labor while maintaining political stability.

The scoring of the political practices that, as explained before, shape dominant elite strategies toward labor was presented in Table 2.1. These scores are qualitative as, for example, the limitations on *voting* and *resistance* are of a different nature and have a different evolution in democratic Chile than in authoritarian Portugal. In the same vein, the practice of *recognition*, because of its moral character in terms of inclusion and support for the rights and duties of citizenship, is more fundamental to understanding labor political legitimacy in the post-transition period than are the other practices. Political legitimacy refers to the degree to which labor organizations are valued for themselves and considered right and proper as political actors (Lipset 1959, 71), it has a moral character and is intrinsically related to the practice of recognition, even in a democratic environment. As such, the elite practice of recognizing labor as a political actor would importantly influence whether wage policy is used as a pre-distributive instrument.

The historical evolution of these political practices would inform the Left in the post-transition scenario, as explained in Chapters 4 and 5. The analysis of elites' attitudes toward the empowered inclusion of labor and of how the Left and labor react over the long haul helps explain present-day leftist governments' challenges regarding the use of wage policy as an instrument for distribution; that is, history matters (see Slater and Simmons 2010).

The second component is also a historical comparison of how the unity of the Left affected party-labor relations after the dual transition (see Mahoney and Rueschemeyer 2012). The analysis characterizes the evolution of Left unity, disunity, and disunity structure when appropriate. As emphasized in the Chilean and Portuguese cases, these differences would affect leftist governments' use of wage policy as a pre-distributive instrument. The scoring of the unity of the Left, the second factor, follows the structure presented in Table 2.2, and could be mapped by the combination of two dimensions – the Left bloc organization and the electoral arena – in four quadrants. As previously hypothesized, the presence of an electorally viable challenger from the far Left elevates the cost of empowering labor for leftist governments, which reduces their willingness to use wage policy other than for minimum wage policy.

The third component of the analysis is a within-case analysis of post-transitional leftist government policymaking in the labor relations arena, particularly addressing instances affecting wage policy, the outcome of the analysis. The analysis extends over influential labor and wage policy landmark legislation and reform attempts, both successful and unsuccessful. The scoring of the outcome, as explained above, combines the reform outcomes in terms of centralization and the mandatory character of wage policy included as a pre-distributive instrument by the Left.

Analyzed reforms and political events were selected to reveal party preferences and, as such, to understand intra-Left conflicts over wage policy and the role the perceived tradeoff between employment and salaries plays in each case. In Chile, the 2001 and 2016 reform attempts advanced by the Concertación governments indicate a conflict between sectors within the party coalition. In Portugal, the study of social concertation through the accords signed within the CPCS, the long-lasting process to create the 2003 Labor Code, the 2009 reform advanced by the Socialist government, and the use of wage accord extensions (*portarias de extensão*) by different governments elucidates the conflict between moderate and far left parties. In Uruguay, the analysis of the

2007 labor reform and other relevant policy decisions captures the bargaining process within the FA for balancing employment creation with wage egalitarianism.

Data

The data used for the analysis comes from varied sources. The research for this book began in 2008 and ended in 2019. During these eleven years, I did extensive fieldwork in the three countries, which included collecting an exhaustive set of historical and parliamentary documents and personal interviews. A total of 160 interviews with political and social actors in the three countries – mostly business and labor leaders – were conducted between 2008 and 2019.

Archival research in parliamentary libraries, national libraries, and private libraries of different associations and parties was also part of the data collection strategy. A collection of around 200 documents in total was gathered, most of them referring to labor and wage policy-making. Press research was also carried out in each of the three countries. The strategy used for this was to collect all available press coverage of a particular reform or debate that had been published in prominent newspapers in each country. A total of seven newspapers were regularly consulted for this purpose.

Stylized quantitative data presented in the first chapter comes from The Organization for Economic Cooperation and Development (OCDE), United Nations Economic Commission for Latin America and the Caribbean (ECLAC), EUROSTAT, The International Labor Organization (ILO), and The World Bank. Each analysis details the data used.

3

The Modeling of Elite Strategies toward Labor

[With the Estado Novo], unions were no longer [organized] by industry, but by profession. In other words, in transport, there was the union of drivers. However, at the same time, there could be a union of administrative employees from this same company (...) a transportation company could have three, four, five unions. So, the labor movement was separated geographically by districts. The labor movement was separated by professions. The labor movement had statutes that they had to respect. They had to accept the cooperative organization; there was no national confederation and no international affiliations. The unions themselves had to be approved. They had to be accepted by the Ministry of Corporations. The interests of labor and capital were subordinated to the superior interests of the nation.

(CGTP labor leader, personal interview held in
Lisbon, January 2019)

This chapter addresses the first part of the historicist causal structure of the argument as crafted in the previous chapter: the consolidation of elite strategies toward the empowered inclusion of labor during the first part of the 20th century. *Elite-biased contention, controlled coordination,* and *consociationalism* became dominant during this period in Chile, Portugal, and Uruguay, respectively. The structure of the chapter follows the hypothesis derived from Table 2.1, a simplified version of which is reproduced below as Table 3.1.

The consolidation of these elite strategies was a slow-moving process that occurred while political regimes were changing and consolidating during the first decades of the 20th century. During those decades, attitudes toward labor activism constituted the primary cleavage in terms of labor relations, as Luebbert (1991) and Collier and Collier (1991) have pointed out in their analyses of Europe and Latin America. In other

TABLE 3.1 *Political practices and elite strategies toward labor.*

Political Practices	Elite dominant response regarding each political practice before the dual transition[1]		
	Biased Contention	Controlled Coordination	Consociationalism
Directly related to Legitimation of Labor			
Recognition	Limited	Unlimited	Unlimited
Representation	Limited	Limited	Unlimited
Join	Unlimited	Limited	Unlimited
Indirectly related to Legitimation of Labor			
Vote	Limited	Limited	Unlimited
Resistance	Repressed	Repressed	Tolerated

[1] Based on Table 2.1.

words, organized labor became a pivotal actor, impacting both national politics and other actors' political strategies. Our three cases were not exceptions in this regard. While labor confronted an intransigent business sector in each of the three countries, as it did in Europe at the time (see Luebbert 1991), the relationship between political and economic elites played out differently in the three cases and resulted in different dominant long-run strategies.

An important aspect of the argument is the political acceptance of who, in each case, enjoys legitimacy as a political actor. Elite action in terms of the above-defined five political practices – labor recognition and representation, allowing labor to join representative associations, allowing voting, and tolerating resistance (see Table 3.1) – would craft long-lasting elite strategies. As these strategies became dominant, they allowed or impeded the empowered inclusion of labor. Not only in the short-term but, most importantly, over the long run, they affected labor's political legitimacy.

3.1 COMMON ROOTS OF THE TWO REGIONS AFFECTING ELITE STRATEGIES

Elite strategies in the two regions were influenced by some critical common factors that deserve mention. A central factor in understanding these strategies, common to Southern Cone and Southern European societies, is their historical difficulties in dealing with cross-class conflict and compromise. For example, while Scandinavian countries gradually found suitable coordination mechanisms by the end of the interwar period, and Northern Continental Europe embarked upon a successful coordination path after the demise of fascism at the end of WWII, the Southern Cone and Southern Europe continued to experience major difficulties up until the late 20th century. Elites in these two regions continued to rely during this period on top-down control mechanisms to guarantee an ordered advance toward state-defined goals such as modernization and industrialization.

During early democratization attempts, elites faced the challenge of either accommodating or repelling organized labor, a new and increasingly powerful actor. Labor grew in organizational size and strength during this period in the three cases. However, the opportunities available to it and the gains it achieved in terms of empowered inclusion varied greatly from case to case, mainly due, as noted above, to labor's relationship with political and economic elites. In the context of moving from oligarchies or monarchies toward greater levels of political participation and tolerance, the conflict primarily pitted traditional political elites against new politically mobilized subordinate groups. The political dominance of liberal and conservative elites and the intertwined relationship between political and economic elites became important for understanding long-term elite-labor relations, as explained below for each case.[1]

As shown below, elite strategies usually opposed – or at least hesitated to tolerate – conflict in daily politics (Dahl 1971) or the idea that mutual tolerance between political adversaries is a necessary condition of democratization (see Linz 1978). Among the three cases studied here, Uruguay stands as an exception in this regard.

A second important factor common to the Southern Cone and Southern European states, related to the previous one, is that both regions have historically departed from classical liberal or Marxist approaches to

---

[1] The classic work on Chilean elites at the turn of the 20th century, by Alberto Edwards (1928), points to the undivided character of the elite and its hold on social, economic, and political power, as well as the role of intermarriage in preserving its closed character. By contrast, classic works by Barrán (2004) and Barrán and Nahum (1984) about the Uruguayan elites at the turn of the 20th century portray a politically divided elite and a political class that competes to enforce the new democratic rule on the economic elite. Louçã et al. (2014) describe the Portuguese economic elite as a small group of families, as in the Chilean case, but without a dominant hold on power. The Estado Novo developed a distinct political elite.

conflict, showing a common disdain for (democratic) procedures. There is a diverse literature stressing the importance of Roman Law, medieval natural law, and Catholic social philosophy in shaping the state.[2] Stepan (1978) provides valuable categories for elucidating the conflict in these societies and building the political legitimacy of labor, such as the idea of the importance of the community vis-à-vis the individual and, following from this, the idea of a common societal interest and common good that the state defines and pursues. Stepan proposes that, while the idea of the common good is not intrinsically anti-democratic, it "lends itself to aliberal legitimacy formulas for two basic reasons: being the common good known by 'right reason,' there is no need for procedures. Second, the pursuit of the common good, not elections or representation of group interests, is the measure by which the legitimacy of the state is evaluated" (Stepan 1978, 65). This lack of respect for procedures or for subordinate groups' interest representation directly affected the political practices of *voting, recognition,* and *representation* in many cases.

A third common factor is the persistence of employers' intransigence toward labor for a much longer period than in other western regions. The 20th century witnessed gradual and non-linear processes of labor organization and empowered inclusion in Southern Europe and the Southern Cone, as described in the seminal works of Crouch (1993) for Europe and of Collier and Collier (1991) for the pre-transitional periods. Employers' intransigent attitude toward labor at the onset of the 20th century was widely shared across the Western world. Governments' attitudes toward labor activism based on repression or malicious indifference were also widespread before the first world war, including cases such as Sweden and Norway. However, while repression softened and employers' intransigence moderated in Europe by the interwar period, neither moderated in Southern Europe and the Southern Cone (Collier and Collier 1991; Crouch 1993; Luebbert 1991). This difference has significant consequences for the two regions under study here in terms of the consolidation of mutual distrust and for understanding historical and current power constellations. Employers' intransigence and state repression, in turn, certainly exacerbated *resistance.*

The evolution of employers' organizing efforts in the three countries was consistent with the neocorporatist theory of centralization

---

[2] See Stepan (1978, 57) for a detailed account of this literature up until the beginning of the third wave of democratization. Wierda and McLeish (2001) make a similar argument for the particular cases of Spain and Portugal.

in small economies subject to the perils of the market (Crouch 1993; Goldthorpe 1984; Katzenstein 1985). Employers' efforts to centralize their political interests were fueled primarily by anti-labor sentiment and a strong, almost intransigent, opposition to the advancement of labor rights (Caetano 1984; Crouch 1993; Haindl 2007). In other words, they approached the labor problem strategically, usually in response to state signaling under different governments –governments in which at many points in time they participated, as argued in the previous chapter and shown in this chapter.

Industrial relations, therefore, were dominated by high levels of contestation. With an intransigent business sector fighting the empowered inclusion of labor, in a context of fragile, new democratic experiences and backward production systems based on the primary sector, elites' attitudes toward labor varied in Chile, Portugal, and Uruguay. The dominance of the three strategies did not occur overnight or without challenges. In Chile, for example, labor undeniably benefited from the periods during which a liberal coalition was in office, while in Uruguay, labor repression occurred mainly during periods of conservative rule. However, neither liberals in Chile nor conservatives in Uruguay challenged the legal framework in ways that would either promote or hinder labor's political interests. Therefore, over the long run, the dominant strategies described above became elites' accepted course of action in dealing with the "labor problem."[3]

A fourth common factor is the high degree of economic protection afforded by the state during the period, which had important effects in terms of labor's and employers' coordination strategies. In heavily protected economies, the state became a powerful bargainer to protect domestic sectors from global market perils. The hierarchical organization of associations for employers and labor during this period directly affected these groups' political practice of *joining*. In addition, high levels of protection from external perils and subsidies from the government decreased incentives for employers and labor to cooperate because the

---

[3] Neither this chapter nor the book address the initial causes shaping these long-term strategies, as interesting as these phenomena undoubtedly are. In Chile, for example, elite-biased contestation may have been a consequence of some combination of a unified elite confronting a coherent and united organized labor. Labor power was rapidly growing in strength and finding important allies in the political system; sometimes allying with the military, as in the 100-day Socialist Republic, sometimes with centrist parties, as during the Popular Front coalition, and sometimes even forming a class-based coalition with Communists and Socialists, as during the Unidad Popular period.

protected environment made it possible to defuse distributive conflicts via subsidies and additional protections.

Notwithstanding these commonalities in the two regions' political processes, the contexts of democratic breakthroughs and backlashes, state modernization, and the institutionalization of party competition were highly diverse across the two regions and between countries within each region. This diversity manifested itself in terms of political regimes, political stability, and the source of this stability; namely, whether elites included or excluded from the political arena actors representing demands from subordinate groups (see Huntington 1968) and actors challenging the values upon which political, economic and social orders rested.[4]

The response of elites to labor political activism was mediated by the state. As Luebbert (1991) shows for inter-war Europe, states' response to employers' intransigence toward labor included important variation. This, in turn, shaped labor's organizational trajectory, political inclusion, and ability to build political legitimacy over the long term. These responses varied from case to case but showed critical levels of stability when analyzed as large-scale historical processes. The responses in Chile, Uruguay and, to a lesser extent, Portugal differed from the experience in other regions. For example, in Scandinavia and other parts of continental Northern Europe, responses to labor political activism changed between the pre-war and the interwar years from indifference or outright repression toward labor accommodation under social democracy to violent repression or cooptation under fascism.[5] In Chile, Portugal, and Uruguay, these responses ranged from outright political exclusion to the empowered inclusion of unions, recognizing them as legitimate political actors (Collier and Collier 1991; Crouch 1993; Fernandes and Branco 2017).[6]

[4] For example, Piñeiro and Rosenblatt (2020) provide an excellent discussion of party system adaptation to the incorporation of demands coming from different social sectors in the process of institutionalization with a focus on Latin America.

[5] Luebbert (1991), particularly Chapters 5 and 6, provides an excellent depiction of the development of labor political activism, the evolution of labor parties, and state reactions to these processes during the pre-war and interwar years. In a recent addition to the literature, Rasmussen and Knutsen (2023) show, for the Norwegian case, how labor activism fueled by the Bolshevik Revolution triggered an elite response based on advancing social policy and making concession to labor demands partly as a response to their fear of domestic revolution.

[6] Collier and Collier (1991) have provided the most influential and detailed account of the process of social incorporation in Latin America, with a particular focus on the initial incorporation of the labor movement. This book builds on Collier and Collier to understand the strategies of the Chilean and Uruguayan states toward labor during the first part of the 20th century.

3.2 CHILE: POLITICAL ORDER BETWEEN TOLERATION AND EXCLUSION OF LABOR

A Characterization of Elite-Biased Contention

Chile combines a rather strong democratic record with mild corporatism during the period, consistent with the continuation of the political exclusion of labor as a strategy for maintaining political order. In the words of Collier and Collier (1991, 189), in Chile, the "fear of the threat posed by the working class was very high, and the salience of the social question was probably the greatest of the countries under consideration." Chile did not form a state-dependent elite in an effort to forge a new state-society equilibrium by policies aimed at incorporating salient working-class groups into a new economic and political model (Stepan 1978, 74). This form of corporatism did occur in Mexico, Argentina, and Brazil. In addition, Chile's economic structure, which combined the preeminence of rural haciendas and mining in distant peripheral locations, hindered the ability of unions to position themselves as central political actors.

On the one hand, geographic decentralization made it easier not to include labor as a legitimate political actor. Foreign companies in the mining sector and large haciendas were, in a sense, the state. Large mining firms, for example, owned schools and hospitals. On the other hand, this productive structure made other urban unions heavily dependent on political parties and the state apparatus.

In Chile, elites privileged order over the empowered inclusion of subordinate groups. Conflict in the labor arena fostered repression in a context of a nascent democracy. Consistent with the notion of *elite-biased contention*, elites privileged the maintenance of social and political order by seeking to make subordinate groups acquiesce to their rule. The analysis of the Chilean case shows how this strategy included anti-democratic practices in a democratic context, such as labor repression, disenfranchisement of subordinate group voters, or even handicapping the collective decision capacity of subordinate groups by outlawing their encompassing organizations. Elites' practices within this strategy included, as explained below, limitations to labor political *recognition, representation, voting* and *resistance*. However, in the case of Chile, it did not include limitations on *joining*.

The consolidation of democratic institutions in Chile was, according to Valenzuela's thesis (1999), less in response to pressures from below than as a consequence of inter-elite rivalries and strategies to maximize electoral gain. While conservative and liberal elites alternated in office during the first part of the 20th century, the exclusion of labor from the political arena by various means became a repeated strategy in the Chilean version of conservative modernization. As a general rule, Chilean elites preferred to delay the political participation of subordinate groups, particularly organized expressions of the working class. Such preference signaled a lack of *recognition* despite granting labor the rights to represent themselves and to join representative associations.

In terms of political *recognition*, the tendency to exclude labor from the political arena in Chile has a long history that goes back to the beginning of the 20th century (Collier and Collier 1991). Exclusion has been a dominant strategy for elites to maintain order (see Baland and Robinson 2008; Gamboa and Morales 2015 for similar analyses of exclusionary mechanisms in Chile during the period). Direct repression of labor occurred frequently until at least 1925, including legal restrictions on collective rights and repeated bans on labor confederations during the first part of the 20th century. Even during periods of elite toleration of the labor movement, labor suffered from legal restrictions and eventual repression (see Cavarozzi 1975; Collier and Collier 1991; Valenzuela 1976). Elites did not recognize labor or empower labor as a legitimate political actor. Labor is never embraced but, rather, is simply allowed to exist.

What made Chile so special is that, during this period, the country became a full urban democracy. Therefore, labor representatives participated in the political arena through the Socialist and Communist parties. The urban labor movement became vibrant, carried out strikes, demonstrated, and got involved. Elites tolerated but did not embrace labor. The rural sector, however, remained politically excluded until after 1958. According to Collier and Collier (1991), until 1932, labor was not given the "opportunity to cooperate or collaborate … the repression of existing leadership and unionism was a central component of this [labor] policy" (p. 178).[7] While this direct repression of labor activism illustrates the fact that intolerance of *resistance* was a common practice on the part of the elite, it constituted, only one of three main instruments for the political exclusion of labor.

Limitations on voter enfranchisement, for example, remained a prime instrument for controlling pressures from below in the urban sector.

---

[7] Collier and Collier (1991, 22) propose that the period of labor incorporation in Chile extends from 1920 to 1932.

Voter literacy requirements constituted a powerful indirect instrument for handicapping labor's strategic capacity in the political arena (see Baland and Robinson 2008; Gamboa and Morales 2015). Importantly, voter literacy requirements were not challenged by the liberal reformist coalitions under Alessandri Palma before 1932 or under the Popular Front after 1936; they remained an essential and unchanged tool of exclusion until 1958.

The effects of voter literacy requirements on the empowerment of labor are indirect but significant. They are indirect because they do not affect the constitution of labor unions or the extent to which unions are allowed to lobby for their interests. However, they are significant because they dramatically reduce the electoral effects of political parties' mobilization of subordinate groups in a full urban democracy, Chile for example. As such, literacy requirements also reduced labor leaders' political leverage in bargaining with elites and governments.

Restrictions on the practice of *voting* preclude the empowerment of subordinate groups, adversely affecting the ability of leftist parties to mobilize in pursuit of electoral opportunities and the ability of members of subordinate groups to aspire to elective posts. Legal restrictions on collective rights, such as strikes, adversely affect the practice of *recognition*, which, in turn, limits subordinate groups' access to the rights and duties of citizenship (Table 3.1).

Eventually, a different instrument was employed to directly reduce labor's political power by outlawing labor centrals, unions, or even labor-mobilizing parties such as the Communist party. Legal restrictions on labor political activism, affecting *representation* and *joining* practices, were not challenged by liberal coalitions during the period. While Chile legally recognized the right to unionize early on, it also banned unions and labor confederations during various periods, obliging labor to form new organizations over and over. These actions affected the practice of *representation*, limiting inclusion over time. A ban on the Communist Party also occurred during the 1940s.[8] The use of repression and legal restrictions was not uniform throughout: repression was predominant until the mid-1930s and legal restrictions became more prevalent during the 1940s and 1950s. Restrictions on *voting*, by contrast, remained constant until the end of the period.

---

[8] This ban was contemporary with similar bans in other western countries, such as attempts to hinder the organizing efforts of trade unions during the years before the New Deal in the United States (Griffin et al. 1986).

Despite these limitations, organized labor has been stronger in Chile than in Portugal during most of the 20th century. Under the Labor Confederation (CTCh), the labor movement became part of the coalition supporting the Popular Front and Democratic Alliance governments between 1938 and 1947 and was part of the coalition supporting the Popular Union government between 1970 and 1973. These spurts of political participation were, nevertheless, met by new periods of contention. The essence of elite-biased contention is a struggle between conservative elites seeking to prevent the empowered inclusion of subordinate groups in the political arena and liberal elites open to accommodating the empowered inclusion of the popular sectors.

In a democratic context, the combination of restrictions on *recognition*, *resistance*, *representation*, and *voting* put labor in an unequal position relative to other social actors in terms of its recognition as a political actor. This inequality eroded labor's ability to build political legitimacy over the long term. The contentious relationship between labor and most governments implied that labor was never embraced but tolerated. Labor did not gain the legitimacy it needed to serve as an effective counter to economic or political elites.

The Historical Development of Elite-Biased Contention as an Elite Strategy

The 1891 Civil War in Chile ended with a conservative victory over liberal reformism. This outcome enabled the conservatives to strengthen their exclusionary strategy toward labor to maintain control and order. The period that followed was one of party fragmentation and instability that afforded no political opening to subordinate groups. Consequently, the Liberal and Conservative parties continued to be dominated by the elites. The conservative coalition that ruled during the period nurtured the export-oriented growth model and successfully impeded the expansion of voting and labor rights (Castedo 2001). Conservative governments opposed and repressed labor organizations until 1920 (Haindl 2007).

It took much longer to universalize the vote in Chile than in Uruguay, reflecting the reluctance of Chilean elites to open participation to subordinate groups. While universal male suffrage via secret ballot was sanctioned as early as 1874, a literacy requirement was reintroduced in 1885 and was only lifted in 1969 (Valenzuela 1985). Women were not allowed to vote until 1949. Moreover, Remmer (1984) shows that, well into the 20th century, the wealthy – i.e., those who paid the highest taxes – controlled voter rolls. When turnout went up too much, tax rolls went up to maintain turnout at a lower level.

Despite these constraints, Chile developed one of the most vibrant labor movements in Latin America during the period.[9] Possibly, as Marks (1986b) argued, intense repression produces a shared sense of victimization and working-class unity. From the 1900s to the 1930s, the Chilean working-class unionization process included intense labor activism, particularly during 1907, 1913, and 1918–1919. This activism was met, as noted above, with state repression. While the labor movement developed a centralized structure early on, it had neither political power nor political legitimacy because it was heavily repressed.

The Chilean Worker Federation (FOCh – *Federación Obrera Chilena*), created in 1911, focused on mutualism and had no political relevance until 1916. After 1916, it strengthened its relationship with the Socialist Party, which had been founded in 1912 as the *Partido Obrero de Chile*. This inaugurated a period of social unrest and state repression, signaling the beginning of labor's attempt to gain political recognition and of its direct involvement in politics (Haindl 2007). Anarchist workers also organized themselves in 1917 under the Chilean section of the International Workers of the World but remained a minor actor without political relevance (Carriére et al. 1989; Muñoz Gomá and Arriagada 1977).

The reformist coalition led by the Liberal Party, supported by the middle class, advanced labor legislation and workers' protection, including the legal recognition of labor unions.[10] The 1925 Constitution expanded the vote franchise to all literate males of at least 21 years of age, thus excluding most middle- and lower-class adults and the labor movement's core. Repression softened but did not disappear. Labor did not become part of this ruling coalition (DeShazo 1983; Haindl 2007; Muñoz Gomá and Arriagada 1977). In this regard, DeShazo (1983) shows that the relationship between President Alessandri Palma and the FOCh was not one of cooperation despite the government advancing legal recognition of the labor movement. By the end of 1921, barely two years into Alessandri

---

[9] Statistics provided by the Confederación Sindical Latinoamericana (CSLA) in 1928 show that labor organizations in Chile experienced greater levels of worker participation than did organizations in Argentina and Uruguay (Rama 1976).

[10] The "Parliamentary Republic" was still a presidential system, but with a debilitated president given a series of constitutional reforms after the 1891 Civil War. The President could not dissolve the Congress, and the Ministry of the Interior played the role of the head of government (Castedo 2001).

Palma's first term, repression again began to be used against labor. In a similar vein, Collier and Collier (1991) describe how repression occurred between 1925 and 1931 and argue that politics toward labor was characterized "not by party-centered popular mobilization but by a politics of accommodation between the oligarchy and the reformers" (p. 172). This description illustrates the core of the elite-biased contentious dynamic: liberal elites ultimately accommodated the interests of conservative elites to the detriment of the empowerment of subordinate groups.

The first presidency of Ibañez del Campo, inaugurated in 1927, signaled the end of this brief period of pro-labor reformism and the attempt to move toward a mild version of corporatism. Ibañez del Campo's first term (1927–1931) is, arguably, the period in which the most corporatist features could be identified in Chile. Consistent with the corporatist ideas imported mainly from Southern Europe and adopted throughout much of Latin America, the FOCh was outlawed in 1927. The use of legal instruments to restrict labor political power gained importance during this period. Repression, thus, was paired with legal bans that excluded labor from political participation or hindered the capacity of labor and labor-mobilizing parties to carry out their political strategy. The Ibañez government attacked representation and joining capabilities. After outlawing the FOCh, Ibañez del Campo favored a developmental strategy. Consistent with the corporatist recipe at the time, the Ibañez government attempted to have labor represented by a state-dependent organization, the National Federation of Independent Workers (*Federación Nacional de Trabajadores Independientes*) (Salinas 1980, 146). However, this organization was short-lived, and labor even managed to conduct three general strikes against the Ibáñez government. Democratic and independent unionism returned after Ibáñez del Campo's failed attempt to bring them under government control. Critical for my argument, during the period from the 1930s to the 1950s, the agenda of the working class centered on the failed attempt to alter imposed legal constraints on the political empowerment of labor (Collier and Collier 1991).

The FOCh was replaced in 1936 by the CTCh, during Alessandri Palma's second term (1932–1938). During the period that followed, labor enjoyed partial political inclusion. While access to the vote franchise remained limited, the CTCh participated in the ruling coalition led by the Radical Party governments of Aguirre Cerda (1938–1942) and Ríos (1942–1946). Muñoz Gomá and Arriagada (1977) use press reports to demonstrate that the CTCh organized fewer strikes during the Popular

Front (FP, *Frente Popular*) coalition period than had occurred in the period between 1916–1925, even though strikes were prohibited in the latter, but were allowed in the former (Valenzuela 1976, 156).

Rural sectors remained among the most intransigent concerning labor. The Sociedad Nacional de Agricultura (SNA) had blocked the passage of a 1934 proposal to provide rural workers with a minimum wage.[11] The Aguirre Cerda's government had to negotiate with the SNA the formation of the Corporation of Production Promotion (CORFO, *Corporación de Fomento de la Producción*) (Gomá and Arriagada 1977; Moulián 1989). As a concession to the rural elites during the negotiations regarding CORFO, the government aborted rural workers' unionization attempt as early as 1939. By 1940, the Socialist Party and CTCh broke with Aguirre Cerda (Collier and Collier 1991). By 1946, labor repression resumed it prior intensity. The CTCh participated in the CORFO negotiations, but it would end up with only one member out of 23 on CORFO's board of directors. Labor's restricted participation on the board illustrates how limited its effective political *recognition* was, even during a period in which governments were favorable to labor.

During the Popular Front period, beginning in 1936, labor grew in strength and density alongside gradual gains in political participation and the softening of voting restrictions. However, the increased influence of labor in government did not last. Even during the first years of the Popular Front government, when pro-labor legislation was adopted, there was almost no change to the legal framework (Cavarozzi 1975; Collier and Collier 1991). Political *recognition* of urban labor by elites occurred during those years, but it did not produce lasting institutional change.

In 1942, parliament gave President Ríos the power to break strikes under certain circumstances, a provision that was used frequently and extensively (Cavarozzi 1975, 164–65). During Gonzalez Videla's term in office (1946–1952), the relationship between the government and labor continued its' deterioration until a complete break occurred in 1948, after Videla outlawed the Communist Party (Moulian and Torres 1989). In that same year, González Videla's government imposed additional legal constraints on labor.

In 1946, the CTCh divided itself into two groups, greatly weakening labor's capacity for political action until 1953. The repeated conflicts between Communists and Socialists (1945–46) and participation by

---

[11] A minimum wage in the rural sector was not established until 1954, during Ibáñez del Campo's second term (1952–1958).

the Communist Party in Gonzalez Videla's government also contributed to the division of the labor movement (Moulian 1986a). Labor reorganization began again in 1948, resulting in the formation of the National Commission of Workers Unity (*Comisión Nacional de Unidad Sindical*). More than 2,000 delegates represented thirty-five federations and unions (Angell 1974, 222–26). In 1953, labor centralized its political interests by establishing the Central Labor Confederation (CUT, *Central Unitaria de Trabajadores*) (Moulian 1986a). The CUT would play a crucial role in the center-left coalition under the Unidad Popular (UP).

The prohibition of leftist parties or labor organizations continued during Ibáñez del Campo's second term (1952–1958). Elected by a populist coalition supported by rural sectors and urban industrialists, the Ibáñez government maintained an exclusionary, intransigent attitude toward labor (Moulian 1986a). This new decade, during which labor and the Communist Party were politically isolated, triggered the formation of a powerful class coalition that, by the late 1950s, had united Communists, Socialists, and organized labor. This critical change in the political system, aided by the gradual easing of voting restrictions beginning in 1958, inaugurated a period during which the dominant strategy of *elite-biased contention* rapidly weakened.

3.3 PORTUGAL: POLITICAL ORDER BY AUTHORITARIAN CORPORATISM

A Characterization of Controlled Coordination

Portugal exhibited the characteristics of authoritarian corporatism most notably during the long-lasting Estado Novo period under Salazar and Caetano (Schmitter 1974). The state played a central role in organizing social actors. The failure of democratization combined with the development of a corporatist regime during the Estado Novo period gave rise to a different elite strategy toward labor: *controlled coordination*.

Authoritarian corporatism in Southern Europe became a viable avenue for an orderly pursuit of the state-defined common good in modernizing states with backward economies (Luebbert 1987). Under the Iberian experience of authoritarian corporatism, labor participated in corporations but remained highly restricted in its political action. The Estado Novo bounded social actors' political activity within the framework of corporatist institutionalism. In other words, labor participated in a highly controlled coordination framework with employers, which enabled some continuity of labor participation in the political arena, with specific restrictions imposed by the authoritarian regime.

The state subordinated associations by coopting labor and employers, which distorted *representation* and *joining* practices. These coopted associations served, in turn, as transmission conduits to provide benefits and for coercion (Luebbert 1987, 450). Lucena (1976) and Schmitter (1999) emphasize the role of state-led unions (*sindicatos nacionais*) as substitutes for previously extant autonomous unions, monopolizing coordination. This subordination imposed crucial limitations on *representation* and *joining* practices (Table 3.1), but not on *recognition* vis-à-vis other social actors such as employers. Limitations on *representation* are self-evident as the expansion of inclusion over time and space was severely limited to what the state allowed. The Estado Novo legitimized institutionalized – highly restricted – participation in vertically organized unions (see Fernandes and Branco 2017; Schmitter 1999).[12]

An undisputed authoritarian setting maintained political order through the cooptation of autonomous labor (and employer) organizations. Allowing labor some minimum level of political participation became desirable for a regime in need of legitimization. While the authoritarian state employed repression, top-down control by state-controlled corporations via forced participation was the main instrument for balancing political order and the empowered inclusion of labor. Although this arrangement precluded state-controlled labor associations from gaining political legitimacy, it did allow labor to participate in those few instances in which the regime allowed participation. Thus, the authoritarian regime recognized labor as a legitimate actor while restricting or limiting the other four political practices: *representing, joining, voting* and *resisting*. This was the case in Portugal during the Estado Novo (Madureira 2007; Schmitter 1974, 1999; Wiarda 1973, 1974).

The political *recognition* of labor was born out of continuous political participation in conditions comparable to those of employers, which was instrumental in legitimizing labor as a political actor over the long run. This political recognition was also instrumental in gradually building a culture of coordination that would flourish after the turbulent dual transition and, in contrast to Chile, despite the high levels of political radicalization that occurred during the Portuguese transition.

---

[12] For a seminal work on the differences between authoritarian and totalitarian regimes, and an analysis of political opposition in the two types, see Linz (1978).

Elites extended channels of organizational influence through officially sanctioned compulsory and non-competitive mechanisms. *Joining* practices, consequently, were highly limited. Such limitations relate to the inability of labor to join other associations than those chartered by the state, limiting constituency formation and the empowerment of resistance. However, Fernandes and Branco (2017) explain how some of the Estado Novo institutions, particularly in the electoral and welfare arenas, were somewhat inclusive. Even the repressive institutions created by the Estado Novo for the control of workers allowed the union movement to have some power and pushed workers under the influence of the Communist Party. Workers began to clandestinely participate in the Intersindical labor confederation and strengthened the Communist Party's mobilizational capacity.

Portugal experienced a period of mobilization and partial or temporary inclusion followed by repression during the First Republic, similar to that which occurred in Chile. However, whereas this back-and-forth dynamic continued in Chile, in Portugal, the Estado Novo corporatist regime consolidated, restricting *representation* and *joining* – not to mention *voting* and tolerance of *resistance* – thus controlling labor's political action and institutionalizing its political role. Over the long run, labor – not state-imposed labor associations – gradually built political legitimacy.

The Historical Development of Controlled Coordination as an Elite Strategy

Portugal witnessed the end of the monarchic regime amid great political instability, with 45 governments in 15 years during the First Republic (1910–1926) (Baklanoff 1992). The First Republic began with a reformist impulse that gradually gave way to increasingly more conservative alliances. Labor rights improved during the first years, but repression against labor increased gradually, reaching a notable peak during a brief dictatorship (1917–1918). The First Republic did not decree universal male suffrage as promised and offered the excuse of wanting to avoid the kind of monarchic revolts that occurred in neighboring Spain. Political participation remained restricted to literate males (Costa Pinto 2000). During this period, governments progressively began to exclude an incipient labor movement from the political arena to contain its political activism, resorting to systematic repression. The authoritarian turn of 1926 and the strong influence of Italian corporatism on the first decades of the subsequent Estado Novo period (1933–1974) would abruptly change industrial relations and governments' relationship with organized labor and even with organized employers. Under this new context, the political inclusion of labor into the corporatist regime occurred through state-controlled unions.

During the First Republic, the Portuguese Republican Party (Democratic Party -PDP- since the 1915 election) rapidly became dominant, while conservative forces remained unable to form a viable electoral alternative. The PDP governed for the whole period other than during the coups of 1915 and 1917–18. This political dominance froze conservative elites out of government, which fueled increasingly anti-democratic strategies on their part. The freezing out of conservatives from office through a lack of party rotation accounted for the fragility of the First Republic institutions (see Costa Pinto 2000; Baiôa et al. 2003). This fragile democratic breakthrough would end with the 1926 coup.

The labor movement became highly centralized primarily because of an increasingly repressive state, though it maintained its anarcho-syndicalist profile until the end of the First Republic. The democratization process that began in 1910 legalized strikes and the unions' political role. Labor became active in fighting for the legal regulation of working hours. The 1917 general strike was a high point in labor demonstrations, ending in massive arrests and heavy repression. In 1919, the General Labor Confederacy (CGT, *Confederação Geral do Trabalho*) was founded with an anarchic-syndicalist profile (Teodoro 2003). However, governments became increasingly repressive during WWI due to the growing influence of the new, anti-democratic, employers' federation (UIE, *União dos Interesses Económicos*) (Costa Pinto 2003).

The labor movement developed strong ties with the Portuguese Communist Party (PCP), which was founded in 1921. The PCP was also severely repressed and was outlawed by the end of the First Republic. It was, nevertheless, the only political party to survive the long-lasting authoritarian regime clandestinely until resurfacing for the 1974 revolution. While the CGT maintained its' anarcho-syndicalist profile, its relations with the Communist Party were fluid and unlike those with any other party, until communist union members were expelled from the CGT in 1925, during the final crisis of the First Republic (Teodoro 2003).

The 1926 breakdown and subsequent military coup in Portugal represented an abrupt change in the organizational dynamic for both labor and employers. Beginning in 1922, government repression of labor peaked alongside a conservative reaction, setting back previous labor political *recognition* as well as the tolerance of *resistance*. The CGT was dissolved in 1927 by the authoritarian government. By the end of the First Republic, the government suppressed the right to strike. Unions, as well as political parties, were heavily restricted or outlawed. Political exclusion was the leading strategy governments deployed to reduce labor activism, fundamentally through the instrument of repression. A complete setback to our political practices of interest occurred during this period: dominant elites withdrew support for the practices of *recognition*, *representation*, *joining*, and even for *voting* and tolerance of *resistance*.

Following the 1926 breakdown, the state created bargaining structures to defend the new regime, mirroring Mussolini's Italy (Costa Pinto 2003). The new regime received strong influences from the nascent corporatism in neighboring Italy and from the Catholic movement around the Rerum Novarum and Quadragessimo Anno encyclicals. The 1928 elections had only one contender, Oscar Carmona, who appointed Antonio Salazar as Finance Minister. Salazar deployed a successful program based on state intervention, which extricated Portugal from the Great Depression. This intervention afforded Salazar prestige in conservative circles, including among the military (Costa Pinto 2003).

An authoritarian corporatist regime consolidated in the years that followed, which is crucial for understanding institutional legacies in labor relations and cooperation in the labor relations arena. The Estado Novo modernization program had three pillars: the state, the social role given to the Catholic Church, and the tight control of political and social opposition. The 1933 National Labor Statute (ETN, *Estatuto Nacional do Trabalho*) became the cornerstone of Portuguese corporatism during the following four decades. Spain and Dollfuss' Austria followed similar paths (Crouch 1993). In Portugal, the ETN laid the foundation for highly restricted political participation on the part of labor, albeit through state-controlled unions. Consistent with the role played by Catholic social doctrine, during the initial phases of the Estado Novo, the Union of Catholic Workers (*Círculo de Trabajadores Católicos*) and the Catholic Student Union (*Centro de Estudiantes Católicos*) were key players in the consolidation of corporatism (Madureira 2007).

With the dissolution of previous labor unions, new associations were chartered from the top (Makler 1976; Costa Pinto 2003). Labor was organized in unions called *Sindicatos Nacionais*, which were explicitly intended to subordinate labor interests to the goals and interests of the nation and to oppose class struggle and internationalism. The regime forced previously existing unions to convert to this fascist-style union structure (Barreto 2000), which had a legal monopoly on labor representation during the Estado Novo with only minor changes during Caetano's administration (Barreto 2000). The government's successful cooptation of organized labor in a top-down fashion reflected clearly aliberal elite practices toward labor regarding *representation* and *joining*.

As explained in the previous chapter, while this cooptation did not legitimize labor organizations, it contributed to the *recognition* of labor as a political actor. While labor's political participation in the corporatist regime was highly restricted, the participation of employers from the state-led employer association was also restricted. In this context, labor participation did legitimize labor as a political actor alongside employers. This strategy of *controlled coordination* thus proved a key legacy after the dual transition and contributed to the legitimation of labor as a political actor decades later under democracy.

While employers had decidedly back the 1926 coup, the following corporatist regime would considerably challenge their associations and independence just as it did with labor. Although employers were formally organized in patronal guilds *(grémios)*, major firms and nascent economic groups accepted bureaucratic control by the state in exchange for privileges, that is, rent-seeking (Baklanoff 1992; Makler 1976). Small but influential groups gradually managed to exert influence in the Salazar administration via the stipulated corporatist institutions (Baer and Leite 1992). As Louçã et al. (2014) posit, Salazar's policies gradually hindered industrial competition in favor of dominant groups.

At the summit of the corporatist reorganization of the state, a Ministry of Corporations (*Ministério das Corporações e Previdência Social*) was even created in 1950 to direct the corporatist management of labor relations and production. By then, a growing inflow of foreign direct investment into Portugal accompanied the country's entry to the European Free Trade Association (EFTA), the General Agreement on Tariffs and Trade (GATT), the International Monetary Fund, and the World Bank during the following two decades. These events signaled a moderate but firm initial economic opening process (Baer and Leite 1992; Baklanoff 1992).

After Salazar's successor, Marcelo Caetano, eased labor law restrictions beginning in 1968, the labor movement began a clandestine centralization process under the new Intersindical Nacional (IN) labor central. The fact that the process was clandestine indicates the continuance of aliberal elite practices toward labor *representation* and *joining* and the diminished effectiveness of the previous corporatist order. The gradual and nonmonotonic process of economic liberalization beginning in the 1960s aided the increased labor political activity, guided by the integration of Portugal into Europe and the effects of decolonization on Portuguese domestic politics.

The Estado Novo ended abruptly but its decay, and that of elite strategies toward the empowered inclusion of labor, occurred more gradually in a process that began slowly in the mid-1950s, as proposed above. In the next chapter, the analysis of the dual transition in Portugal emphasizes how it affected elite strategies toward the empowered inclusion of labor.

3.4 URUGUAY: POLITICAL ORDER BY CONSOCIATIONALISM

A Characterization of Consociationalism

A third strategy for balancing political order and the empowered inclusion of labor, illustrated by the Uruguayan case, was "*consociationalism.*" This strategy was possible in a context of a solid democratic record and the presence of two catch-all parties through which a divided elite was able to channel conflict over the inclusion of subordinate groups in politics. In Uruguay, parties historically have been the main catalyzers of societal conflict (Real de Azua 1984), relying on informal but continuous dialogue and consultation with employers and labor leaders.

Unlike in Chile or Portugal, the analyzed period in Uruguay begins with the robust political domination of a liberal reformist coalition within the Colorado Party ideationally oriented toward pre-war Europe. The liberal character of this coalition was closer to the British or even Swiss experience than to Chile or Portugal. However, by the mid-1920s, the influence of fascist corporatism on conservative elites shifted this liberal ethos by the 1930s toward a mild version of corporatist aliberalism.

Early recognition of labor by the liberal coalition within the Colorado Party that dominated the country's politics between 1903 and 1933, which coopted labor leaders by appointing them to government positions – obviated labor's need for resistance. Labor lacked an incentive to centralize their political interest under an encompassing association, instead maintaining representative associations along ideological lines with a strong divide for most of the period between anarchists and communists. Labor enjoyed unrestricted representation prerogatives except during the authoritarian impasse between 1933 and 1942. Individuals' ability to join autonomous labor organizations was not seriously challenged in Uruguay during the period either.

Universal suffrage for males was granted in 1918 and for women in 1934. Therefore, unlike in Portugal or even in Chile, males in Uruguay acquired the right to vote and stand for election as early as 1918 without any other restriction. No franchise restrictions for any subordinate group have been imposed in the years since. In 1943, wage coordination became mandatory and semi-centralized at the sector level, reinforcing tripartite concertation and fostering deliberation. This consociational strategy was sustained by informal linkages between party and labor leaders instead of being institutionalized from the top down as in Portugal.

A *consociational* strategy with the crucial participation of political parties became dominant. Conservative sectors, nevertheless, were able to slow the pace of such reformism and even neutralize it during three periods: between 1916 and 1919, between 1933 and 1938, and, finally, beginning in 1958. Neither liberal nor conservative governments controlled associations *strictu-sensu* or legally restricted political participation on the part of labor. Centralized wage coordination allowed an underorganized labor to strengthen the building of its long-term political legitimacy.[13] The combination of these sustained liberal practices toward labor assured early political *recognition* and, as such, enabled labor to build political legitimacy over the period. *Resistance* was only activated following the demise of the liberal coalition in power by 1958, amid the strengthening of leftist parties and the centralization of labor political interests for the first time during the 1960s.

While the structural conditions for corporatism were absent in pre-dual transition Uruguay, consociationalism served a similar function because interest concertation provided levels of cooperation that promoted social well-being (Streek and Kenworthy 2005). The corporatist experiments of the 1930s and 1940s in Latin America, Stepan argues, served the purpose of recreating a new hegemonic base for support for the state to include subordinate groups after the 1929 crisis (Stepan 1978, 55).

While the influence of corporatism in Uruguayan politics is undeniable, it is also clear the country's experience differed from that of countries such as Argentina, Brazil, and Mexico, whose experiences provided the lens through which the region was characterized. Uruguay is a divergent case in this respect, because it did not exhibit any of the four characteristics the literature identified as favorable to the emergence of corporatism in Latin America at that time (Stepan 1978, 78–95). During the first decades of the 20th century, Uruguay exhibited a high level of development of independent political parties and interest groups, high

---

[13] See Steiner and Ertman (2002) for similar experiences in the European context.

levels of polarization with political mobilization around two catch-all parties, critical advancements in welfare legislation and structural reforms between 1911 and 1928, and relatively low state-resource capacity alongside symbolic and coercive dimensions. A divided elite mobilized by the two main political parties had not invested in strengthening state symbolism or even in creating a well-trained military.

During this period, the close relationship between party and labor leaders at the top minimized conflict until the final demise of the dominant liberal coalition in the Colorado Party (between 1958 and 1964). Labor, though weak and divided, began participating in politics in a very liberal state that progressively adopted corporatist-like systems of shared decision-making in which commissions and cabinets included government-appointed members alongside employer and labor leaders.[14] Overall, during this period, elites *recognized* labor as a political actor, allowed and tolerated *representing* bodies and freedom of association, eliminated *voting* restrictions and, for most of the period, tolerated *resistance.*

The Historical Development of Consociationalism as an Elite Strategy

In the face of growing labor activism, political stability was achieved in Uruguay via a consociational strategy toward labor political activism that strongly resembled the French, British, or Swiss liberal experiences. In Uruguay, the 1904 Civil War ended with the victory of the liberal Colorado Party (PC, *Partido Colorado*) over the conservative National Party (PN, *Partido Nacional*), which triggered a period of major social reforms up until 1916. The Colorado Party's highly dominant liberal reformist coalition supported labor rights and organization. It passed universal male suffrage as early as 1918. During the period, nevertheless, there was some mild repression, mainly between 1907 and 1911 (Caetano 1984; Yaffé 2001).

Between 1903 and 1915, Uruguay enacted significant pro-labor legislation, such as the right to strike and the 8-hour workday (Caetano 1984). Yaffe (2001, 10) demonstrates how, during the period, governments abandoned the traditional repressive response to labor activism, effectively marking a turning point in elite attitudes toward social conflict.

---

[14] For a detailed account of consociational democracies in Europe, read Ertman and Steiner (2002). Afonso (2013) revisits the conceptualization and use of social concertation in Europe in the 21st century.

Union leaders were coopted by the government, but their organizations did not develop formal linkages to the PC. The building of consociation-alism occurred through personal relationships between party and labor leaders, a feature that would endure in Uruguayan politics. In contrast to the situation in Chile and to Portugal, the Uruguayan political and eco-nomic elites comprised different individuals. Because these political and economic elites competed with one another, they mobilized labor earlier (Real de Azua 1984).

The labor movement grew fragmented in a context of a high level of governmental tolerance of its political activism. The concentration of the main unions in an urban setting (Montevideo), in contrast to the situation in Chile or Portugal, facilitated this activism. With no connections to polit-ical parties, the labor movement embraced anarcho-syndicalist strategies that encouraged neither organizational nor political growth. The anarchist-oriented Uruguayan Regional Workers Federation (FORU, *Federación Obrera Regional Uruguaya*), the socialist-oriented General Workers Union (UGT, *Unión General de Trabajadores*) and even a Catholic-oriented con-federation (CUGO, *Confederación de Uniones Generales de Obreros*) were founded in 1905. Although the CUGO and the UGT did not last long, the latter played an important role in the foundation of the social-democratic-oriented Socialist Party in 1910.[15] The Communist Party was founded in 1921, splitting from the Socialist Party; both parties remaining electorally weak throughout the period. In 1923, the anarchic-syndicalist Uruguayan Syndicalist Union (USU, *Unión Sindicalista Uruguaya*) was created (see Rodriguez 1966), and in 1929 a Communist bloc left FORU to create the Uruguayan General Labor Confederation (CGTU, *Confederación General del Trabajo del Uruguay*), led by the Communists.

Elite strategy toward labor political activism remained largely the same after 1916, when the liberal coalition witnessed a conservative reac-tion – influenced, somewhat, by Italian and Spanish corporatism – dur-ing the inter-war period. The conservative coalition was bipartisan and formed by non-liberal sectors in the PC and the conservative PN. It was formed during the 1920s and governed between 1930 and 1942. Between 1916 and 1933 there was a retreat from reformism, though labor did not suffer from systematic repression or legal bans (Caetano 1984). During the authoritarian interlude between 1933 and 1938, labor suffered from more sustained repression (see Caetano 1984; Caetano and Jacob 1987;

---

[15] See Zubillaga and Balbis (1985) for a detailed history of the Uruguayan labor movement at the turn of the 20th century.

Porrini 2003). Tolerance of *resistance* fell among the dominant political elite at the time, but neither *recognition* practices nor *joining* or *representation* changed markedly. No restrictions on *voting* occurred. The 1934 Constitution established females' right to vote.

This conservative coalition had a fascist and corporatist ideological foundation. A series of parliamentary initiatives during the 1920s and 1930s illustrates this ideological orientation. In 1925, a project was introduced in parliament to create state unions, mirroring Mussolini's initiatives in Italy (Rodríguez 1966). The project, which would have severely restricted representation and joining practices, did not pass. However, it illustrates the extent to which early Southern European experiences with authoritarian corporatism influenced Uruguayan politics. It also shows how fascist corporatism became influential throughout the two regions and, particularly, in the three cases studied here.

In contrast to the experience of labor in Chile and Portugal, labor in Uruguay remained weakly organized, fragmented along ideological lines, and without strong ties to the main parties (Alexander 2005). During the strengthening of the conservative reaction, during the 1920s, the Communist Party and labor movement united under the CGTU. The Communist Party remained small and electorally unsuccessful during the period. In 1934, labor united for a general strike following the President's self-coup. Their unity did not last. The General Workers Union (UGT, *Unión General de Trabajadores*), a new Communist-led labor organization, was created in 1942.[16] However, as in 1933, and despite initial success, it was hampered by internal divisions (Porrini 2003; Rodríguez 1966).

Overall, during the period, a divided organized labor movement was only able to centralize its members political interests in ad hoc fashion (Porrini 2003; Rodríguez 1966). Employers faced the same challenges during the period, organized in industry-related chambers and unable to centralize their political interests. Similar to experiences in western Europe, Uruguay's non-repressive and even accommodating climate toward labor prevented the formation of a coherent working class. During the period, the primary political cleavage remained a middle-class divide instead of a cross-class cleavage.

The conservative reaction to the liberal reformism weakened between 1938 and 1942. Conservative sectors failed to maintain incumbency in the 1942 election. Between 1943 and 1951, Uruguay consolidated its ISI and nationalized foreign-owned utilities under a new reformist coalition,

---

[16] This union is not related to the short-lived socialist leaning one mentioned before.

once again within the PC. A wave of nationalizations and the sanctioning of mandatory and semi-centralized wage coordination encouraged a period of labor unionization in the public and private sectors (González 1999; Lanzaro 1986).

Consociationalism continued to be the dominant elite strategy toward the empowered inclusion of labor during inward-looking industrialization. While dialogue between labor leaders and political leaders had been promoted during the previous liberal period through the Colorado governments' cooptation of labor leaders, centralized wage coordination became a mechanism that reinforced consociationalism until its' suspension in 1968 (Bogliaccini et al. 2021).

The Communist and Socialist parties gained some political relevance during this period by exploiting their parliamentary alliances with the reformist sector of the Colorado Party (see Lanzaro 2013, 237). Nevertheless, this late liberal-labor alliance ("Lib-Labism") did not yield better electoral outcomes for the two leftist parties.

In accordance with the corporatist tendencies that prevailed at the time in Europe and in the Southern Cone, and amid a divided and politically weak labor and an uncoordinated rent-seeking business sector, the PC reformist coalition unsuccessfully attempted to coopt organized labor by creating a pro-government confederation: the Labor Batllista Action (AGB, *Acción Gremial Batllista*) (1947–1950) (Rodríguez 1966). However, labor resisted this corporatist-like top-down initiative and remained divided and independent, only entering a process of interest centralization during the 1960s, once the reformist coalition became greatly debilitated (González 1999; Lanzaro 2004). This attempt on the part of governing elites, had it succeeded, would have hindered the pluralist practices of *representation* and *joining*.

Conservatives within the PC once again formed a coalition with the conservative sectors in the PN. Together, conservatives advanced a constitutional reform to replace the Presidency with a National Government Council (*Consejo Nacional de Gobierno*), a collegiate executive of nine members – five from the majority party and four from the minority party – that would redistribute power between winners and losers. The reform, adopted in 1952, dispersed authority,[17] allowing conservative factions within the PC and PN to slow or block the reformist agenda.

---

[17] Because Council members were distributed within each party based on how many votes each faction received, the faction that received the most votes held only a proportional majority in the Council.

In 1958, the PN won the national election, which signaled the beginning of the end of the PC reformist coalition. Consociationalism withered due to several causes. With the weakening and eventual demise of the reformist factions in the PC came a decade-long political realignment.

Alongside this process, two other phenomena contributed to the weakening of the dominant strategy toward labor. On the international front, the Cuban Revolution contributed to a polarization of labor relations and in the domestic arena, repression toward labor increased (Alonso Eloy and Demasi 1986). These processes prompted labor for the first time to centralize its political interests under an umbrella organization, the National Labor Central (CNT, *Central Nacional de Trabajadores*). These processes also promoted the parallel unification of the political Left, including the Socialist and Communist parties, under the Frente Amplio umbrella.

As an elite strategy toward the empowered inclusion of labor, consociationalism failed to retain its dominant character as the reformist factions of the PC weakened beginning in 1958. The economic stagnation and political turmoil of the 1960s also contributed to the demise of this strategy.

4

The Unity of the Left and Adaptation of Elite Strategies

Each generation has its epic. Our epic was to throw Pinochet away and to do it with Pinochet alive. I tell my Spanish friends that "you pontificate a lot, but you waited for Franco to die to do something. We did it with 'Franco', alive and as Commander in Chief for eight years". Can I tell you how our transition was in an anecdote? It was a state visit of President George Bush to President Aylwin back in 1993. They start talking. There were five hundred people in La Moneda. Well, on that visit, Bush asks Aylwin: "Tell me, was it in this palace that President Allende committed suicide? Could you tell me where it was?" Aylwin responds: "Yes, of course, dinner ends, and I will show you." Dinner follows, and Bush asks Aylwin: "What happened to the widow of President Allende?" [Aylwin answers] "There she is, over at that table." [Bush] "Is she here?" [Aylwin] "Yes, of course, because she is the widower of a president, she is invited by protocol." The conversation continues. [Bush] "And what about Pinochet? What became of him?" [Aylwin] "Pinochet is over at that table, over there. [Bush] 'Here? Pinochet in La Moneda?" [Aylwin] "Of course, because he is the Commander-in-Chief of the army. It is up to the Commander of the Armed Forces to be present at a State dinner." That is our transition, "Tencha" [Allende's widow] here, Pinochet there.

(President Ricardo Lagos, personal interview held in
Santiago de Chile, September 2019).

This chapter presents the second part of the historicist causal structure of the argument. It first analyzes the historical underpinnings of the unity – or disunity – of the Left. Second, it shows how pre-dual-transition elite strategies toward labor – described in the previous chapters – weakened in the face of emerging tensions but ultimately adapted to the new democratic and open market circumstances.

Over the course of the dual transition, Chile, Portugal and Uruguay experienced deep transformations in their production regimes, though with different characteristics. As Kuznets (1960) and, before him, Polanyi (1944) proposed regarding the effect of rapid economic change on political institutions, all three countries succumbed to a process of rapid economic deterioration. Rapid social change and mobilization of new groups into politics accompanied these changes, which, as Huntington (1968) proposed, produced political instability. Political regimes eventually collapsed, no longer maintaining an equilibrium between political stability and the inclusion of subordinate actors into the political arena.

A strengthened political Left played varying roles in the political conflicts of the day, depending on the national context. In Chile, an experiment with democratic socialism was interrupted by the 1973 military coup, which harshly repressed politicians from the Left and organized labor in the subsequent years. In Portugal, there was a unilateral Communist radicalization, in alliance with organized labor and part of the military, at the onset of the Carnation Revolution. This attempt to establish socialist authoritarianism was openly opposed by the Socialist Party, establishing a deep and long-lasting divide between the two main parties of the Left at the time. In Uruguay, neither the Communist nor the Socialist Party, which remained united alongside labor but refrained from engaging in any regime-destabilizing activities, backed the guerrillas. Thus, the guerrilla movement was not directly related to either the political Left or to the labor movement.

The unity of the Left was affected by two main factors. First, it was affected by the extent to which divisions over political strategy appeared within leftist parties during the period. For example, the PCP and the PSP in Portugal differed over the direction of the political transition after the Carnation Revolution (Costa Pinto 2008; Fernandes and Branco 2017). The second factor was the images that the political Left and organized labor constructed – that is, the narrative they told – regarding the role they had played during a period of violence and harsh repression on the part of their political opponents.

Employers experienced great distress during the dual transition and varied in their capacity to adapt. In Chile, for example, the military government pushed for harsh liberalization backed by a competitive and internationalized business sector. In Uruguay, however, employers tried to hold on to their rent-seeking strategies while attempting to influence a military government that did not have the decisiveness or clear objectives of their Chilean counterparts. In Portugal, after the abrupt end to the Estado Novo, an aggressive nationalization process greatly weakened traditional economic elites. As a result of these three distinctive trajectories, explained in detail below, labor and leftist parties in the three different countries found themselves with different challenges and opportunities for gaining political power – jointly or separately – in a general context of uncertainty.

Organized labor changed its trajectory in the three countries both before and during the dual transition, strengthening its relationship with the political Left. Labor participation in the political arena also increased during the period as regime change in the three countries weakened the previous political order and created opportunity for participation from below.

Analysis of this period is critical, therefore, for understanding how these events affected the post-transitional unity of the Left in each country. In Chile, a division occurred between the center-left parties forming the Concertación coalition and the Communist Party. The Concertación did not attempt to renew the pre-transition close linkages with the labor movement. In Portugal, a division occurred between the Communist and Socialist parties, as did a divide in the labor movement between the two main labor unions. In contrast to Chile, the two blocs within the political Left maintained close relations and strong societal linkages with one of the labor unions. In both Chile and Portugal, though for different reasons, an inner-party system,[1] from which the Communist Party was excluded, was formed in the post-transitional period (see Bosco 2001; Roberts 1995). In Uruguay, the political Left remained united and gradually nurtured its' relationship with an undivided labor movement. These differing scenarios, in turn, yielded different post-transitional paths for solving the perceived employment-wages tradeoff and for how long-term elite strategies and intra-left relations shaped distributive strategies. The unity of the Left had crucial effects on the Left's ability or willingness to mobilize subordinate groups in the political arena and even on their decisions about how to pursue, as political actors, the empowered inclusion of these groups, mainly organized labor.

Elite strategies toward labor, in turn, have shown striking continuity in all three cases between the pre- and post-dual transition periods in their approach toward the empowered inclusion of labor. In Chile,

---

[1] Morlino (1986) coined the concept of "inner-party systems" to depict how in post-transitional environments, pro-regime parties may exclude parties that are perceived as anti-regime by government coalitions, marginalizing them from decision-making and resource management instances.

the legal framework inherited from the authoritarian period featured a series of important provisions for limiting labor's political participation, including restrictions on individual and collective labor rights. The design of electoral institutions, particularly the return to voluntary registration and the binomial system, also constituted voting-related practices that, although adapted to the new democratic context, still lessened the political participation and political representation of the less privileged. In Portugal, the new democratic state recognized labor's political legitimacy even during a severe economic crisis, continuing to use institutionalized participation mechanisms for limiting labor's capacity to pursue its political strategy. In Uruguay, dialogue between social actors and political actors continued to be the main mechanism for articulating order and empowered inclusion under the auspices of a state that had returned to playing a mediating role between employers and labor. These continuities in the three help explain the influence of long-lasting elite strategies in shaping the constraints and opportunities for leftist unity and left-labor relations after the dual transition.

The historical analysis of the period, which follows, connects the dots to explain how the political rise of the Left, the growing importance of class politics, and the disproportionate levels of political violence during the dual transition affected the post-transitional unity of Left, particularly the relationship between Communists and Socialists. The analysis also elucidates the linkages between the dominant elite strategies of the earlier period, during the first half of the 20th century, and the strategies elites consolidated in the three decades following the dual transition. This continuity, in turn, suggests significant levels of path dependence, which I analyze in Chapter 5 through the lens of labor reforms.

4.1 CHILE: A DIVIDED LEFT AND ELITE-BIASED CONTESTATION

Franchise Expansion and Left Political Mobilization of Labor

Elite-biased contestation became less and less effective in Chile's rapidly changing circumstances. A first important change was the elimination of voting restrictions, which contributed directly to the empowered inclusion of subordinated groups and indirectly to the political legitimacy of labor as a collective actor, allowing citizens and constituencies to elect their representatives from their constituencies and to veto disfavored policies. In fact, only a decade after the beginning of these reforms, a political coalition comprising the Communist and Socialist parties would win the Presidency. The electoral reforms of 1958 represented the first step in a decade-long process of increasing voter participation. The 1958 electoral reform made the vote more effectively secret and in 1962 voter registration became mandatory.[2] Illiterates were allowed to vote and the voting age was reduced in the 1969 electoral reform from 21 to 18 years.[3] Because of these reforms, registration increased from 40 percent to 74 percent of the eligible population. Voter turnout almost doubled from 35.4 percent of adult population in 1961 to 62.9 percent in 1964 (Moulian and Torres 1989), increasing to 82 percent between 1971 and 1973 (Moulian 1986b). Overall, in just a few years, the electorate increased by around 240 percent (Moulian 1986b, 23).

The Communist Party was also legalized in time to present a candidate of its own for the 1960 municipal election. The reincorporation of Communists to political life, alongside the significant reforms to the electoral landscape, was a game-changer. Opportunities for labor political activism grew between 1964 and 1973 when Christian Democrats, Communists, and Socialists competed for the working-class vote. The reincorporation of the Communist Party, *per se*, lifted some limitations on the practice of *representation*.

During the 1950s and 1960s, the Christian Democracy Party (DC) replaced the Radical Party as the representative of the middle-class. The Radical Party, in turn, moved to the right and formed electoral alliances in support of right-of-center candidates. The Christian Democrats, positioned at the center of the electoral preferences, strongly competed with the Communists and Socialists for the political allegiance of labor (Collier and Collier 1991; Luna et al. 2014; Raymond and Feltch 2014). This change was accompanied by growing political instability and conflict during a period of elite division.

The legalization of rural unions in 1967 during the Christian Democratic government (1964–1970) (Arriagada 2004, 111), another lifting of limitations on *representation* and an advance in tolerating *resistance*, further strengthened a united labor movement under the CUT, which gained enormous political power and also political legitimacy during that period. However, it did so in the context of increasingly acrimonious industrial relations as inward-looking industrialization stagnated. Labor organization in Chile by the 1960s resembled the British Trades

---

[2] Law 12.918 from June 1958. For a detailed analysis of the 1958 reform, see Gamboa Valenzeula (2011).

[3] Law 17.284 of January 1970.

Union Congress (TUC) in that it had reasonable levels of centralization and a high level of union membership.[4]

Overall, an expanding electorate posed fundamental challenges to the existing parties, which struggled to represent an increasing set of demands. This opened the door for party realignment or renovation. The Christian Democratic party's refusal to form a coalition with either the Right or the Left had important consequences (see Luna et al. 2014)[5] and produced a three-block party system. Elections during this decade reflected this situation, dividing the vote into three more or less equivalent parts.

After winning the 1964 election, internal conflicts between the "moderates" and the "rebels" within the Christian Democrats ended with the latter splitting to form the Popular United Action Movement (MAPU, *Movimiento de Acción Popular Unido*) (Moulian 1986b). The DC strategy of not partnering with any leftist or right-wing party created an opportunity for a class coalition uniting Communists, Socialists, and the CUT that crystallized during the 1960s and won the 1970 election by a narrow margin.[6] This coalition of the Socialist and Communist parties, together with other minor parties, formed the Popular Union (UP, *Unidad Popular*) by the end of 1969 as an electoral coalition. It was a class alliance with the explicit goal of socializing means of production and increasing popular participation (Bitar 1995). The CUT's role in voicing labor concerns grew, and its political power also increased until 1973.

Unidad Popular explicitly excluded the Radical Party, with which left-of-center parties had formed alliances in the 1930s and 1940s. MAPU entered the UP alliance for the 1970 election. This electoral union, which had the enthusiastic support of the CUT, prevailed in a highly competitive election in 1970 (Valenzuela 1995). The Allende government (1970–1973) then began a radical plan for moving Chile toward a democratic socialism.

In terms of recognition, the inclusion of the CUT in the cross-class alliance formed with the UP provided legitimacy to labor for advancing collective bargains and compromises. This brief period, between 1967 and 1973, would position Chile in the empty quadrant in Table I.1 in that

---

[4] See Luebbert (1991) for a detailed account of the British TUC at the time.

[5] The electoral vote for the Christian Democrats increased steadily from 6.37 percent in 1956 to 22.8 percent in 1963, while the Radical Party received on average 22 percent of the vote and the Right (the Liberal and Conservative parties together) received 24–31 percent of the vote (Moulián 1989).

[6] Christian Democracy (1956) originated from the Falange Party (1939) that seceded from the Conservative Party.

it featured both a united Left and labor political legitimacy. However, this would be a brief period, after which the conservative reaction that followed withdrew recognition of labor's political legitimacy and would, in part, produce a long-lasting division between the Communist and Socialist parties.

The Response from Civilian Elites and the Military

The 1967–1973 period witnessed a series of critical changes for employers (see Arriagada 2004). The expansion of the voting franchise proved to be particularly damaging for the political Right. The traditional Liberal and Conservative parties shrank their vote share drastically, obtaining a combined 12.5 percent of the total vote in the 1965 parliamentary election. For the next electoral period, these two parties merged along with other minor parties to create the Nacional Party (Moulian and Torres 1989). This inchoate party successfully endorsed an independent candidate for the 1970 election, supported Pinochet's coup, and promoted military continuity in the 1988 plebiscite.

The land reform that was initiated by a Christian Democrat government (1964–70) and expanded under Allende (1970–73) threatened rural property rights not simply because of land expropriation but also because of illegal occupation of some land (Arriagada 2004; Haindl 2007). State participation in the economy increased after Christian Democrats created the National Planning Office (ODEPLAN, *Oficina de Planificación Nacional*), increased taxes, partially nationalized mines, and extended the land reform. That marked a departure from the previous government's liberalization attempt (1958–64) and the advice of the Klein-Saks mission during that government (Haindl 2007). Chilean governments under the DC and UP were abandoning a long-held tradition of Chilean elites to remain within the United States' zone of economic influence, a custom the military government restored under Pinochet after the coup.[7]

The electoral victory of the Unidad Popular Left-labor coalition further polarized the political landscape. The UP government (1970–1973)

---

[7] In 1925, Alessandri's government asked the US economist William Kemmerer to serve as an economic adviser, which resulted in the creation of the Central Bank (1926) and the short-lived re-instauration of the Gold Standard (1925). The importance of the Kemmerer Commission does not lie in its immediate results but in how it illustrates the geopolitical center of reference for Chilean elites during the 20th century. Pinochet's regime would move Chile under the United States' influence once again in seeking the advice and policies recommended by the so-called "Chicago Boys."

engaged in rapid economic nationalization to move toward democratic socialism. This radical plan elicited high levels of domestic opposition from elites and international opposition from the United States – a heavy investor in Chilean copper – in a Cold War context. The Cuban Revolution had turned significant attention to Latin America (Silva 1993, 1996). The Allende administration's nationalization of industries threatened economic elites. In 1970, there were only 79 public firms, but by 1972 Allende's government had expropriated 202 private firms and appointed interveners in another 350. CORFO became responsible for administering these businesses, controlling 561 firms at its peak (Haindl 2007).

An anti-socialist coalition crystalized (Silva 1993). Threats to private property encouraged interest convergence between capitalists, landowners, the middle classes, opposition parties, and the military. A violent military coup ousted the governing coalition in 1973 and a harsh military regime imposed not only high levels of repression but a radical move toward a neoliberal market economy (Bitar 1995; Linz and Stepan 1978, 1996; Madariaga 2020).

The Bureaucratic Authoritarian government (1973–1990) followed a well-designed plan toward a markedly liberal integration into the global market mirroring the Anglo-Saxon model.[8] Without exception, large business organizations favored gradualist liberalization and supported the military regime between 1973 and 1975. This gradualist period conformed to classical observations about authoritarianism in Latin America. At the same time, radical internationalist groups (Monday Club and the Brick, Chicago Boys) challenged the gradualists between 1975 and 1978 and eventually gained the military's support (Silva 1993). In the mid-1980s, the government created a strong alliance with organized business through the CPC and the novel right-of-center parties National Renovation (RN, *Renovación Nacional*) and Independent Democratic Union (UDI, *Unión Democrática Independiente*). All five political practices analyzed – *recognition, representation, join, vote and resistance* – became limited once again under the authoritarian regime.

Disunity of the Left and the Return to Elite-Biased Contestation

The Unidad Popular coalition experienced internal tensions between "Radicals" (*rupturistas*) and "Bargainers" (*negociadores*) as soon as the

---

[8] For detailed and complementary accounts of the neoliberal transformation of the Chilean economic model, see Silva (1993) and Madariaga (2020).

Allende government put in motion its plan to move Chile toward democratic socialism (Moulian and Torres 1989). These tensions deepened amidst the economic downturn that preceded the coup. For instance, the Socialist Party opposed the government's decision, in 1972, not to expropriate firms that had not yet been expropriated (Bitar 1995).

After the coup, harsh repression followed. Both labor and the Communist Party suffered in terms of political legitimacy during the dual transition. The labor movement was strongly repressed and outlawed during the authoritarian period, with union density and labor's political power declining dramatically. Labor rights, in turn, were reduced severely by a new set of labor laws in 1979.[9] These restrictions included limitations on the right to strike, weakening collective bargaining capacity within a firm by allowing employers to replace workers during a strike, or even to lock down the firm (Frank 2002). While the labor movement – as in Portugal and Uruguay – remained active clandestinely, its relationship with left-of-center parties, particularly the Socialist Party, became distant.

During the democratic opening, between 1988 and 1990, the previous class alliance between organized labor and the Left gave way to a new center-left alliance – the Concertación (*Concertación para la Democracia*) – between Christian Democrats and Socialists as well as other minor parties. This coalition explicitly excluded the Communist Party (Roberts 1995) and cut linkages with the labor movement and grassroots (Luna and Altman 2011; Navia 2006; Pribble 2013; Roberts 2013). That decision resulted from retrospective analyses of the Allende government experience by Socialists who had been leaders in the Unidad Popular and in the Allende government. As many important political figures from the Concertación stated in personal interviews held in Santiago between 2008 and 2019, the electorally successful center-left coalition that governed the country for twenty years after the dual transition was "born out" of the failure of Allende's Unidad Popular (Popular Unity – UP). As such, this political organization sought to avoid class-based conflicts, prime among which is the distributive conflict. The pre-1973 class alliance would not reemerge.

The resolution of the dual transition was a controlled democratic opening. The military set the pace and extent of the transition to safeguard the

---

[9] A set of four decrees were passed in 1979, radically changing labor organization frameworks and collective bargaining. These were Legal Decrees No. 2756, 2757, 2758, and 2759. The book discusses the detail of such changes in Chapter 5 in the analysis of labor reforms.

inherited neoliberal model (see Madariaga 2020; Siavelis 2001). The military did so by imposing a set of so-called authoritarian enclaves, which had the purpose of limiting the capacity of left-of-center governments to implement their strategy (Moulián 2003; Oppenheim 1993; Siavelis 2001). As the quotation by President Lagos at the start of this chapter illustrates, the military remained a powerful actor. The legal constraints imposed by the military and conservative elites on the political Left and, especially, the labor movement show how pre-dual transition elite strategies based on biased contestation reemerged and adapted to the new democratic environment. Some of these authoritarian enclaves relevant to understanding the relationship between the Left and labor are discussed in Chapter 5 while analyzing the Concertación's labor reform attempts.

The Concertación faced a growing internal divide over labor issues beginning in 1997 in the context of a failed labor reform attempt during Frei's last year in office (1994–1999) and in the wake of the Lagos administration (2000–2006).[10] This divide, and the debate structuring it, gradually became central to Chilean politics, particularly among the center-left coalition (Kaiser 2011; Ominami 2009). This conflict, which divided Socialists, members of the Party for Democracy (PPD), and Christian Democrats alike, unfolded just a year before Frei's reform proposal of 1999 and was still relevant at the time of the Lagos election. Several interviewees have referred to the "two souls" of the Concertación and have observed that the division was not between the parties composing the government coalition but mainly between technocrats and politicians within the coalition.[11]

It is important to note that, because of the legal limitations labor faced and the conflictive relationship with the Concertación governments, the

---

[10] This divide was grounded in two manifestos, written and signed by Concertación members in 1998 (Bogliaccini 2020; Fuentes 1999; Montecinos 1998; Navia 2006; Pribble 2013). A first manifesto, entitled "Renewing the Concertación: the strength of our ideas" [*Renovar la Concertación: la Fuerza de Nuestras ideas*], was signed in May by 59 party members and rapidly became known as the "self-Complacent" manifesto. As a response, another manifesto entitled "People is right: thoughts on the Concertación's responsibilities during current times" [*La gente tiene razón: Reflexiones sobre las responsabilidades de la Concertación en los tiempos presentes*] was signed in June by 146 party members and relevant figures from academia, unions, and culture. This second manifesto was rapidly labeled the "self-flagellants" manifesto. The two manifestos put in writing a growing internal debate in the Concertación. This debate centered around the manifestos' distributive achievements during the Aylwin and Frei administrations and the future distributive strategies.

[11] Personal interviews with three ex-Labor and one ex-Finance Secretaries during the first and second Bachelet administrations, held in 2019.

labor movement also became increasingly conflicted internally. This conflict led to the formation of competing labor confederations amid a remarkable weakening of the CUT (Bogliaccini 2020; Roberts 1995). An inner-party system also formed, as in Portugal, excluding the Communist Party from the governing center-left coalition. The following quotation from a personal interview with an ex-Minister of Labor for the Concertación governments illustrates the divide within the Left as well as the influence of technocratic elites in the Concertación's internal struggles over labor policies:

Look, I think that the Concertación lacked the old Communist Party, the Communist Party of 1973. In Chile, we used to say that when it rained in Moscow, the Chilean communists took out their umbrellas; it was a party that had a very interesting institutional configuration. The Chilean Communist Party was very, very, very Allendista, more than the Socialists. That party would have been vital during the transition, where the center strongly imposed itself on the Left, a divided Left. (…) I would say that within the scope of the coalition, the hegemony of the center was strong. I think that greatly affected the labor issue. Then, there were some very important economists (…), who had a technical link with some economists in the socialist world, who formed a strong opinion, that was very influential in the political field, about the importance of being very careful in labor issues. (ex-Labor Minister, personal interview held in Santiago de Chile, September 2019)

Despite this adverse scenario at the time of the democratic transition, the Concertación had great electoral success, uninterruptedly governing between 1990 and 2010. However, disunity among the Left framed the Concertación position on the employment-wage tradeoff. While the Concertación succeeded in achieving macro-economic stability, it was less successful in redistributing wealth (Muñoz Gomá 2007). The divide among the Left in Chile is directly related to the role pre-distributive policies – wage policy specifically – should have in affecting the growth model inherited from the military period and successfully nurtured during the Concertación governments for the following two decades. As stated by several interviewees, wage policy was a difficult issue to bargain over with the Right. The following excerpt from a personal interview held in Santiago, in 2010, with a Socialist parliamentarian illustrates this point: "Labor relations have been the hardest topic to negotiate with the Right during the post-Pinochet period. Both the political Right and business have retrograde views on labor relations." (Interview with Socialist Congressmember held in Santiago de Chile, July 2010).

From a long-term perspective, the Chilean experience in terms of the relationship between the political Left, organized labor, and conservative elites is an alternation between tolerance and repression. A long-lasting strategy of *elite-biased contestation* led to two decades of political instability, conflict, and repression after the lifting of voting limitations, and the electoral scenario changed abruptly. The radical movement toward democratic socialism during the Allende government led to a renewed strategy of political exclusion during the Bureaucratic Authoritarian period, based once again on heavy repression, the out-lawing of the political Left and labor, and the imposition of legal restrictions on labor's political action after the democratic transition (Linz and Stepan 2017; O'Donnell 1996). While voting limitations had been lifted -albeit vote registry was rolled back to a voluntary character once again, some of the authoritarian enclaves, such as the imposition of a binomial electoral system, lessened the electoral aspirations of the Communist Party. These enclaves also distorted parliamentary major-ities, because the creation of institutional senators provided a means of limiting the empowered inclusion of labor, imposing clear limita-tions on the practice of *representation*.[12] When faced with the challenge of empowering inclusion, the Concertación governments followed the steps of the Liberal government during the 1920s and the Broad Front later on: accommodating the interests of conservative elites in order not to challenge the political order.

4.2 PORTUGAL: A DIVIDED LEFT AND THE EMPOWERED INCLUSION OF LABOR

The Political Mobilization of Labor at the Dawn of a Social Revolution

During the 1960s, Portuguese labor began strengthening due mainly to an initial softening of the previous Salazar regime by his successor and to the initial economic opening, as explained in the previous chap-ter. The country's productive structure suffered significant transforma-tions between 1960 and 1973. The percentage of the labor force in the primary sector dropped from 44 to 28 percent of the total labor force while the percentage in the secondary sector grew from 29 to 36 per-cent and in the tertiary sector grew from 28 to 35 percent (Baklanoff

---

[12] Institutional senators, also denominated "designated senators", existed in Chile between 1990 and 2006. These life-long senators were appointed under the provisions of the 1980 Constitution.

1992). These concomitant processes generated new dynamics in the labor arena, increasing the labor force in the secondary sector by developing an export-oriented manufacturing sector (Baer and Leite 1992; Macedo 2003).

In contrast to Chile and Uruguay, Portugal had colonial territories overseas. By the end of the 1960s, the political situation in the African colonies became unstable, and the period known as the "Colonial Wars" began. That placed an increasing strain on public finances, affecting the overall equilibrium in the public budget and eroded public support for the Estado Novo (Baer and Leite 1992).

These two factors fueled political instability. The replacement of Salazar by Caetano as Prime Minister in 1968 created a gradual – albeit incomplete – opening in political participation. In 1969, the Caetano government allowed Sindicatos Nacionais to grow beyond the district-level and to limit state interference in unions (see Barreto 1990). These measures facilitated coordination among labor leaders to better escape the monitoring of the corporatist state. While still present, limitations on *resistance* and *representation* began to weaken.

This strengthening of organized labor mobilization, although clandestine, provoked a reaction on the part of Caetano's government. The beginning of the 1970s were years of growing conflicts between labor and the government in a context of substantial expenditure on warfare because of the colonial wars (Baer and Leite 1992) and low investment in welfare provisions (Huber and Stephens 2012). For instance, the Portuguese expenditure on Africa was almost half of its GNP (Lloyd-Jones 2001). Furthermore, as Fishman states (2019), further demands led to further repression once Cateano's liberalization attempts failed. In contrast, by the end of the period, the welfare state in Portugal was much weaker than were those in the Southern Cone of Latin America (Huber and Stephens 2012).

In October 1970, in this context, labor clandestinely established the Intersindical Nacional (IN) labor central, which would centralize labor's political activity against the dying Caetano government. Labor also strengthened its relationship with the Communist Party. Soon after, in 1971, Caetano's government prohibited the IN, although it remained clandestinely active until it became the CGTP right after the 1974 revolution (Barreto 1990).

As political violence increased, a social revolution in which the military, labor, and the Communist Party played major roles ousted the regime (see Bermeo 1987; Fishman 1990a, 2011). This social revolution rapidly displaced old Estado Novo cadres while opening the door for disputes over regime changes that were both political – for example, democracy or a new authoritarian rule – and economic – for example, socialism or capitalism. This tripartite coalition radicalized and attempted to move the political transition toward a new left-leaning authoritarian regime.

No party, employer association, or even labor association from the Estado Novo survived the dual transition, except for the Communist Party (Bruneau and Macleod 1986). Because of the radicalization of the CGTP and the Communist Party during the 1974 revolution and the weakness of employers' organizations, there was no effective tripartite bargaining either, despite the marked corporatist character of the revolution (Crouch 1993).

The Divided Left at the Twilight of the Social Revolution

The political Left in Portugal became dominated by the newly founded Socialist party (PSP) and the Communist Party (PCP). After the dual transition, a narrow and radicalized alliance between the Communist Party and organized labor (CGTP), which sought to block the democratic opening process at the onset of the 1974 Carnation Revolution, closed the door to a wider alliance with a center-left Socialist Party that had a strong democratic orientation and office-seeking oriented (Costa Pinto 2008; Fernandes and Branco 2017; Kitschelt 1994; Smith 2012).

The revolutionary transition to democracy, as Campos Lima and Naumann (2011) argue, produced a long-term politicization of unions. This process of early radicalization even ended up breaking the labor movement because of UGT's apparent socialist leanings. The CGTP also experienced strong internal divisions between pro-communist and pro-socialist labor leaders due, in part, to the changing political orientations of the revolution. The CGTP remained closely linked with the PCP while the UGT aligned with PSP and with the center-right Social Democratic Party (PSD). As the two parties severed relations, the conflict deepened between the two labor centrals (see Smith 2012; Wiarda and Mac Leish Mott 2001).

The PCP played an essential role in labor politics during the transition, even managing to convince the military government (MFA, *Movimento das Forças Armadas*) to pass the *unicidade sindical* law. This law officially recognized the IN-CGTP as the sole officially-sanctioned labor central with a monopoly on worker representation (Bruneau and Macleod 1986). This PCP strategy was a significant force in the split between the PCP and the PSP (Smith 2014). As early as November 1974, the Socialist Party tactic was to create a union movement to compete with the Communists (Harvey 1978).

Shortly after democratic restoration, the Socialist Party realized its' vote share largely surpassed that of the Communist Party, making an alliance unnecessary (Smith 2012). The Communist Party was excluded from the inner-party system, and legal steps were taken to allow the formation of alternative labor centrals (see Bosco 2001). The revocation of *unicidade sindical*, by the 1976 constitution, made it possible to create the pro-socialist and social-democratic General Workers Union UGT (União Geral dos Trabalhadores) as early as 1978.[13] The UGT, since its creation, was wary of strikes and demonstrations (Bruneau and MacLeod 1986). The relations between the two labor centrals have been marked, from the beginning, by sharp conflicts and little to no coordination. While political recognition of labor remained unlimited, the democratic restoration restored legitimacy to social actors and their organizations. Democratic restoration also lifted limitations on the practices of *representation, voting, joining and resistance*.

Between 1976 and 1984, Portuguese labor relations were contentious in the midst of a process of firm nationalization in which employers were greatly weakened (Dornelas 2010; Fishman 1990b). This period would firmly shape power constellations in the post-transition scenario. In contrast to Chile, however, employers in Portugal remained divided, weak due to the heavy losses nationalization imposed on them, and lacking strong ties with the political Right. Party-employer relations have been weak, as in Uruguay, because employers have supported different parties. Although right-wing parties have maintained, during specific periods, a more robust grasp on representation of employers' interests, the PSP has also maintained strong linkages with employers. For instance, almost all Socialist governments have had more ministers and state secretaries with ties to employers than without such ties (Louçã et al. 2014).

Employers developed their umbrella organizations, by sector, after the revolution. These new associations also confronted significant conflicts in their attempts to centralize employers' political interests. The

---

[13] See Dornelas (2010) for a detailed and complete description of the different periods of the Portuguese industrial relations system until 2009.

Industrial Confederation (CIP, *Confederação da Indústria Portuguesa*) was formed mainly by big business, with weak roots at the local level. Severe internal conflicts of interests were present during the early years of the Agrarian Confederation (CAP, *Confederação dos Agricultores de Portugal*) (Bruneau and Macleod 1986). As noted above, the wave of nationalizations in the aftermath of the revolution greatly weakened the business sector. This changed during the liberalization process carried out by Prime Minister Cavaco Silva's government (1985–1995) (Crouch 1993). As in Uruguay, employers were unwilling to centralize their political interests under an inter-sectoral umbrella organization.

The Socialist Party, with a clear office-seeking strategy (Kitschelt 1994), held office during most of the first decade after the revolution, although usually in minority governments, while the Communist Party remained in opposition. Unlike the PCP, the PSP became an inner-system party (Smith 2014; Bosco 2001). The center-right political space accommodated two parties: the Social-Democratic Party (PSD, *Partido Social Democrata*) and the Center Social Democratic Party (CDS, *Partido de Centro Democratico Social*). Unlike their left-wing competitors, these parties attempted to build ad hoc coalitions, some of which were electorally successful, such as during the 1979–1980 Democratic Alliance (AD, *Alianza Democratica*) government. The Left Block (BE, *Bloço de Esquerda*), born in 1999, occupied, along with other minor parties, the rest of the left-of-center political spectrum.

In terms of labor relations, the post-revolutionary scenario was highly favorable to labor because nationalizations, the 1976 constitution, and labor law were highly protective. As early as 1976, with inflation having reached 50 percent, the Socialist Party (PS) in government together with the votes of the center-right PSD and the rightist CDS liberalized lay-offs (Decreto-Lei n.o 841-C/76 1976). Policy expanded the list of admissible causes for lay-offs and, quite notably, eliminated the need for unions' approval before a dismissal. By 1977, the government allowed for the hiring of temporary workers (Decreto-Lei n.o 781/76 1976)[14]. Firms did not need to justify the use of temporary workers, who could be offered renewable three-year fixed contracts. Workers hired under these temporary contracts accounted for around 12 percent of the total labor force during the 1980s (see Watson 2015, 139). That same year, the government issued another decree that allowed

[14] https://dre.tretas.org/dre/12470/decreto-lei-781-76-de-28-de-outubro

firms with financial hardships to be excused from collective bargaining agreements (Decreto-Lei n.o 353-H/77 1977)[15].

Conflicts in the labor relations arena increased between 1981 and 1983 as the new Democratic Action (AD – *Acción Democrática*) government formed by the center-right PDS and the rightist CDS passed the so-called *"paçote laboral"* which heavily cut employment protection and unemployment benefits. The labor movement called for two general strikes in 1982. Violent confrontations with the police occurred during the second one, even resulting in deaths (Watson 2015).

The divide among the Left consolidated in Portugal – both in the political and labor realms – by the time of the country's accession to the European Community in 1986, even after CGTP's strategic shift and PCP's abandonment of its revolutionary stance by 1989 (Watson 2015, 168). This divide features vertical ties between CGTP and PCP and between UGT and PSP (and, until 2003, between UGT and PSD).

Over the long term, party-labor relations evolved along ideological lines and with a permanent divide between the Communists and Socialists at the party level and between the CGTP and UGT at the labor level. Unions and parties were closely attached as Portugal union leaders could run for the Assembly under a party label or be an active member of a party. Union leaders ran within the PCP, PSP, and even the PSD (Bruneau and Macleod 1986). The PC-CGTP alliance has been strong and enduring over several decades; the PS-UGT alliance facilitated coordination rather than a stable coalition. During the 1980s and 1990s, the UGT also had strong linkages with the PSD. These linkages weakened after the 2011 crisis.

In 2015, the Communist Party broke the inner-party system barrier, joining a leftist governing alliance comprising the Socialist, Communist, and the Left Block (BE, *Bloço de Ezquerda*) parties. That only occurred after the hardships of the 2011 crisis and the movement to the right by the governing PSD. For the first time, the PSP sought an electoral coalition with the PCP and the BE, breaking the idea of an inner-party system. However, this was merely an electoral coalition, not even a governing one as BE and PCP had independent bilateral accords with PSP. Several actors from the three parties acknowledged this view in personal interviews conducted in 2019. The PS negotiated with each of them separately, subject to electoral performances.[16]

---

[15] https://dre.pt/pesquisa/-/search/240853/details/normal?jp=true/en
[16] Three interviewees, the PSP, BE, and PCP leaders, confirmed the short-term perspective of the leftist coalition. Interviews were held in Lisbon in January–March 2019.

The Consolidation of the Left Divide and State-Led Concertation

The depth of the Portuguese Left divide precluded the type of neocorporatist policymaking present in other European countries and in Uruguay after the dual transition. Notwithstanding this divide, elites returned to promoting coordination among employers, and labor continued advocating for greater political participation. Governments began adapting labor regulations from the Estado Novo and revolutionary periods. A gradual process of transformation in labor relations began amid a period of high economic distress but with the prospect of joining the European Economic Community. Labor resisted the increase in flexibilization, with the CGTP and the UGT even managing to coordinate with each other to stage two general strikes in 1982.

The post-revolutionary period required a strong coordination commitment between the different actors in the political arena (Fishman 1990b; Lloyd-Jones 2002). The military gradually withdrew from the political scene beginning in 1976. The new parties from the Left and the Right began to build their coalitions (Bruneau and Macleod 1986). While governments were volatile under the new parliamentary system, multiple accords between 1982 and 1985 allowed for a new period of gradual but continuous dialogue between the political system, labor, and employers. In 1984, the coalition government of Socialists and center-right Social Democrats created the Permanent Council for Social Concertation (CPCS, *Conselho Permanente de Concertação Social*), a corporatist institution for facilitating dialogue between the government and social actors (Royo 2002).

State-led concertation is an attractive alternative to coalitional politics in contexts of a divided Left, where labor is a legitimate political actor. Under contentious politics, institutionalizing social concertation with direct control exerted by the government becomes attractive. Portugal meets these conditions. Fishman (2011, 2019, 29) argued that corporatist institutions facilitated a legal continuity during the transition toward democracy in Portugal. This book looks at the institutional basis of social concertation as a critical element of state-led concertation. Institutional binding of labor power insulates governments from unwanted wage militancy.

The CPCS aimed to boost coordination between governments, employers, and labor. It is important to note that the criterion for choosing this type of institution was based on the capacity of organizations to influence decisions regarding collective bargaining rather than representativity

(Dornelas 2003). On the side of labor, UGT and CGTP participate in the CPCS; while on the side of employers, the CIP, the Commerce and Services Confederation (CCP, *Confederação do Comércio e Serviços de Portugal*), and the CAP participate from the beginning. Later, the government invited the Tourism Confederation (CTP, *Confederação do Turismo Português*) to participate as well. Labor and employers have an equal share of votes in the CPCS.

By 1986, a first accord was signed in the CPCS, initiating a long-lasting tradition of social dialogue. Fishman (2017, 2019) underlines the importance of social forces having the ability to initiate collective action, in addition to having organizational strength and resources, as critical features that distinguish the Spanish and Portuguese democratic practices. The CGTP refused to participate in the CPCS until 1987, despite having a chair at the table from the beginning. The CPCS ultimately allowed both the communist-leaning labor central CGTP and the socialist-leaning UGT to participate actively in institutionalized decision-making. As Watson (2015) posits, the CGTP's decision to recognize the legitimacy of CPCS was a turning point in its overall strategy. Since 1987, CGTP has actively participated in the CPCS but hardly ever signs accords. However, according to Schmitter and Grote (1997), from 1987 to 1992, CPCS mirrored what Northern European institutions had done in the previous decade by exchanging wage moderation and flexibility for social measures and labor legislation. This decision-making institutionalization mechanism, which will be analyzed in-depth in Chapter 5, posed different opportunities and challenges for labor and employers' organizations. It also institutionalized labor's political legitimacy. The institutionalization of political participation by labor under the CPCS helps to combine the empowered inclusion of labor and political stability. It also gives a clear advantage to the PSP in terms of governability.

From a long-term perspective, the Portuguese experience regarding the relationship between the political Left, organized labor, and economic elites is one of mutual recognition of the other party's legitimacy as a social partner (*parceiro social*). A long-standing strategy of controlled coordination did not legitimize pre-revolution labor organizations. It did, however, legitimize labor. The corporatist strategy of controlled coordination adapted to the newly democratic context. Controlled coordination became institutionalized consociationalism in the context of the CPCS. Labor gained enormous political leverage from the 1976 Constitution, but governments, even PSP ones, employed corporatist institutions to bind labor's political power while recognizing its political legitimacy. Cooperation became institutionally bounded instead of controlled. While state-led concertation is entirely democratic, and controlled coordination is not, both are similar in their use of institutions as a prime instrument for binding labor political activism.

4.3 URUGUAY: LEFT UNITY AND THE CRAFTING OF A LEFT-LABOR COALITION

The Demise of Liberal Reformism and the Strengthening of Labor Mobilization

Consociationalism weakened in parallel with the exhaustion of the PC liberal coalition. That, in turn, signaled the need for labor to centralize its political interests to gain political leverage, which opened the door for the political Left to gain political relevance. Consociationalism, however, legitimized labor as a political actor. It also established a path-dependent culture of dialogue between labor and political parties on both the left and the right.

The 1958 election signaled the end of the second reformist PC coalition's political dominance. Consociationalism weakened as the ISI model began to stagnate by the end of the 1950s, opening the door to a gradual increase of class-based coalitions on the Left and growing repression from the government. Politics entered a period of instability. No incumbent party faction was reelected between 1952 and 1966, illustrating the inability of the political system to cope with economic and political problems, which, in turn, fueled a growing social discontent. An increase in working-class coherence, in turn, was paired with the surge of a labor-mobilizing party.

The Uruguayan experience with centralized wage coordination between 1943 and 1968 departed from a pure non-coordinated wage setting mechanism. However, the state's role in a highly protected environment did not foster a strengthening of autonomous coordination between labor and employers, as did happen in northern and continental Europe during the period (Katzenstein 1985). Centralized wage coordination accompanied a development strategy where politics would trump economics. Because the country remained a liberal democracy, political stability was aided by tripartite coordination. However, the stagnation of the ISI put enormous pressure on this concertation-based model.

The end of the second PN conservative government in 1962 marked a period of party realignment, characterized by strong fractionalization (González 1991, 1993). The party system began a process of change with the PC moving to the right after the demise of its reformist coalition, the PN moving toward the center, and the foundation of the center-left Frente Amplio (see Lanzaro 1993; Yaffé 2005).

Organized labor, which had remained divided along ideological lines, began a process of interest centralization, which yielded the foundation of a new labor central, the National Workers' Confederation (CNT, *Convencion Nacional de Trabajadores*).[17] Concomitantly, the Frente Amplio was founded in 1971 by a merger of the Left Liberation Front Party (FIDEL, *Frente Izquierda de Liberación*), the Communist Party, the Socialist Party, the Christian Democratic Party, "Lista 99" – a faction that defected from the Colorado Party – "Lista 41" – a faction that defected from the National Party – and other minor groups.[18] The newly formed Frente Amplio obtained 18 percent of the popular vote in the 1971 election, ending a 150-year period of two-party dominance in Uruguayan politics. However, the military coup of 1973 prevented the potential consolidation of an electorally successful left-labor alliance during the period.[19]

The government replaced wage councils, in 1968, with the Council on Wages and Prices (COPRIN, *Comisión de Productividad, Precios e Ingresos*) (Doglio et al. 2004).[20] Employers also began to participate in electoral politics within party lines more directly and influenced government by increasing their participation in elected posts (Stolovich et al. 1991; Bogliaccini et al. 2020). Rural employers recovered their capacity for political strategy after a period of decay during the neo-Batllista era, with the formation of the Federal League for Rural Action (*Liga Federal*

---

[17] The Uruguayan labor movement at the time is comparable to the contemporary French, Italian, and even Finnish cases – although the Finnish movement had higher levels of centralization at the time. High fragmentation levels follow from ideological tensions among labor groups (Crouch 1993).

[18] See Doglio et al. (2004) for a detailed account of the politics of the formation of the Frente Amplio and the interest centralization of the labor movement.

[19] For the 1971 election (the first one after the CNT formation), the combined working-class vote for the PC and the PN came to slightly over 50 percent. The FA vote composition for that election included 43 percent of upper- and middle-class voters (Collier and Collier 1991).

[20] COPRIN comprised five delegates from the Executive branch of government, two from organized business, and two from organized labor. However, the government appointed labor delegates from a six-candidate list these organizations submitted.

de Acción Ruralista) by the mid-1950s. As in Chile, rural economic groups were more enthusiastic about economic liberalization than were industry and urban business groups (see Doglio et al. 2004; Zurbriggen 2006). Unlike in Chile, the two main parties from the previous period, the PC and PN, continued to represent business sectors and channeled their political demands.

The increase in political violence during the 1960s did not help consociationalism. Political violence increased, as did government repression toward labor. The conservative PC administration (1967–1972) repressed labor protests against significant decreases in real wages. The government even incarcerated workers during strikes (Notaro 2016). As a result, prior to the 1973 democratic breakdown, labor was actively contesting the measures taken by the PC's government (see Demasi 2016). The political practices analyzed – *recognition, representation, join, voting and resistance* – became limited under the authoritarian regime.

The Consolidation of a Left-Labor Alliance

The closeness of labor to the Left goes back to the end of the 1960s. The two organizations were born in the process of interest centralization leading to the creation of the CNT (which later became the PIT-CNT) and the FA. The Chilean UP was an early model for the two organizations regarding their ability to unite and be electorally successful. However, the Bureaucratic Authoritarian regime that emerged only two years after the FA's first electoral participation interrupted the political strengthening of the newborn party and the labor central. Political parties and the labor movement were outlawed, civil liberties heavily restricted, and repression further increased.

In contrast to the situation in Chile or Portugal, neither the FA nor the CNT was a vehicle for political radicalization and violence. On the contrary, the main party leaders remained pro-democratic actors, joining most Blanco and Colorado leaders in the clandestine fight against the dictatorial regime. The labor movement and the Frente Amplio strengthened their political legitimacy during the authoritarian period by joining the political opposition to the regime while strengthening their ties clandestinely (see Yaffé 2005). Moreover, Yaffé (2005) shows how, even during the last years of military rule, the outlawed Frente Amplio voiced many demands through the labor movement.

The military regime did not accomplish much. It neither revitalized the ISI model nor decidedly turned to a neo-liberal model, as happened in Chile. ISI stagnation continued while some liberalization was attempted by the military but without any success. The Council of Wages and Prices, which had functioned since 1968, was replaced by an even more authoritarian corporatist-like body for setting price, the National Directorate of Costs, Prices and Income (DINACOPRIN, *Dirección Nacional de Costos, Precios e Ingresos*). Even in an authoritarian setting, there was still formal wage coordination, though it was often inefficient or rigged.

FA and CNT leaders continued their political activity clandestinely. The post-dual transition setting provided a new common enemy against which these two actors could present a united political front: "neoliberalism". The alliance between the Left and labor strengthened under military rule and the post-transition opposition to right-of-center governments during the 1990s. Within the general opposition to government reforms, the labor relations arena became a cornerstone for forming and consolidating the long-lasting alliance. The suspension of mandatory, centralized wage coordination in 1991, affecting union density levels for more than a decade, was vocally opposed by the FA. During the next three elections, the reinstatement of this wage policy instrument became a central issue in the FA electoral platforms. This policy issue elicited little conflict within the party, which speaks to how the FA embraced the relationship between employment creation and wage-egalitarianism. A year into its' first-ever mandate, in 2006, the FA reinstated collective wage councils. By 2008, comprehensive reform to the 1943 law was on its way. The approval of the reform occurred only three and a half months after its arrival to Congress. The PIT-CNT played an active role in the public debate. Employers won only two concessions in the bill: the exclusion of any regulation of a firm's occupation by workers and the incorporation of a "peace clause" stating that labor cannot strike on previously agreed issues.

Labor leaders in the PIT-CNT are, when affiliated with political parties, usually affiliated with the Communist and Socialist parties, and, in a less organic form, with the Tupamaros (mainly in the Popular Participation Movement, MPP-FA), all of which are within the Frente Amplio. In contrast to the situation in Chile and Portugal, the Communist Party remained united with the center-left in the Frente Amplio, strengthening the Left bloc and its relationship with the labor movement. The Communist influence in the labor movement remained as high as ever during the late 1980s and the 1990s (see Doglio et al. 2004, 258; Rodríguez et al. 2006, 80). In the 1989 election, the Communist Party obtained 46.9 percent of the vote the Frente

Amplio received. Lanza (2013) argues that the Communist Party invested in the Frente Amplio by moderating its discourse at the critical moment of the demise of the Berlin Wall, which signaled a moment of crisis for the Communist Parties worldwide and in particular in our two regions.[21] The Frente Amplio, Lanza (2013) argues, may well have served as a corset for the tensions inside a Communist Party experiencing an ideological crisis amid a very successful election turnout in 1989.[22]

The left-labor alliance strengthened to the point that, once the Frente Amplio won the 2004 election, many labor leaders obtained positions in government. The Frente Amplio has evolved during the last two decades to become a labor-backed party, augmenting labor's political strategy capability (Lanzaro 2011). As an example, and in contrast to Chile where most Labor Ministers from the Concertación governments have been economists, all Labor Ministers in the three FA administrations have been ex-labor leaders.

When FA won the election in 2005, it took away good and strong leaders from PIT-CNT. (Interview with FA MP and ex-beverage union leader held in Montevideo, March 2010)

Uruguay is the only one of the three analyzed cases where the political Left did not experience harsh internal conflicts during the dual transition. Not having government experience or participating in political violence during that period enabled the FA to remain united and carry out important clandestine activity. The Communist Party remained a vital part of the Frente Amplio, which became a privileged channel, though not the only one, for dialogue between the party and organized labor (see Senatore and Yaffé 2005).

The Return of Dialogue between Elites and Labor and the Birth of Neocorporatist Policymaking

By 1985, after the democratic transition, the elected government reestablished centralized wage councils. No intra-left conflicts divided the Frente Amplio or even weakened the relationship between the FA and labor. To the contrary, the labor movement became a prime political ally for the Frente Amplio after the dual transition. The two formed a

---

[21] See Bosco (2001) for an analysis of Communist Parties at the time in Southern Europe.
[22] See Lanza (2013) for a detailed history of the Communist Party during the post-dual transition.

robust coalition (see Bogliaccini 2012; Doglio et al. 2004; Etchemendy 2019; Pérez Bentancur et al. 2019; Rosenblatt 2018).

During the first democratic administration, under the PC (1985–1989), labor relations resumed in the form they had before 1968, with the reinstatement of centralized wage councils. The main challenge for the labor movement during those first years of democratic rule was a perceived need to moderate the rhetoric and confrontational attitude from the previous period (Filgueira 1988; Monestier 2007). Organized labor rapidly gained in membership and increased its ability to affect political decisions vis-a-vis a still-fragmented business sector.

This rapid rebuilding of pre-1973 institutions, even in a challenging international context favoring neoliberal policies, resembles similar processes under a comparably challenging international scenario in post-WWII Germany and Austria (Crouch 1993; Keohane 1984). After 1990, the novel PN government attempted to liberalize the political economy by falling into line with the regional trend at the time (Alegre and Filgueira 2009). The PIT-CNT density shrank, and the increasing over-representation of the public sector in the overall membership did not help labor moderate its approach to collective bargaining during those years (Monestier 2007). Unionization rates plummeted to around 14 percent. Only with the return to centralized wage-setting in 2005 did unionization figures increase again, peaking at 37 percent in 2011 (Rodriguez et al. 2001).

The suppression of wage councils between 1990 and 2005 followed the impulse to shape liberal market institutions. However, three alternative mechanisms to regulate wage coordination, some formal and others informal, were put in place during the conservative PN administration (1990–1994) or directly by sectoral organizations. These mechanisms show the influence of long-term elite-led consociationalism, even during periods that witnessed aggressive attempts at liberalization, and the political legitimacy of the labor actor. First, some sectors continued to participate in bipartite centralized bargaining. That was the case for the construction, metallurgic, transport, health, and banking sectors. The usual condition for the continuity of collective bargaining in these sectors was the existence of a strong union. In most cases, there was a period of strong conflicts following the 1990 suspension of wage councils.

Second, "bargaining tables" were instituted by the PN administration to negotiate the salaries of workers in public firms, though not of workers in the central administration, for whom collective bargaining mechanisms had not previously been available. These were not formal bargaining mechanisms but informal dialogue and consultation mechanisms. This initiative followed from bitter conflicts between the previous administration and public firms (1985–1989). These informal mechanisms remained until the passing of a public sector collective bargaining law during the first Frente Amplio administration (2005–2009).

Third, after suspending the wage councils and witnessing a steady drop in salaries, President Lacalle Herrera asked government officials to establish informal negotiations with the PIT-CNT to stop and then reverse the decline (see Bogliaccini 2012). These negotiations were in place between 1993 and 1995. The second PC administration (1995–1999) called for a three-year "National Dialogue," organized by the Labor Ministry, with the participation of labor and business, aimed at creating a new labor relations framework. There was no final product since the business sector favored voluntary firm-level wage bargaining and labor favored a return to the sectorial-level wage councils.

From a long-term perspective, the Uruguayan experience regarding the relationship between the political Left, organized labor, and economic elites is mutual recognition of the other party's legitimacy and strong vocation for dialogue and negotiation. A long-lasting consociational strategy made its way through the dual transition. Labor's legitimacy as a political actor was not challenged by the dual transition or even by the liberalization period during the 1990s, though it did experience a sharp decrease in union density and a consequent decay in political power. Governments did not abandon dialogue even under decentralized wage mechanisms. Thus, labor remained a legitimate political actor even during the neoliberal period. The Left did not divide itself or distance itself from organized labor. The PIT-CNT continued to be the unchallenged dominant labor umbrella organization. Overall, the liberalization reforms during the 1990s greatly weakened the labor movement, even though informal bargaining between labor and center-right governments persisted and remained fundamental vehicles for dialogue between conservative governments and the labor movement. That is not to say conflicts disappeared. Beginning in 2005, a successful government coalition between the Frente Amplio and labor moved industrial relations toward a type of neocorporatist policymaking.

5

The Usage of Wage Policy for Pre-distribution

We never stopped negotiating salaries with SUNCA [construction sector's union], with good and bad years, from 1985 up until today. We had a fierce conflict back in 1993, an 87-day strike that included the burning of trucks. After that conflict, we decided to get together and bargain over salaries, and we did it until the Councils were reinstated in 2005. (...) We have an ongoing relationship with SUNCA and have put together a set of sectoral social programs: the Housing Fund, the Social Fund—which has been in place for fourteen years—the Dental Plan, the Vision Care Plan, and several school-enrolling support plans for workers' children. We administer them jointly, and both parties contribute to their funding. We have also launched a plan for skills formation with the direct support of President Mujica. We have 1,000 workers in training now and expect to have 3,000 by 2012. SUNCA and CCU [Construction Trade Association] fund 50 percent of the program and the government provides the other 50 percent. Workers in training work 6 hours a day and complete 3 hours of training twice a week.

(ex-CCU leader, personal interview held in
Montevideo, April 2010)

This chapter analyzes the inclusion of wage policy as a pre-distributive instrument in distributive strategies by leftist governments in the post-dual transition period. The analysis of wage and labor reforms brings together the elements theorized as central for explaining the use of wage policy as a pre-distributive instrument: a large-scale and long-lasting elite strategy toward the empowered inclusion of labor; the cohesion – or lack thereof – among the political Left; and the approach left-wing governments have taken toward the perceived trade-off between employment and wage-egalitarianism as an anchoring factor. The chapter shows how wage policy – aside from the setting of minimum wages – is only used as a pre-distributive instrument when governments can comfortably combine their office-seeking strategies with the strengthening of political action by labor. That, in turn, is a consequence of any process that involves moving wage-setting mechanisms from a decentralized and individual-level setting toward centralized and, eventually, mandatory settings.

Employers and labor tend to have opposed preferences regarding wage policy with respect to centralization and their mandatory or voluntary character. The relative ability of each group to build political support ultimately defines the role wage policy plays as a pre-distributive instrument in each country. Labor's ability to gather political support for its cause is strongly related primarily to its empowerment and its strength vis-à-vis employers. The divisiveness or unity of the Left becomes a central factor in labor's lobbying ability. Because of this, the chapter begins by mapping power constellations for the three cases. The analysis builds from there to understand the outcomes of wage reforms and policymaking. It does so by analyzing each country's experience with wage-policy reforms and outcomes separately.

Our cases exemplify change amid continuity. In Chile, there was little room for wage policy in the Concertación's distributive strategy, as there was no room for the empowered inclusion of labor. The Chilean Left has been unable to reconcile both goals, following a *third way* leftist liberalism. The chapter shows how different attempts toward social concertation occurred during the Lagos and Bachelet terms. However, divisiveness among the Left and the Concertación's lack of roots in the labor movement in the context of labor's lack of political empowerment ended up tilting the field toward the status-quo favored by employers and center-right parties. The chapter also shows how conservative elites use electoral and labor legislation to adapt the old restrictive *voting* practice to a democratic environment to prevent labor empowerment. It also shows how restrictions in terms of *representation* and *resistance* adapted through the persistence of the 1979 Labor Code, and how the Concertación ended up accommodating to this status quo.

In Portugal, *state-led concertation* allows empowered inclusion of labor under conditions that give PSP governments – and those of other parties – leeway to increase minimum wages and decree government-controlled collective accord extensions. The PSP found a viable route through institutionalized decision-making, promoting state-led concertation, primarily through the CPCS, and a discretionary mechanism for extending voluntary agreements within sectors via administrative decrees (*portarias de extensão*), which avoided coalitional politics and bounded the empowerment of labor within certain institutional limits. As the chapter shows, PSP and PSD governments used wage policy in different ways. Similarly, the chapter shows how the PCP and the CGTP have been critical to the CPCS and its role in managing political dissent.

In Uruguay, the FA built a distributive strategy based on a semi-centralized wage-setting process and made it mandatory, grounded in a durable coalition with the PIT-CNT. With few institutional checks and balances to political action on the part of labor, party-labor relations remained vital for maintaining a virtuous equilibrium. Neocorporatist policymaking is, then, grounded in a long-standing culture of dialogue between political and social leaders, requiring cooperation between governments, unions, and employers. The chapter shows the importance of dialogue in Uruguayan politics by analyzing government-labor relations during the tenure of the PN and PC center-right governments between 1985 and 2004.

5.1 CONTEMPORARY POWER CONSTELLATIONS

After the dual transition, Chile, Portugal and Uruguay entered into an already four-decades-long experiment with democracy and open-market capitalism. Economic and political performance have undoubtfully improved during this period, but not without partial setbacks. After two decades of continuous growth, Chile has experienced, since 2011, growing social discontent with political elites and parties as representation vehicles. In October 2019, a spontaneous social upheaval decimated Santiago – and Chile in general – in only a few days, amid chaos, repression, and takeovers, resulting in over 30 deaths. At the time of writing, the increasing social upheaval of the last decade has slowly begun to provoke Chile's political system toward replacing the 1980 Constitution, which it inherited from the authoritarian period.

Along with the rest of Southern Europe, Portugal suffered a massive economic crisis in 2008, the Sovereign Debt crisis. This crisis provoked the intervention of the European Commission (EC), the European Central Bank (ECB), and the International Monetary Fund (IMF)–the *troika*–in the domestic management of the crisis. Even Uruguay, with its comparatively rich democratic record featuring, for the first time, 35 consecutive years without a democratic breakdown, had to confront its worst economic crisis on records in 2002. The sudden devaluation of the Argentinean Peso provoked the need for the Uruguayan government to borrow money from the IMF and the United States. Thus, countries in the two regions have remained vulnerable to political and economic difficulties. At the same time, their political and economic institutions continue gradually to strengthen and adapt to the new demands of changing societies. In these vulnerable contexts, leftist governments have had to build long-lasting distributive strategies, and did so successfully.

Power constellations shape these distributive strategies and the use of wage policy as a pre-distributive instrument in them. Labor, more or less empowered, and the (united or divided) Left interact among themselves and employers and the political right. Power constellations slowly stabilized after the democratic transition in each case, adapting to the new democratic environments and their legal boundaries and the challenges and opportunities imposed by the global economy. Table 5.1 describes how employers and labor entered the post dual transition period with respect to their organizational strength, political organization, linkages with political parties, and the legal contexts in which they operated.

Elucidating power constellations and the balance of power during the aftermath of the dual transition is essential for understanding labor relations and labor-reform outcomes, particularly those concerning wage policy. In Chile, the authoritarian enclaves and legal restrictions on individual and collective labor rights is an additional factor obstructing the reconstruction of the pre-Pinochet period relationship between labor and the Left. In Portugal, the revolution and the disempowerment of employers during the nationalization period facilitated the reconstruction of consultative organs. In Uruguay, the employers' divisiveness and an imposition-free transition to democracy facilitated dialogue as a central feature in Uruguayan politics.

The political salience of the perceived economic tradeoff between wages and employment also depends on the historical legacies of elite-labor interactions and power constellations in the present period. Therefore, the articulation of this tradeoff is shaped by domestic conflicts over distribution, links to history, and the political constraints the Left faces in each country. The relative strength of employers vis-à-vis labor to build political support shaped power constellations. In the three countries, employers consistently have opposed the centralization of wage coordination and efforts to make it mandatory whenever a reform proposal put this issue on the table. The following three quotations illustrate employers' interests during key labor reforms in the three countries. In Chile, employers' opposition to the 2006 labor reform advanced by Lagos' government was fierce, as evidenced by the CPC President's speech at a national forum:

TABLE 5.1 *Power constellations and legal environment at the end of the dual transition*

	Labor			Employers		
	Chile	Uruguay	Portugal	Chile	Uruguay	Portugal
Organizational centralization level	Labor has two rival union since the CAT formed in 1995. In a legally hostile context, three rival labor unions (CUT, CAT, and UGT) are active by the end of Lagos' period (2006).	The PIT-CNT will maintain itself as the only and uncontested labor union in Uruguay during the period.	Labor is in two rival union, the CGTP and the UGT.	CPC is the uncontested business-encompassing organization since Pinochet's regime forced employers to centralize their demands and lobbying activity.	Employers have not had a peak level organization since the COSUPEM (1991–2002) broke apart. Conflicts between sectors were present during this encompassing attempt.	Employers do not have a peak-level organization. The CPCS allows for coordination among the primary sectoral organizations (CIP, CCP, CAP, and, later on, CTP).
Legal restrictions for collective action	Labor faces legal constraints on collective action imposed during Pinochet's regime.	Labor faces no legal constraints.	Labor faces no legal constraints, and the CPCS provides a privileged institutional arena for concertation.	Employers face no legal constraints.	Employers face no legal constraints.	Employers face no legal constraints, but the economic nationalization process, until 1979, debilitated their structural power.

(continued)

TABLE 5.1 (*continued*)

	Labor			Employers		
	Chile	Uruguay	Portugal	Chile	Uruguay	Portugal
Coverage / Density levels	Organized labor represents between 9 and 11 percent of the labor force during the period.	The unionization rate is around 33 percent during 1985–1991, gradually dropping to 14 percent by 2004. After the reinstitution of collective bargaining (2006), it stabilizes at around 37 percent.	About 60 percent of the labor force is unionized by 1980. Union density drops until stabilizing at less than 20 percent after the Sovereign Debt crisis (2011).	CPC sectorial member organizations represent more than 50% of firms in their sectors (as reported by CPC). Small firms are underrepresented.	Sectorial Trade Associations represent more than 50 percent of firms in their sectors (as reported by the different chambers). Small firms are underrepresented.	Sectorial Trade Associations represent around 50 percent of firms in their sectors (as reported by the different chambers). Small firms are underrepresented.
Linkages with political leaders	Labor relations with political leaders are distant.	Labor relations with political leaders in the Frente Amplio are close and ongoing.	CGTP and PCP leaders are close, while UGT leaders remain close to the PSP and PSD. UGT-PSD ties loosen after 2009.	CPC's relationship with political leaders is close and ongoing.	Sectorial Trade Associations' relationship with political leaders is distant and ad hoc.	Sectorial Trade Associations' relationship with political leaders is distant and ad hoc.

This reform the government is proposing is obsolete and has been removed in different countries. This reform emulates European countries that have high levels of unemployment and many labor subsidies. It would be much better to apply a modern labor reform, like that in the United States, which has low levels of unemployment and important growth levels each year. (CPC President, Mr. Ariztia, speech in the forum "Generación Empresarial", cited in La Tercera, March 23rd, 2001, page 24).

In addition to opposing any departure from the inherited status quo in wage policy, as illustrated above, the business sector has consistently lobbied against any attempt to reform the 1979 Labor Code. Employers in Chile have successfully centralized their political interests and remain strong as political actors.[1] The following excerpts from a press interview with former CPC President Mr. Riesco in December 2000 and a business leader at a National Business Forum that same year clearly illustrate employers' closeness to the economic model and wage policy in particular:

Logically, businessmen have a sense of loyalty and great respect for the person who was President of the Republic [Pinochet], and who led the country not only to restore normalcy but also gave it a new path to development through a true economic revolution. (La Tercera 2000a, 23).

Lagos must choose between the distributive illusion and the telluric power of growth, (...) between commanding a government which either slows down the private sector or strategically allies with business. Pedro Ibáñez, President of Corpora SA, at National Business Forum 2000 (ENADE 2000). (La Tercera 2000b, December 9th).

In Uruguay, employers decidedly opposed the centralization of wage-setting mechanisms in 2005. In a document presented to the government, signed by the main business associations, employers stated that the norm that regulates this aspect of labor relations "must promote bilateral collective bargaining, without state intervention, (...) the Wage Councils should only intervene in the determination of the minimum wages." The document notes that "all other issues related to the regulation of working conditions should be left out of collective bargaining" (La República 2009). However, differently from Chile, employers in Uruguay did not centralize their political interests. Their relationship with political parties has been less organic, and their lobbying capacity less effective.[2]

---

[1] For detailed accounts of different aspects of business power in Latin America, and particularly in Chile, see Schneider (2004), Fairfield (2015), Madariaga (2020), and Pérez Ahumada (2021).

[2] For a detailed account of business political interest's centralization and its' relationship with political parties and the political system during and after the dual transition, see Bogliaccini (2019) and Bogliaccini et al. (2020).

In Portugal, the debates regarding the 2003 labor reform that created the Labor Code also showed employers' preferences for completely decentralized wage setting or, eventually, semi-centralized but voluntary wage setting. This latter option became part of the 2003 labor reform. Employers, as in Uruguay, have remained divided, and their lobbying capacity with the government has been weak. After the revolution and the cooptation process during the Estado Novo, the nationalization process did not promote the development of employers' power or influence, except for that of big business, as described by Louçã et al. (2014). According to Valdez (2020), employers' position on liberalization is shaped by sector and firm-size production strategies and binding associational commitments. Big business has usually stood for greater decentralization of wage-setting. Consider, for example, the statement of Pedro Ferraz da Costa, an ex-President of an industry trade association (CIP) and prominent businessmen, to one of the widely-read newspapers at the time:

We do not have any advantage in terms of a centralized wage policy. When I was president of CIP, I defended the idea that we should end Social Concertation. Centralized bargaining means treating all people in the same way, which is not realistic in economic terms (Correio da Manhã 2002).

By contrast, labor has consistently lobbied for greater centralization of wage-bargaining during such reforms in the three cases, as illustrated by the quotations below. For Chile and Uruguay, the first two quotations not only express labor's interests regarding wage policy but allow us to grasp, from the perspective of labor, the power balance at the time and the effective influence employers and labor had on the leftist – Concertación and Frente Amplio – governments. In Chile, the President of the most important labor union regrets that the Lagos administration has sided with employers on two of the most pressing issues labor has lobbied for since the return to democracy. In Uruguay, by contrast, the expressions of the PIT-CNT ex-Coordinator reflect almost perfectly the soul of neocorporatist policymaking.

At the end, pressure from business and right-wing parties on government ended by convincing the Concertación and the government (...) with the weakening that the government applied to key issues as inter-firm bargaining and the elimination of the employer's right to replace a worker during a strike, this reform is not good for us. (Mr. Martínez, CUT President. Cited in La Tercera, 2001, March 23rd, page 23)

We would have preferred the final draft to have more support from business and the opposition parties. (...) That [collective wage-bargaining] law came to stay, and any government attempting to remove it will have to confront the labor movement. (Fernando Pereira, PIT-CNT Coordinator, to El País, July 25th, 2009)

The two following quotations, for the case of Portugal, express labor's preferences in the wage policy arena and the more combative position of the CGTP and the more conciliatory posture of the UGT. As explained in the previous chapter, the two unions have distant relations and strong vertical linkages to the Communist and Socialist parties, respectively.

Even so, in these 16 years, there have already been 40 conventions that were extinguished administratively by the Ministry of Labor. Even today, it is proven that the justification [for ending *caducidade*, i.e., allowing employers to withdraw unilaterally from existing agreements] that was presented by the Right in 2003, that it was necessary to boost collective contracting, given the numbers and facts, was invalid. Today we can say that, comparing the dynamics of collective bargaining in the mid-1990s with that which we have today, there were more collective bargaining agreements, there were better conditions for workers, and at the same time, there was also a greater regularity in the annual update of wages. (Personal Interview with an ex-CGTP General Secretary, held in Lisbon in January 2019).

Collective bargaining in Portugal is essential. It is part of, and a fundamental component of, the system of labor relations. It has always been so. There was already a collective bargaining system before April 25th [1974]; it has adapted over time, but it always remains. Collective bargaining is a union's right. (Personal Interview with an UGT ex-General Secretary, held in Lisbon in February 2019).

The CGTP General Secretary defends the pre-2003 reform equilibrium, mainly regarding how to end a collective agreement, which since 2003 requires only one of the two parties, mainly the employers, to ask for its termination.[3] By contrast, the UGT Secretary-General strikes a more conciliatory tone and focuses on the right of labor to bargain collectively, pointing out precisely the continuity of collective wage setting before and after the 1974 revolution.

Overall, as emphasized in Table 5.1, the variations in the empowered inclusion of labor and unity among the Left analyzed in Chapters 3 and 4 are consistent with the different degrees and strength of opposition from employers. In the following sections, the analysis compares labor's

---

[3] A detailed explanation of these policy changes is offered below in this chapter.

and employers' strengths and their ability to influence policy from right-wing and left-wing parties when in government. The analysis provides a picture of power constellations and of how they influence leftist governments' use of wage policy in each case.

5.2 CHILE: THE MAKING OF LEFTIST LIBERALISM

A Disempowered Labor and the Failure of Social Concertation

The democratic transition in Chile occurred in a context of relative strength on the part of the military vis-à-vis the civilians and on the part of employers vis-à-vis labor. The military set the pace of the transition (see Linz and Stepan 1996). The conservative forces' strong position allowed the outgoing regime to design institutions and rules to prevent the new governments from jeopardizing the economic order they were about to inherit. It also allowed for a more than two-decade-long post-transition political vetoing of proposed changes to the previous order, known in the literature as authoritarian enclaves (see Siavelis 2000). In other words, the military instituted legal provisions that limited effective bottom-up political participation, such as proscribing minor disruptive parties like the Communist Party. The military and its conservative political allies prepared the state for effective use of an old and long-standing strategy of limiting empowered inclusion under the new and – for the military – threatening democratic regime. Moreover, they succeeded for a quarter of a century. If one considers that unions' ability to organize and strike is determined beyond the market by the state (Marks 1986b, 13), then the Chilean state, in this sense, maintained stability by limiting political participation and the empowerment of subordinate groups.

One of the rules the outgoing conservative regime imposed was the binomial electoral system, which remained in force from the democratic transition until 2017 and hindered the electoral ambition of small parties, such as the Communist Party. Left outside the Concertación coalition, the Communist Party vote share during the period 1989–2009 was around 5 percent, which, under the binomial system, was not enough to elect any member to Congress. By 2009, during the first electoral coordination between the Concertación and the Communist Party, the latter elected three House members with a 2.5 percent share of the popular vote. As seen in Chapter 4, voluntary voter registration, also enacted during the transition, disproportionately decreases voting in non-elite groups, a limitation in terms of the practice of *voting*. In 2012, during Sabastián Piñera's (2010–2014) conservative administration, Chile reverted to automatic voter registration but switched to voluntary voting.

As explained in the previous chapter, the weakness of Chilean organized labor during this period is partly the consequence of the provisions of the 1979 Labor Code, also approved during the authoritarian period. Three major labor reform attempts, in 1999, 2001, and 2016, discussed the limitations on the right to strike, the limitations to collective bargaining even within a firm, employers' ability to replace workers or even lock down a firm during a strike. Legal regulations are an essential link between organized labor's activities in the labor market and its political activities. These restrictions directly damaged labor's political empowerment.

The Concertación made a strategic decision, early in the democratic transition, to keep labor at arm's length because organized labor maintained a close relationship with the Communist Party. Although labor reforms were always on the Concertación agenda, little progress was made in advancing this agenda (Bogliaccini 2020; Cook 2007; Pribble et al. 2010).

As early as the Aylwin administration (1990–1994), the government approved a comprehensive reform eliminating the most flagrant authoritarian regulations. As Sehnbruch states, the Concertación under Aylwin and Frei considered the generation of social agreements to be first among its labor policy priorities for fostering cooperation between employers and labor (Sehnbruch 2006, 59). This goal would remain central to the governments of Lagos and Bachelet as we shall explain, albeit with low success as it was the case during the Aylwin and Frei terms.

The Aylwin reform, nevertheless, affected positively the practices of *recognition, representation*, and *resistance* in the new democratic environment. Unions were legalized and the requirements to form them were eased (Frank 2002). However, collective labor rights remained restricted. The right to strike continued to be heavily regulated and was legal only under certain conditions. The employer retained the right to replace the striking worker for the duration of the strike ("replacement issue") or to close the firm for 30 days (lockouts), in which case workers were not allowed to benefit from unemployment insurance. This is a restriction in terms of tolerance toward *resistance*. Wage coordination remained completely decentralized at the firm and individual levels. This reform passed under the close watch of the military and right-wing parties. The military secured roles in the Executive and a majority in the Senate due to the institution of lifetime Senate appointments, which affected the practice of *representation* precisely by distorting electoral majorities in the Senate.

A second attempt to reform the Labor Code occurred in 1999, during the last year of Frei's administration. This initiative failed to pass in the Senate because of the votes of two institutional senators. The proposed reform included eliminating the "replacement issue" and the extension of collective bargaining to the industry level (Campero 2007). Although government senators voted in favor of it as a bloc, there is evidence that the bill provoked internal conflicts among Christian Democrats, who accounted for two-thirds of Concertación's members of Parliament between 1997 and 2002 (La Tercera 2000e, 2000f). This reform attempt also left a strong mark on right-wing parties, as Fairfield (2015) documented in her analysis of tax reforms.

The third reform attempt came six months into Lagos's term when the Executive sent a bill to Congress. While the 1999 election did not give the Concertación a majority in the Senate because of the institutional senators, the Concertación had an unparalleled window of opportunity because it held a majority in both chambers between August 2000 and March 2002 due to the combined application for the lifting of immunity for opposition Senators Pinochet and Errázuriz. This parliamentary change revealed the genuine preferences of the Concertación party officials. Government and opposition parties recognized this majority during the debates (Law 19759 History of the Law 2001; El Mercurio 2000, 2001a; La Tercera 2000f). This reform was meant to prohibit the replacement of striking workers. However, at the end of the day, the reform failed to incorporate such a change in the law, due once again to the Concertación's internal conflicts in the context of considerable pressure from business (Frank 2004). Nonetheless, the 2001 reform did introduce some measures that protected unionization. Although the unionization rate rose from 16 percent in 2001 to 19 percent in 2005, unions remained marginal political actors (Pribble et al. 2010).

Similar to previous Concertación candidates, President Bachelet campaigned in 2009 on a platform that called for a new reform to the nation's labor laws. This reform was never even taken up by the Congress because of internal differences among the members of the Concertación. In two personal interviews held in 2019, two ex-Labor Secretaries who served during the first and second Bachelet administrations stated that internal coalition divisions around the topic were the primary reason President Bachelet did not send a bill to Congress.

I believe that "Bachelet I" had no conviction regarding the labor issue. It was not the government's central axis (...) Moreover, I did not believe that it was time to create change around the labor issue. "Bachelet II" [Bachelet's second term] was the appropriate time, and she did. (Ex-Labor Minister, personal interview held in Santiago de Chile, September 2019).

There are also dissensions within the Concertación regarding how to face this [labor] issue. I was a minister in the first government of President Bachelet, and we made a project of collective bargaining, but we did not even make it to Parliament. Furthermore, the dissensions were not because we had an adversary in Parliament, as we had a majority, but basically, the decisions were made by the Executive. Here the Finance Secretary institutionally plays a very important role and plays it in all areas, particularly in this area [labor]. (...) I believe that controversy originated within the government bloc as to how far to advance. There is no agreement about negotiation by branch [at the sector or industry levels] even in the New Majority [post-Concertación left-wing coalition]. (Ex-Labor Minister, personal interview held in Santiago de Chile, September 2019).

Important advances regarding the three conflictive issues were made during Bachelet's second term, although under a different coalition named "Nueva Mayoría," which included the Communist Party in a coalition for the first time since the return to democracy. Incorporating the Communist Party into the leftist coalition requires us to distinguish the Concertación period (1990–2010) from this second Bachelet presidency (2014–2018). The 2016 reform expanded collective bargaining coverage and the right to strike while establishing a baseline for collective negotiation. It also eliminated an employer's right to replace a worker during a strike. Overall, the reform helped advance the political empowerment of labor. Nonetheless, an essential feature of the intended reform – a monopoly on representation for unions, that is, the exclusive right of unions to negotiate to the detriment of non-unionized negotiation groups – was overturned by the Constitutional Tribunal (Candia and Campillay 2018). This reform also was the subject of significant intra-government conflicts, according to individuals who served as Finance and Labor Ministers during the period (see also Marambio et al. 2017).

Social dialogue as an instrument for social concertation has been weak in Chile, although there were two crucial dialogue experiences during the Concertación governments. Upon taking office, Lagos put together a tripartite Social Dialogue Council with opposition parties, employers, and labor. This Council was tasked with reaching agreement on a wide array of reform proposals in a context in which the

Concertación had a majority in the House but fell just one seat short of a majority in the Senate (La Tercera 2000d).

This Council met during the first months of the new administration and reached agreement on several aspects of the proposed labor reform, chief among which was an agreement not to include provisions for extending collective bargaining (La Tercera 2000a). However, the government unexpectedly found itself with a majority because of the lifting of immunity for Senators Pinochet and Errázuriz at the end of August. This majority remained unchanged until the mid-term elections of December 2001. This unexpected situation changed the nature of the political negotiations (see BCN – History of the Law 19759 2001, 115,665,675,690; El Mercurio 2001b, 2001c; La Tercera 2000c). However, early agreements reached by the Council proved important in settling the intra-Concertación conflicts over labor issues. While the reform became law, neither of the "hard topics" was included in the bill, in accordance with the agreement made prior to August 2001. The inclusion of labor in the social dialogue instance is strong evidence of the recognition of labor as a political actor by the Concertación government, a recognition of its legitimate role as a social partner. However, this instance was not institutionalized; similar instances did not occur until more than a decade later.

A second important experience with social dialogue occurred with respect to the 2016 labor reform during the second Bachelet presidency. This reform enacted the Superior Labor Council as a formal institution for overseeing labor relations (CSL – *Consejo Superior Laboral*). The Council is a consultative institution; it has no formal decision authority on any matter. In this sense, it mirrors the Portuguese CPCS. However, instead of including all three labor confederations – CUT, CAT and UGT – only the CUT was invited to participate. As the quotation below illustrates, this government decision was highly conflictive among workers and ended up being decided in the courts. The decision undermined the representativeness of the labor movement in the Council. It gave the center-right second government of Piñera (2018-) grounds to engage in informal dialogues with the other confederations and to avoid sending labor-related proposals to the CSL, as three members of the CSL each argued in separate personal interviews held in 2019.[4]

---

[4] Interviews were held in Santiago de Chile with three members of the labor councils during the Bachelet's and Piñera's terms.

A conflict was generated among the workers' organizations. Because at that time we had three workers' centrals and we discussed which was the most representative. There was a problem with determining how many members each organization had. That even went to the Supreme Court. In the end, the CUT was ratified as the most representative. (Ex-member of CSL. Personal interview held in Santiago de Chile in September 2019)

The main task the law gives the CSL is to monitor the implementation of the 2016 labor reform through a series of yearly briefs for the government. The initial effects of the reform seem to have been a moderate increase in unionization, in the percentage of female workers unionized, and a reduction of organizational dispersion. However, as mentioned, the use of the Council as a consultative organ is too recent and uneven. While the Bachelet administration consulted with the CSL on many labor initiatives, the Piñera administration has ignored the Council. Members of the Council have declared that it has become problematic to present proposals to the Council. As in Portugal, there tends to be a tension between parliaments and these councils in terms of perceived competition for jurisdiction over reform proposals. In Portugal, the CPCS has gained preeminence with respect to the Assembly. Any important proposal is discussed in the Council first, and, therefore, elected officials perceive the Assembly's room for maneuver as greatly reduced. In Chile, by contrast, this new Council lacks the legitimacy of its' Portuguese counterpart. Therefore, proposals have, on many occasions, arrived at a point in the parliamentary debate where it is hard for the CSL to make valuable recommendations.

Chile has not nurtured a tradition of broad social dialogue. Rather, it has nurtured a tradition of dialogue at the top between elites. The main strategy continues to be elite-biased. While the Concertación during the Lagos administration (2000–2005) and the Nueva Mayoría during the second Bachelet presidency (2014–2018) made interesting attempts to promote and even institutionalize social dialogue in the Portuguese tradition with clear support for political participation by labor, these attempts have not yet prospered. While the Left and the Communist Party successfully incorporated important leaders of the 2011 student movement (Von Bülow and Bidegain Ponte 2015, 181), the massive protests of 2019 seem more challenging to harness by a political system lacking healthy societal linkages. The fragmentation of the party system in Chile in recent years, even after the election of the center-left government of Gabriel Boric (2022–present), also hinders the building of those linkages.

A Wage Policy Limited to the Setting of Minimum Wages

The Left entered the new democratic period deeply divided. The Concertación has progressively detached itself from the historical, social bases of the Left and organized labor. The Concertación governments between 1990 and 2010 were characterized by the left-turn literature as an example of the "moderate" Left (Castañeda 2006; Flores-Macías 2010, 2012; Levitsky and Roberts 2011; Weyland 2009b). These governments expanded welfare to a greater degree than any other country in the region (Castiglioni 2005; Garay 2016; Huber and Stephens 2012; Pribble 2013). However, this unprecedented expansion of social expenditure was grounded in a liberal-like framework for labor relations inherited from the authoritarian period (Cook 2007; Cook and Bazler 2013; Muñoz Gomá 2007; Sandbrook et al. 2007; Taylor 2006), in the clear style of *third wayism*.

Wage policy has been a particularly conflictive issue for the Concertación governments because of the divide among the Left, a conflictive character of Left-labor relations, and how the employment-wages tradeoff has permeated a strong technocratic elite within the Left. The following excerpts from the 2001 labor reform debate under the Lagos administration illustrate, once again, this internal conflict.

What we need is an accord between Concertación senators and deputies for collective bargaining provisions in order to send a modification to Congress (Labor Minister, Ricardo Solari, La Tercera 2000c).

It seems that these issues [collective bargaining and replacement of striking workers] should not have been raised at that time [Santiago I meeting], because I do not think that when a government sent a project two weeks ago, why open the discussion again? The issue today is unemployment. (...) Therefore, the only central issue in this country in the next year is employment (DC Senator Foxley, La Tercera, 2000g).

This divide continued to influence labor and wage policy during the two Bachelet administrations. During the 2016 Bachelet reform, the conflict moved to the Executive, between the interests of the Labor Minister and her Finance counterpart for the advancement of centralized wage coordination. In the end, once again, the issue was decided in favor of the latter by President Bachelet.[5]

---

[5] They were confirmed in interviews with both Labor and Finance Ministers at the time. Interviews were held in Santiago de Chile in September 2019. There is also a growing stream of literature analyzing the role social movements had in changing the balance between these two groups within the Concertación and, later on, Nueva Mayoría. See Raitzin (2017), Palacios-Valladares and Ondetti (2018) and Fábrega et al. (2018).

Although Bachelet [during her second administration] has had three [Finance Ministers], every one of them is very strong in the cabinet, very decisive. Whenever one wanted to promote any measure, they always had to go through the treasury. (Ex-Labor Minister. Personal interview held in Santiago de Chile in October 2019)

The employment-wages tradeoff, in turn, deeply rooted in the Concertación, heavily limited the use of wage policy. That became self-evident in the analysis of the debates leading to the 2001 and 2016 labor reforms. Chile has a highly technocratic elite, an outlier in the Southern Cone and Southern Europe. After the dual transition, this technocratic elite treasured essential aspects of the inherited and well-functioning economic model (Centeno 1993; Joignant 2011; Markoff and Montecinos 1993; Muñoz Gomá 2007), in the vein that Mudge (2018) analyzes for Europe.

The explicit objective of not jeopardizing growth and competitiveness, shared by center-right and center-left parties, in combination with the Left's preference to avoid political conflicts, has reduced the Concertación coalition's distributive strategy to the sole use of redistributive policies and the setting of minimum wages. It has focused on macroeconomic stability, economic growth, employment, poverty alleviation, and human capital investment as their primary goals (Pribble et al. 2010; Weyland 2010). This point is illustrated in the following quotation from a personal interview with a Concertación (and Nueva Mayoría) legal advisor to the 2001 and 2016 reforms, referring to the 2001 reform process:

Many leaders talked, some maintained their support, others were against the project. Those who were finally detractors, more than due to generational issues, were the economists, a group of economists who never looked favorably on the reform. (Personal interview held in Santiago de Chile, September 2018)

Wage policy in Chile, then, was limited to the raising of minimum wages, which, as analyzed in Chapter 1, was a consistent policy during the Concertación governments. The ex-Finance Minister during the second Bachelet administration and the 2016 labor reform, Rodrigo Valdéz, stated that "It is important to recognize that labor regulation is a public policy in which objectives of efficiency and productivity easily collide" (Valdéz 2018).[6] The form of the intra-Concertación divide is consistent with the argument about how leftist cadres perceive the political challenges imposed by the tradeoff between employment and wage-egalitarianism and its relevance for structuring the debates over labor and wage policy. It

---

[6] Ex-Finance Minister Valdéz confirmed the existence of a conflict within the Concertación over wage policy as a distributive policy, from his experience during his tenure, in a personal interview held in Santiago de Chile in September 2019.

is also consistent with the idea that economic policy is crucially affected by the selection of certain types of economic policy-makers (see Hallerberg and Wehner 2018). While I do not argue that the conflict remained static during the period from 1997 to 2019, evidence suggests a sustained impact of the perceived tradeoff on the development of the Concertación's distributive strategy during more than two decades.

Chile emerged from the military regime with an independent central bank, limiting the opportunity for political use of an expansionary monetary policy that may endanger the well-functioning economic model. Constraining monetary policy in this way was the military government's explicit goal in adopting this policy just two years before the transition. As Ondetti (2021) stated in analyzing the evolution of taxation in Chile, the conservative reaction to the Allende years produced a strengthening of anti-statist actors that endured post-democratization and have self-perpetuated during the past three decades.

An independent central bank could have been an asset in the design of a semi-centralized wage policy for the center-left, (see, e.g. Iversen and Wren 1998; Rueda and Pontusson 2000). However, the issue of having an independent central bank that could make credible threats in response to eventual wage militancy strategies on the part of labor in a semi-centralized wage setting was never a bargaining chip for labor-policy reform, either during the 2001 reform nor during the 2016 one. Proponents of a centralized wage setting did not use this argument during the discussions. In Uruguay, where wage coordination was effectively centralized under a mandatory regime in 2005, the issue of the relationship between wage policy and monetary policy was not on the table either, even in the absence of a divide among the Left regarding wage policy. The consequences of a lack of credible threat regarding non-accommodating monetary policy are discussed below for Uruguay.

Wage-bargaining centralization, while it remained voluntary, entered the discussions concerning three labor reforms: the Frei initiative in 1998, which did not pass in Congress due to the vote of two institutional senators; the 2001 Lagos reform; and the 2016 Bachelet reform. In the latter two cases, the intra-Concertación debate over wage policy centered around the proposed tradeoff, as depicted in the quotation from Bachelet's Finance Minister Rodrigo Valdéz that serves as the epigraph to chapter 4:

Although it was not one of the so-called "structural reforms of the government program, the changes to the Labor Code gained great prominence in 2015 and became a new focus for business mistrust after the tax reform. The logic of the original project was simple: give unions more power to negotiate, incentivize unionization and eliminate mechanisms considered as attacks on workers" rights.

The rationale was that with stronger unions, better income distribution and, possibly, more social peace could be obtained. (...) It is important to recognize that labor regulation is a public policy in which objectives of efficiency and productivity easily collide with those of equity. (Valdéz 2018)

Technocrats within the Concertación pushed similar arguments against the reform within a 15-year window. Both the literature and the evidence from interviews presented above affirm the strength of the divide among the Left on this issue, the importance of employers' fierce opposition to these policies, and the way the tradeoff became internalized by Chilean politicians and technocrats. In 2010, a former presidential advisor to Lagos made a similar argument, illustrating the importance and stability of this political challenge in the minds of influential political elites:

The correct way of negotiating collectively is about redistributing productivity. That is why wage bargaining should occur at the firm level; you gain nothing with centralized collective bargaining except price distortions (Personal Interview, held in Santiago de Chile in July 2010).

Overall, the lack of success in the use of wage policy as a pre-distributive instrument is directly related to the three factors identified above: elites' long-standing agonistic attitude toward labor, the intra-left divide in a context of solid business opposition to altering the inherited economic model through wage-policy reforms, and the political challenges imposed by the perceived wages-employment tradeoff. The Concertación, therefore, was not able to reach consensus internally about promoting a more centralized wage coordination and, consequently, did not incorporate wage policy, other than increases in the minimum wage, into its distributive strategy. Nevertheless, individual-level rights were advanced gradually from a very restrictive departure point (see Boylan 1996; Murillo and Schrank 2005). In addition, expenditures post-tax and transfers have been highly progressive, though they are not the most generous in the region (ECLAC 2012; Huber and Stephens 2012).

5.3 PORTUGAL: THE MAKING OF STATE-LED CONCERTATIONISM

State-Led Concertation as a Strategy for Consolidating Social Partnership

Portugal is a pivotal case informing the two regions. It combines long-standing authoritarianism with a social revolution. Both processes are structured by corporatism and a state that, through corporatist institutions, nurtures the idea of the importance of social partners' participation in decision-making. Corporatism bridges the authoritarian Estado Novo and the post-transitional democracy. However, the concertation strategy and how subordinate groups' political participation is regulated differ markedly in the two scenarios.

The combination of a favorable attitude among the left-wing elite toward the empowered inclusion of labor and a deep conflict between political partners on the Left made it possible for two labor unions – CGTP and UGT – to consolidate and endure by nurturing relations with either the PSP or the PCP. This context also nurtured the importance of institutions for binding political participation by an otherwise divided and potentially conflictive labor movement. The scenario of a divided Left and a divided labor precluded the opportunity for the development of coalitional politics.

The corporatist heritage canalized labor's political participation and curved down the increasingly conflictive environment. By 1983, the newly elected Central Block government formed by the center-left PS and the center-right PSD became decisive in institutionalizing dialogue between employers and labor. It did so by adapting controlled coordination to state-led concertation.

In a context of profound social and political conflict, the government took decisive steps toward higher levels of institutionalized political participation for labor, a year after liberalizing collective lay-offs and further expanding admissible causes for lay-offs in 1983 (Decreto-Lei n.o 398/83 1983).[7,8] The context in which the CPCS was created and evolved was one in which Portugal was adapting its labor relations institutions to the country's accession to the European Economic Community and to the new global environment in which it had to compete. It was also a context of re-privatizations, which placed the state in a relatively strong position vis-à-vis employers.

The literature agrees that the CPCS was instrumental in forging consensus among the social actors for facilitating concertation during a period in which the formation of viable social pacts was difficult due to the

---

[7] https://dre.tretas.org/dre/5944/decreto-lei-398-83-de-2-de-novembro

[8] Portugal experienced a major shift in its economic transition toward the open market economy with the European Community accession in 1986 and the constitutional reform of 1989, opening the door to re-privatizations. During this period, the country made a clear shift from direct state intervention and ownership to an open market orientation, ushering in a sizeable re-privatization program and ending the previously dominant labor-protecting strategy based on substantial public sector employment, high employment protection legislation but weak unemployment protection (see Bermeo 1999; Branco and Costa 2019; Clifton et al. 2005)

acrimonious political relations of the time (Dornelas 2003; Royo 2002). The CPCS's leading function was to formalize participation mechanisms for employers and labor, which had a significant impact on labor relations for the decades to follow (see Schmitter and Grote 1997). Even for the CGTP – which initially did not favor cooperation – recognizing the CPCS legitimacy caused an essential shift in the confederation's strategy (Watson 2015). Social partners in Portugal were – and continue to be – weak and divided, as there were no employers' or labor-encompassing associations. The creation of the CPCS and the government investment in securing better levels of cooperation and coordination between the social partners is evidence of the political legitimacy of labor and its' recognition as a political actor.

The CPCS is a government-led instance of social concertation (see Dornelas 2010; Campos Lima and Naumann 2000), consistent with the state's central role in Southern Europe and the Southern Cone in structuring the relationship between organized social actors. Conflicts occurred between employers and labor in the context of the CPCS over the decades. Social concertation has shaped the relationship between employers and labor. For example, Valdez (2020) shows how, as late as 2012, during the Sovereign Debt crisis, when the Portuguese government set restrictive conditions on the extension of agreements to the sector level to allow wages to adjust (downwards) to improve firm productivity, employers became overwhelmingly against it.

When the Communist Party did not participate in the inner-party system, and the CGTP remained highly critical of any government, the CPCS enabled the CGTP – and the PCP through the labor union – to voice to labor and bind its political participation, consolidating the CGTP's political legitimacy. While the CGTP refused to participate in the CPCS until 1987 – with the blessing of PCP (Watson 2015) – the UGT did participate as a representative of labor. The difference between the strategies of the two labor unions – CGTP initially being reluctant to participate in the CPCS and remaining, until today, reluctant to sign most accords while the UGT participated from the beginning and has signed every accord since – contributed to the long-standing divide and mutual recrimination between the two labor unions. Nevertheless, the CGTP's participation in CPCS, beginning in 1987, despite being not-cooperative for the most part, signaled its decision to recognize the legitimacy of corporatist cooperation under democracy (see Campos Lima and Naumann 2000, 29; Watson 2015, 169). The CGTP and UGT value the CPCS in different forms, consistent with their overall strategy toward state-led concertation. While the

CGTP considers the CPCS a government instrument for moderating labor demands, the UGT considers the CPCS a vehicle for concertation. These differing conceptualizations surface in the following two extracts from personal interviews with leaders in the two organizations.

A problem of consultation and the change in labor legislation. What happened was that the CPCS became the place destined by governments to legitimize government policies that normally undermine workers' rights and accentuate the favoring of employers' pressures (CGTP leader, personal interview held in Lisbon, January 2019).

So, the CPCS gains much strength and today is a fundamental component of democratic Portugal. The government, tripartite, (...) the share of votes in the CPCS which is the same for government, labor, and employers (UGT leader, personal interview held in Lisbon, January 2019).

Reform coalitions have historically included the UGT, to whom Campos Lima and Naumann argue (2011) governments and employers have made concessions disproportionate to its power. UGT's continuous participation in CPCS has been an important cause of its capacity to participate in such coalitions. The PCP, in line with CGTP, has a much more critical view of the role the CPCS plays in Portuguese politics. It views the CPCS as cushioning the divisiveness among the political Left and labor unions and in moderating far-left actors' demands. This view appears in the following quotation from an interview with a Communist parliamentarian:

We have the Constitution and some rules. In my opinion, these rules are against the Constitution. That is why the government does not need the agreement in the CPCS to defend the workers. The government does not need an agreement in the CPCS to increase the minimum wage. There is no need for agreement in the CPCS to reduce working hours. It does not need an agreement in the CPCS to reduce precarity. The government can just do it. (MP Communist Party, personal interview in Lisbon, January 2019)

The CPCS produces social pacts or accords, some of which have had significant effects on wage policy and explain how the tradeoff between employment and wage-egalitarianism presented itself to the governing Left and how the latter attempted to solve it.[9] The role of the CPCS in shaping wage policy comes from its early days. As early as 1986, its first accord agreed on fixed wage increases at 7 percent, adjusted for inflation (see Campos Lima and Naumann 2011), which decidedly

---

[9] See Dornelas (2010) and Campos Lima and Naumann (2011) for a detailed analysis and classification of social pacts under the CPCS between 1986 and 2010.

contributed to curbing inflation (Royo 2002). Furthermore, many of the agreements signed since 1990 are guided by a wage moderation principle (Dornelas 2003).

In parallel with the CPCS or within it, Portuguese labor relations institutions continued to carry out significant transformations until the adoption of the 2003 labor code. To begin with, the 1989 constitution eliminated references in the previous 1976 constitution to "socialism" while privatizing the media and other firms. It also legislated against employer abuses such as not paying compensation to laid-off workers. The Socialist Party backed the new Constitution at a time when the Communist Party was greatly weakened. There was also a decree improving unemployment benefits that same year (Decreto-Lei 79-A/89, 1989)[10].

At this point, Portugal's collective wage bargaining is classified as limited by Crouch (1993, 264), though it continues to grow at a sectoral level. In comparative terms, Crouch states that the Portuguese system is the least institutionalized wage-bargaining system within the European Community. Union density, at the time, was estimated at around 30 percent (Crouch 1993), which is comparable to the figure for Uruguay right before the 1991 suspension of the centralized wage councils. As in Uruguay, employers' coordination in Portugal remained weak.

Coordination through social pacts occurred not only in Portugal at the time but also in Spain and Italy, to set acceptable wage increases and commit to the European Community's nascent monetary union (EMU – European Monetary Union). Hassel (2014) shows how this type of state-led concertation is characteristic of *Mediterranean market economies*, as the literature on varieties of capitalism has termed the proposed Southern European model (see Hall and Soskice 2001)

The role of the CPCS as an instrument for social concertation consolidated during the 1990s, as the Cavaco Silva government presented the *Programa de Progresso Económico e Social para os Años Noventa*, a comprehensive road plan for labor policy, to the social partners at the CPCS (see Royo 2002). After stiff negotiations within the CPCS, UGT and employers' associations signed the *Economic and Social Agreement* (AES) in 1990. This program was the first of a series of encompassing social pacts on labor market adaptability and wage moderation signed in 1996 (*Acordo de Concertação Social de curto Prazo*, ACSCP, 1996) and in 1997 (*Acordo de Concertação Estrategica*, ACE). The AES was signed in 1990 by all social actors except CGTP. However,

---

[10] https://dre.tretas.org/dre/23127/decreto-lei-79-A-89-de-13-de-marco

CGTP actively participated in negotiations during the PSD government of Cavaco Silva to make labor legislation more flexible to catch up with EEC countries (Dornelas 2003). The AES proposed reducing the workweek from 48 to 44 to 40 hours by 1995, and proposed capping wage increases at 13.5 percent and annually revising the national minimum wage. In 1992, the signature of a new accord by the UGT and employers' associations had wage policy moderation as its central goal. While the CGTP did not sign the accord, it did participate in the prior negotiations. This accord set the maximum annual wage increase at 9.75 percent, and an increase of minimum wages at 11 percent. These two key accords, signed in the CPCS in 1990 and 1992 during a center-right government, underline the growing importance this institutionalized body had for political participation by labor, even when the divide between the two labor unions undermines labor capacity to pursue its political strategy.

The ACSCP (1996) and ACE (1997) were signed under the PSP government of Antonio Guterres (1995–2002) and became a centerpiece of the PSP wage policy, as analyzed below. Overall, the CPCS became soon after 1985 a privileged setting for state-led concertation in Portugal. There, an electorally successful PSP coordinated with the social partners, particularly a divided labor movement. The CPCS served the purpose of moderating the labor divide both in terms of social protests and in terms of the ability of the political system, not only PSP governments, to reach social pacts over wage policy and labor relations in general.

This institutional binding of labor's political participation helped PSP governments, allowing wage policy to be used as a pre-distributive instrument by restraining the scope of potential conflicts. However, CPCS was not instrumental for promoting labor cohesion, as several scholars have pointed out (see Dornelas 2010; Campos Lima and Naumann 2000). In the CPCS, the UGT and CGTP each can unilaterally sign accords with employers and with the government; intra-labor coordination is not required.

The Administrative Management of the Political Challenges Created by the Perceived Tradeoff

Wage policy in Portugal is usually limited to setting minimum salaries, which are updated annually by the parliament, under a government proposal. This allows for wage increase differentials within firms, and essential participation from the government in deciding when sectorial or firm-level accords will be extended. The Labor Ministry's prerogative to extend these voluntary agreements (*Portarias de Extensão*) to whole sectors has usually favored employers as the Ministry can pick and choose among several agreements to extend, moderating wage growth when necessary. However, the right to extend agreements has also allowed the government to favor unions at their discretion by extending only certain agreements that they considered desirable for economic and/or political reasons (Watson 2015).

Wage policy varies in its use as an instrument in the PSP distributive strategy. The three PSP governments between 1995 and 2020 have used wage policy as a pre-distributive instrument but in different forms. Social pacts within the CPCS, born from tripartite agreements, are used for policymaking in this arena, as they were in the 1996, 1997, and 2006 accords (see Dornelas 2010). PSP governments also decreed increases in minimum wages or in public sector wages, or decreed extensions of collective agreements, as noted above. Even the 2006 accord within the CPCS used a sustained annual increase in minimum wages between 2006 and 2011, resulting in a 30 percent increase over five years, as its primary strategy.

How did these PSP governments perceive and reacted to the proposed tradeoff between employment and wage-egalitarianism? When the Socialists returned to office in 1995, a new concertation agreement over wage policy took place within the CPCS, albeit once again without the signature of the CGTP. The 1996 and 1997 ACSCP and ACE accords for the 1997–1999 period included a contractual distribution of productivity gains (see Royo 2002, 87) and a wage growth policy consistent with maintaining Portugal's competitiveness in the international context, in particular within Europe (Rhodes 2011; Traxler 2003, 2004). The ACE accord of 1997 exemplifies especially well the tradeoff as it was perceived by the new Socialist government, because it covered most areas of macroeconomics, wages, and social policy:

The articulation between economic growth and the distribution of income, which is fundamental for the reinforcement of social cohesion, in addition to giving rise in this agreement to a specific and autonomous reference to income policy, deserves from the subscribers an agreement on the guidelines for the definition of a medium-term wage norm that, taking into account, in the priority framework of guaranteeing growth that allows the real convergence of our economy and the income generated in it, both the need to carry out structural adjustments of relative prices and the need to maintain a low level of inflation, which are fundamental for promoting the competitiveness of companies and activities exposed to competition. (Conselho Económico e Social 1996)

The ACE accord was based on a three-year scenario that included joining the common currency (Euro) by 1999 and overall estimations of a 3.5 percent annual growth and a 7 percent annual increase in investment. As stated in the accord (see pages 45 to 47), the expected growth for the European Union and for the world were 2.8 percent and 4 percent, respectively. The main employment objective for the three years, based on forecasted annual economic growth and productivity increases of 3.25 percent and 2.375 percent, respectively, was an annual increase of 0.875 percent, equivalent to creating 100,000 new jobs over the three years. The prospects for integrating into the common European currency and the new open market environment placed the alleged tradeoff at the center of the PSP distributive strategy.

Collective bargaining is described in the accord as "the most appropriate and efficient means of adapting labor regimes to the reality of sectors and companies, to improve the quality of employment and productivity" (page 84 in the accord). In the context of an overall process of gradual flexibilization of labor relations, the accord emphasizes the need for voluntary collective agreements and the need for the social partners "to strive to streamline collective contracting processes, to adapt their content to the reality of sectors and companies and improve their competitiveness" (page 85 in the accord).

By the second half of the 1990s, Portugal prioritized meeting the macroeconomic targets required for joining the Euro (see Schwartz et al. 2003). Divisions within the labor movement and a wage policy that lacked rules of representativeness in the collective bargaining system (Dornelas 2003), made it challenging to implement the strategies defined in the social pacts. Wage policy was also inflexible given the ultra-activity (*sobrevigencia*) provision, under which old collective accords would continue indefinitely until a new accord was signed. *Sobrevigencia*, which was considered a labor movement triumph by the CGTP and the UGT, in the context of ceding monetary policy to the EEC, was a severe problem and a great source of division between the PSP and the labor movement.

In this context, the Socialist government of Guterres (1995–2002), through the ACE accord, began to signal its' intention to reform the country's fragmentary labor legislation. Portugal did not have a labor code as such after the end of the Estado Novo. In 2000, the Commission for Labor Law Systematization began to work, and discussions concerning the future labor code occurred in the CPCS. In that Portuguese context, the PSP acknowledged, as clearly suggested in the text of the ACE accord, the perception of a tradeoff between employment and wages and prioritized employment during the labor code debate over the following years. PSP's strategy has been aided over the decades by the UGT predisposition to approve the accords in the CPCS, while the CGTP has maintained an aggressive strategy.

The labor code was passed in 2003 with the support of employers and the UGT and the votes of the center-right PSD and CDS parties, under the PSD government of Barroso (2002–2004) (Lei n.o 99/2003 2003). Campos Lima (2019) states the Code was a unilateral initiative of the center-right coalition between the PSD and the Social and the CDS. The GCTP and the leftist bloc – PSP, PCP, and BE – opposed the code, which became a game-changer regarding wage coordination for several reasons. First, it allowed employers to withdraw unilaterally from existing agreements, while previously an agreement would end only when all signatories agreed (*caducidade*). Second, it allowed for collective accords that included less favorable conditions than those established in the law (Código do Trabalho 2003, Art. 1; Palma Ramalho 2013). Third, it ended the *sobrevigencia*, which established the requirement for an accord to end only when a new one is signed (Código do Trabalho 2003, Art. 556 Art. 557). In the new scenario, when no new agreements occur, the end of an accord would result in the continuity of labor relations without any collective accord. Employers took advantage of this change to avoid signing new accords they perceived as unfavorable. Fourth, non-unionized bargaining groups were authorized to sign firm-level agreements with employers independently of unions (*acordo geral de empresa*), which unions saw as a challenge to their ability to maintain their membership and their political strategy capacity.

The objective, contrary to the government claim, is not to reduce collective bargaining agreements. It is to eliminate existing contractual rights. It eliminates the representation of unions that do not submit to employer demands and enables employers' entities to directly and indirectly manipulate workers. A collective bargaining structure can never allow for an employer's manipulation of workers' options in the definition of the construction or application of a collective bargaining agreement. That is one of the fundamental issues. (CGTP delegate discourse to the General Assembly on January 15th; Assembleia da República 2003)

[The Code] creates favorable conditions for strengthening collective bargaining. Several matters are addressed in the code but do not respond to the real needs. The problem of mandatory expiration as formulated may kill collective bargaining. (UGT delegate discourse to the General Assembly on January 15th; Assembleia da República 2003)

The 2003 labor reform suggests that concertation only works with support from the government, and the rightist PSD-CSD government did not want to use it. This episode resembles the one in Chile in which the Piñera administration (2018–2022) strongly downplayed the political role of the Superior Labor Council (CSL) for social concertation.

The 2003 Code introduced important changes that reinforced, in favor of employers, the natural asymmetry between capital and workforce, disrupting a previous equilibrium which was favorable to unions as set by the 1976 constitution (Campos Lima and Naumann 2000, see 2011). As an illustration of this, by 2004, unions faced a 60 percent reduction in the number of workers covered by new collective agreements (Dornelas 2010). While PSP governments introduced a law in their subsequent terms in office that was intended to moderate some of the effects of the 2003 code, it is fair to conclude that it did not challenge the labor relations architecture set by it.

The 2003 Code also set the legal bases for wage policy and labor relations in general during the following two decades. This code was modified on three main occasions since then, in 2006, 2009, and during the Troika years in 2011. However, the changes to wage policy did not add new instruments and, for the most part, is limited to – nonetheless significant – changes in conditions and duration of the extant provisions.

The 2006 Code reform – during the PSP Socrates majority government – reestablished a period of *sobrevigencia* during negotiations after any party rejects a collective agreement. The 2009 code reform – during the PSP Socrates minority government – targeted a loophole in the 2003 code, prohibiting cessation clauses (OECD 2017). The 2011 Code reform, under the PSD Passos Cohelo government, was the most comprehensive of the three. It was carried out during the debt crisis with critical international pressure from the EU and multilateral organizations. It focused on austerity in state spending and economic growth to promote job creation (see Stoleroff 2013).

The 2011 reform set more restrictive conditions for the use of collective bargaining extensions *(portarias de extensão)*, which already had been suspended during the PSD Barroso and Santana Lopes governments (see Figure 5.1). Insiders' employment protection and unemployment benefits moved downwards toward the Eurozone average, as Cardoso and Branco (2017) show. Finally, as measured by the ILO Index, wage coordination centralization converged to the European Zone average of 2.5 from a previous value of 3.75 (Visser 2015), dating from before the 2003 reform.

The importance of the employment-wages tradeoff has been salient during periods of economic stress, as in the mid-1990s or the Sovereign

Debt Crisis. Regarding this latter period, Valdez (2020) argues that austerity and labor market reforms in Portugal between 2011 and 2015 reflect competition between the interests of technocratic policymakers and those of capital – a divided elite. However, in contrast to Chile, there has been no monolithic opposition from technocrats to wage policy over the period. The use of the extension ordinances, as explained below, supports this argument.

In Portugal and in many other countries in Europe, collective agreements can cover workers not initially involved in them through governmental decrees. These government-issued extensions widen the reach of collective agreements beyond the original signatories to all firms and workers in the same sector. This extension ordinance is the administrative mechanism for extending the scope of collective agreements, and it has great administrative importance due to the potential number of employers and workers it reaches (Baer and Leite 1992). Unlike in Uruguay, where collective agreements automatically affect a whole sector, in Portugal, this extension may depend on the government's decision.

Therefore, as established in Portugal, collective bargaining extensions provide governments with a critical administrative tool to control wage policy and, possibly, decide how important wage policy should be in its distributive strategy. Indeed, it is possible to observe different strategies regarding collective bargaining extensions between the PSD and PSP-led governments since 2003. The PSD governments of Barroso (2002–2004), Santana Lopes (2004–2005), and Passos Cohelo (2011–2015) have not used collective bargaining extensions. In 2004, collective bargaining extensions were suspended (see Figure 5.1), while in 2012, the Passos Cohelo administration made conditions for allowing governments to extend agreements even stricter than they had been (see Decreto-Lei n.o 90/2012 2012). The PSP governments of Guterres (1995–2002), Socrates (2005–2011), and Costa (2015–2024), in contrast to the approach taken by PSD governments, have extended collective agreements much more frequently during their tenures. Figure 5.1 shows the variation in the use of the instrument. From the figure, it is clear how the use of extensions has been quite different during PSD and PS governments. It is evident that extensions form part of the PS wage policy. That is consistent with the argument that the controlled use of wage policy serves as a pre-distributive instrument.

There are few case studies about the effect of the government extension of collective bargaining agreements on employment and wages in

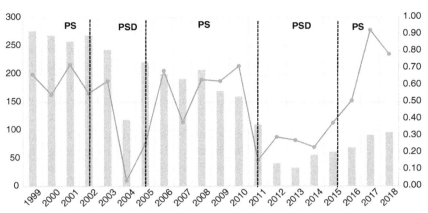

FIGURE 5.1 Collective agreements and extensions (1999–2018).
Notes: Bars indicate the number of collective agreements made in a specific year; the dots indicate the ratio of administrative extensions issued by the government to the number of agreements made that particular year.
Sources: Data from Direção-Geral do Emprego e das Relações de Trabalho (DGERT 2020) and (Hijzen and Martins 2016).

Portugal. These studies show mixed results regarding the effects of extensions on employment. Unfortunately, these studies do not involve comparisons with other countries, which would add important information in two respects: first, extensions in Portugal are arbitrary in the sense that governments have discretion over them, potentially distorting the market. Second, the few studies concerning the effects of these extensions on employment are for the period encompassing the 2011 crisis, which created a very particular environment for employment. With these two caveats in mind, Hijzen and Martin (2016) find that extensions hurt employment growth, in the context of the 2011 crisis, in those sectors that imposed austerity due to high deficits and debt. In turn, Martins and Saraiva (2019) find that between 2005 and 2012, collective bargaining extensions effectively increased wages in those sectors but produced a trade-off in terms of employment losses – which the authors estimate at 2 percent on average and 25 percent higher in small firms.[11] By contrast,

---

[11] The high labor informality rate in Portugal, Chile, and Uruguay vis-à-vis Western European economies illustrates the perils of a "dual" economy. Labor markets are dual when "insiders" and "outsiders" experience different labor market conditions and social policies, as Valadas (2017) and Cardoso and Branco (2018) show for Portugal. See ECLAC (2012) for a comparison of productive structures in Latin America with Portugal included in the comparison.

recent work by Card and Rute Cardoso (2021) on the effect of centralized wage coordination on employment in Portugal finds no evidence of employment responses to wage floor increases.

Overall, the PSP's long-term distributive strategy uses wage policy as a pre-distributive instrument but retains significant levels of political discretion over its use, setting minimum wages as mandated by law, but decreeing extensions of collective contracts to the sector level only when considered appropriate.

5.4 URUGUAY: THE MAKING OF NEOCORPORATIST POLICYMAKING

From Party-Led Consociationalism to Neocorporatist Policymaking

Uruguay combines long-lasting democratic rule with a central role for political parties in building labor's political legitimacy. Dominant elites developed, during the 20th century, a strategy of dialogue and political participation. While corporatist institutions did not develop as in neighboring Argentina or Brazil, corporatism as a system of interest representation remains an essential feature of Uruguayan politics. While the state nurtured the idea of the importance of social partners' participation in decision-making, social dialogue between the partners was less bounded by overarching institutions such as the CPCS in Portugal. Commissions and institutions, whose boards of directors became tripartite with direct participation of employers and labor in decision-making, consolidated between the 1930s and 1960s (Bogliaccini 2012, 2019; Zurbriggen 2006). However, in contrast to authoritarian Portugal, in Uruguay, the role of political parties in politics as effective coordinators, channeling highly diverse demands because of their catch-all structure, reduced the need for binding institutions or the cooptation of social actors. Political parties effectively moderated and channeled demands from labor and employers to governments. However, the lack of institutions for binding political participation by labor does not undermine the centrality of the state in Uruguayan society. Wage coordination remains tripartite, with a central role of government in defining the wage-increase boundaries under a ratified agreement. Even bipartite accords reached in the context of mandatory wage coordination rounds need to be ratified by the government to be valid.

Political stability, while allowing labor's political participation in Uruguay, is (and has been) anchored to party-labor relations. Political parties were decisive actors for the construction of the state. Parties had already acquired a considerable centrality in the early 19th century and continue to be central actors in Uruguayan politics during the 21st century, with high levels of stability and institutionalization. Elites' long-term strategy for the empowered inclusion of labor has relied to a large extent on parties' and party leaders' ability to act in concert with labor and employers. In this context, Batllista-led consociationalism during most of the 20th century gradually gave place to FA's labor-mobilizing strategy beginning in the 1960s (see Etchemendy 2019; Pérez Bentancur et al. 2019). In the post-transitional period, the solid neocorporatist style of the coalition between the Frente Amplio and PIT-CNT stands out. However, the analysis shows how governments of the three main political parties after the dual transition – Frente Amplio, Colorado, and Blanco – have maintained, independent from their wage policy preferences, important channels of dialogue with the labor movement (Lanzaro 2013).

With the restoration of democratic rule, centralized wage coordination returned until suspended once again in 1991 by the PN (1990–1994) conservative government during a period of high and increasing inflation levels. The suppression of wage councils meant that wage policy would return to a decentralized and voluntary firm-level equilibrium. However, voluntary agreements could still be reached at upper levels whenever employers and labor agreed to establish bipartite pacts. The suspension of collective wage coordination remained in place during the center-right PC governments between 1995 and 2004. In 2005, the FA administration reintroduced centralized wage coordination, including previously excluded – and largely informal – groups such as rural and domestic workers.

Between 1991 and 2005, some sectors voluntarily continued bargaining bilaterally. These sectors included the construction sector and the metallurgic, transport, health, and banking sectors. The conditions associated with the continuity of collective bargaining in these sectors typically included the presence of a strong union and, in most cases, a period of fierce conflicts following the suspension of Wage Councils.

In some of these sectors, the continuity of bipartite collective bargaining allowed the relationship between labor and employers to mature. In some cases, such as the construction sector, bipartite bargaining led to the development of valuable mechanisms for welfare and skills formation. After 2005, the Frente Amplio administration of José Mujica (2009–2014) aided this initiative with government funds. This experience in the construction sector supports the argument advanced by Hijzen et al. (2017) about the importance of nurturing high levels of trust over time between social partners as an instrument for successful long-term wage coordination.

Independently from the autonomous bipartite initiative in specific sectors, the PN administration offered two alternative wage-setting mechanisms, formal and informal. First, "bargaining tables" were instituted as a consultive instance in the process of wage-setting for workers in public utilities and in the oil company for whom collective bargaining mechanisms had not previously been available. While these "tables" were only occasions for informal dialogue and consultation, they represented a new participatory opportunity for workers in public firms. As in the private sector cases previously mentioned, this initiative followed bitter conflicts between the previous PC administration (1985–1989) and public firms' employees. The two quotations below from a personal interview with an ex-PIT-CNT leader held in Montevideo illustrate this point. These informal mechanisms remained until the passage of a public sector collective bargaining law during the Frente Amplio's first administration (2005–2009).

Public workers had a discussion table with MEF [Economy Ministry], MTSS [Labor Ministry], and OPP [Planning and Budget Office] held at the MTSS. They were not bargaining tables, but they were a place where workers could express their interests. Mr. Lacalle gave an excellent impulse to public firms' bargaining tables. (Oil Public Firm [ANCAP] and PIT-CNT leader, and FA MP, personal interview held in Montevideo in April 2010)

During Sanguinetti's first term, we [ANCAP] began to "close the gas tap." It was excessive, and the government did react to it, declaring the service essential [which precluded the union from striking] (Oil Public Firm [ANCAP] and PIT-CNT leader, and FA MP, personal interview held in Montevideo in March 2010)

A second initiative by the PN administration came after seeing a steady drop in salaries. Government officials established informal negotiations with the PIT-CNT in order to stop the decline and turn it around. These negotiations took place between 1993 and 1995.

During the second PC administration (1995–1999), a three-year "National Dialogue" was organized by the Labor Ministry with labor and employer participation aimed at creating a new labor-relations framework. There was no final product because while employers favored voluntary firm-level wage setting, labor favored a return to collective wage coordination above the firm level.

The third PC administration (2000–2004) offered no initiative on labor topics, but its two Labor Ministries continued a conciliatory policy in labor relations. It is important to note that the two PC governments between 1995 and 2004 gave the PN, acting as the minor coalition member, the Labor Ministry.[12]

> During my term as Labor Minister, around twenty percent of my activity was to call businessmen to ask them to rehire fired labor leaders. I had no legal provisions for pursuing this goal, but I called them anyway. (Ex-Labor Minister, personal interview held in Montevideo in April 2010)

Dialogue between elite and subordinate groups, as a long-standing strategy, took place even amid liberalization. Conflict was present, as explained above, but, ultimately, labor is a legitimate and politically included actor in Uruguay and even conservative governments recognize it as such.

During this period, there was no serious attempt to derogate the 1943 Law. An Executive decree sufficed to reinstall centralized wage settings during the first year of the first FA administration. The relationship between the FA and PIT-CNT strengthened before 2005, allowing for a strategy based on neocorporatist policymaking while in office (2005–2020).[13] The combination of a labor-inclusive state strategy and a cohesive leftist bloc within the FA contributed to the unity of a labor movement heavily involved in helping the FA govern. As a result, after two wage-bargaining rounds (2006 and 2008), the reform of the 1943 Law began to be discussed in parliament.

Uruguay, then, has nurtured a culture of social dialogue with political parties playing a central role in channelizing labor demands. As in many European countries, the relationship between parties and organized labor evolved. The latter gained strength while labor-mobilizing parties (FA) replaced 19th century liberal parties (PC) as the main partner for organized labor. This change and the absence of conflicts within the Left made it possible to shift from consociationalism to neocorporatist policymaking.

The Centralized and Mandatory Character of Wage Policy Defies the Proposed Tradeoff

This decentralized equilibrium in wage coordination remained unchallenged until after the 2002 crisis, which enormously delegitimized the

---

[12] See Doglio et al. (2004), Senatore and Yaffé (2005), or Pucci et al. (2014) for relevant chronologies and historical accounts of the relationship of the labor movement with different governments between 1985 and 2005.
[13] See Pérez Bentancur et al. (2019) for a detailed analysis of the evolution of mobilization by the Frente Amplio.

ruling center-right coalition and allowed for a profound change in labor relations with the inaugural electoral victory of the center-left FA. There was little dissent in the FA about restoring mandatory and centralized bargaining. Nor was there much dissent about the 2009 law, which was approved only three-and-a-half months after the Executive message to Congress. There was no party divide over the issue, as there was in Chile. Technocratic sectors within the FA, as mainstream as any, were explicitly in favor of combining centralized wage coordination with a general macroeconomic equilibrium. In this sense, the alleged employment-wages trade-off was not perceived as irreconcilable.

During the first FA administration (2005–2009), the 1943 labor law was reformed in two important aspects: First, it reorganized bargaining groups and added rural workers and domestic service workers as new groups. These changes sought to decrease informality, particularly in the rural and service sectors. Second, it eliminated the exclusive prerogative of the Executive to open a negotiation round, which made possible the 1968 and 1991 suspension of collective bargaining. In both cases, President Sanguinetti in 1985 and President Vázquez in 2005 reinstated sectorial-level collective bargaining simply by calling for a negotiation round. The 2009 Law allowed any interested party to ask the Executive to call for a bargaining round whenever a collective agreement could not be reached. In such a case, the government has 15 days to make the call (Law 18566). The reform did not modify an important aspect of the previous law: the compulsory *ad hoc* arbitration role of government in cases where bipartite negotiations reached an impasse. As shown in Table 5.2 (columns d, f and g), this tends to occur albeit infrequently.

A legacy of consociationalism and dialogue between employers and labor helped the FA decide to use wage policy as an instrument in its distributive strategy. As shown in Chapter 1, gains in wage egalitarianism as a pre-distributive outcome followed from the centralization of mandatory wage coordination in a context of rapid growth. Therefore, PIT-CNT had an active role in supporting the process and lobbying in Congress. The only issue the government opposed was the exclusion of any regulation of a firm's occupation by workers. The government's draft excluded that as one of the two concessions made to employers, the other being incorporating the previously mentioned peace clause by which labor cannot strike over previously-agreed-upon issues.

The political opposition, which had preferred a liberal type of industrial relations, did not remain idle in the face of this the initiative. However, the FA majorities in both legislative chambers probably operated as a disincentive for the opposition to take serious issue with the reform. In distress after the 2002 crisis, the PN and PC did not strongly oppose the 2009 reform. The PN members in parliament voted for the overall proposal and opposed some articles. The PC members in parliament voted for some articles but opposed the overall proposal.

Business opposition to the labor reform was strong, but its political strategy capability was weak given its conflictive relationship with almost all political sectors. This is yet another important way in which Uruguay differs from Chile. Macroeconomic and, in particular, monetary policy in Uruguay responded to government needs in handling inflationary pressures during the first decade after the dual transition. The containment of three-digit inflation during the early 1990s became a prime goal for the PN administration (1990–94). Consistent with the Washington Consensus recipe at the time, the government discontinued mandatory and centralized wage coordination. However, as explained above, the decentralization of wage coordination at the firm level was matched with different ad hoc initiatives for wage coordination that showed some disconnection between monetary and wage policies during the period, as illustrated by the following excerpt from an interview with a high-ranking official in the PN administration.

There was a lack of coordination among the economic team. The Central Bank subscribed to orthodox monetarism. Real wages had dropped tremendously in the first months, induced by the government. There was no element in the real economy fundamentals that required a 15 percent drop. There was no logic for it, but it was helpful for fiscal balance in the short term. Lacalle's government popularity dropped immensely because of the salary drop. Lacalle then asked a group of us to initiate an informal dialogue with PIT CNT to recover some salary. Neither the Economy Ministry nor the Labor Ministry knew about this initiative at the beginning. We used to meet in an apartment in downtown Montevideo. We reached an agreement to recover real salary in two years. (ex-OPP [Budget and Planning Office] high-rank official, personal interview held in Montevideo in May 2010)

Macroeconomic stability was a prime goal for the first FA administration. However, the government did not attempt to increase central bank independence or set other mechanisms to insulate macroeconomic policy while restoring collective bargaining institutions. During the following decade, the economy minister took on the responsibility of defending monetary policy choices and enforcing guidelines for maximum wage increases for each round. In other words, it is clear from debates concerning the 2009 labor law that the intersection between wage coordination and monetary policy did not form part of the initial conditions for centralizing wage coordination. That, in turn, is consistent with Uruguay's less-institutionalized and more-informal consociational practices.

Uruguay departs from theoretical expectations regarding an allegedly necessary combination of (1) institutions that make the adoption of non-accommodative monetary policy credible when necessary and (2) semi-centralized bargaining institutions (Iversen and Wren 1998; Pontusson 2018). Credibility comes from a strict alignment between the President and the Economic Minister, which was the case during the two FA administrations under President Vázquez (2005–2009 and 2015–2019), but not during the FA administration under President Mujica (2010–2014). An accommodating policy regime did not help budget containment or even wage moderation during Mujica's term. This example illustrates the perils the system may confront in contexts of political division within the governing party or coalition.

The potential risks in the Uruguayan model for containing wage militancy – and the potential tradeoff between employment and wages – are self-evident. In the absence of institutional safeguards guaranteeing, when necessary, a credible threat from the government regarding a non-accommodating monetary policy regime, wage militancy on the part of a labor movement with relatively low unionization rates in comparative terms, if it occurs, becomes a significant threat to the sustainability of the system. While wage restraint may be a preferred long-term strategy for labor, short-term incentives for higher wages are expected. As Calmfors and Drifill (1988) and Iversen (1999) have argued – see Chapter 1 – semi-centralized wage-setting institutions combined with low-to-medium rates of unionization are a potentially risky combination. Furthermore, when wage coordination is mandatory, the risk of wage militancy may materialize during scheduled bargaining rounds. Coalitional politics are key for managing these risks under an economic slowdown scenario.

Inflationary problems became more critical as the commodity boom slowed down. There is no evidence relating inflationary risks to wage militancy, though some militancy did occur in the public sector. While the economic cycle continued upward, fueled by the commodity boom, the government did not confront major inflationary problems. However, as inflationary pressures mounted with the slowing down of the boom, wage coordination became more acrimonious (see Bogliaccini and Queirolo 2017). A gradual upward inflationary trend followed, from around 5 percent to above 10 percent over the five-year period from 2010–2015. Since 2015, the FA government has moved to a conservative, non-accommodating monetary policy and a conservative wage guideline to contain inflation. Table 5.2 shows how bipartite conflict increased during bargaining rounds as the commodity boom ended. Column (b) shows the percentage of wage agreements reached by mutual consent between labor and employers, which is above 80 percent of the total number of agreements between 2006 and 2015. Column (e) shows how employers and labor reached agreements without government consent during the last two rounds, which is the case when the agreement is outside (over) the government-proposed wage-increase boundaries. That may have fueled wage-led inflation.

Table 5.2 also shows that the FA governments have not influenced wage policy to any great degree by disproportionately siding with any partner, but only by issuing the boundaries for wage increases. However, this instrument seems to be less effective under conditions of economic slowdown and the need for wage moderation. The third FA administration (2015–2019) made a great effort to credibly commit to a non-accommodating monetary policy paired with restrictive wage-increase goals. Employers and labor responded by reaching accords over the government-signaled limits. The government, in turn, responded with strict measures about delaying inflation correctives in salaries for between 12 and 18 months.

The scheme for inflation-corrective measures initially proposed by the government was complied with within the private sector, particularly in tradable sectors of the economy. However, in several of the non-tradable sectors, deferred adjustments over a shorter term were negotiated. There was even the extreme case of the state company for alcohol production (ALUR, *Alcoholes del Uruguay*), which negotiated inflation corrections every two months. The FA administration took exemplary measures against this incipient wage-militancy by annulling the ALUR agreement and even replacing people on the board of directors (see Bogliaccini and Queirolo 2017)

During bargaining rounds, sector-by-sector tables are scheduled progressively over a period ranging from 12 to 18 months. This is potentially prejudicial for periods of economic hardship, which does not help wage restraint. This is so because the outcome of the first sectors strongly signals the mood during the latter ones. Therefore, the government needs to be consistent and effective in their approach from the beginning to avoid accords outside the proposed range of allowable wage increases. Rodríguez et al. (2015) offer a detailed analysis of the negotiations during Round 6 (2015–17), which describes how the government had to ease the salary schedule offered regarding corrections for inflation,

TABLE 5.2 *Wage coordination rounds and outcomes.*

	Bargaining tables (a)	Accords by consensus (%) (b)	Accords without consensus (c)	Accords by executive decree (%) (d)	Accords without consensus (c)		
					Signed by employers & labor (%) (e)	Signed by gov. & employers (%) (f)	Signed by gov. & labor (%) (g)
Round 1 (2005)*	182	90	5	5			
Round 2 (2006–07)*	192	85	10	5			
Round 3 (2008–09)*	222	84	11	5			
Round 4 (2010–13)	222	85	12	3	0	9	3
Round 5 (2013–14)	132	92	9	0	3	2	4
Round 6 (2015–17)	144	63	35	2	27	7	1
Round 7 (2018–19)	115	51	47	3	37	3	7

*There is not available data on columns (e), (f), or (g) for those rounds.

Source: Instituto de Relaciones Laborales – Universidad Católica del Uruguay.

which was at the time the main dispute between the government and workers. This flexibilization in the government schedule, which implied a less restrictive proposal regarding inflation compensation, produced a downward change in the trend of non-consensual agreements. The outcome, a second-best for the government, managed to mitigate the effect of wage militancy.

This equilibrium of higher rates of non-consensual agreements, in which labor and employers avoid following government guidelines during bargaining rounds, is hardly beneficial to labor over the long run. It arguably weakens the political trust in the instrument but provides short-term incentives in the form of higher wage increases.

Overall, the FA distributive strategy includes the use of wage policy, retaining some control over its use within the realm of collective wage agreements. However, this control remains strongly dependent on a non-institutionalized dialogue between government, labor, and employers. Uruguay's neocorporatist policymaking strategy, as shown, decidedly incorporated wage policy as a pre-distributive instrument. Wage policy decisions occur within the walls of mandatory wage coordination rounds where labor and employers attempt to reach bipartite accords at the sector level under the negative incentive of ad hoc arbitration on the part of the state.

Conclusions

> If the erosion of the minimum wage since the 1970s has been partially responsible for the total decline in real wages among low-wage workers, why didn't politics prevent this from happening? One reason is the decline of unions, especially in the private sector.
>
> (Deaton 2013, 224)

Democracy took root in our three countries in the decades after the dual transition, though it has not been a smooth process. Periods of democratic normalcy and significant growth have been followed by deep economic and political crises. Open market capitalism has posed continuous challenges in terms of productivity and innovation to Southern Europe and the Southern Cone of Latin America, two regions that have remained laggards in developing workforce skills since the second half of the 20th century. Macroeconomic management has been uneasy in the context of a globalized economy, albeit none of these countries has abandoned orthodoxy in the face of hard times, as have other Latin American countries (see Flores-Macías 2010). Countries in the Southern Cone successfully curbed hyperinflation during the 1990s. However, inflationary risks remain and challenge the gains achieved in social expenditure to meet social vulnerabilities. Entering the Eurozone further challenged Southern Europe's already problematic fiscal balances, which produced growing deficits and debts until the sovereign debt crisis hit the region beginning in 2009. The post-COVID-19 years have challenged inflation control in the two regions. However, aside from the case of Argentina, whereas of 2023 the annual inflation rate forecast is about 90–100 percent as this book goes to print, the other countries in the two regions experienced upward pressures but as of 2023 have been able to moderate or reverse increases, with peaks not exceeding 12 percent in each case.

Inclusion remains incomplete and uneven. Inflationary tendencies hurt the poor disproportionately, with negative impacts on the purchasing power of median salaries. Moreover, the increasing impact of narcotraffic in the two regions during the last decade and drug-trafficking opportunities for sectors vulnerable to social exclusion has been eroding the gains of the previous decade and exacerbating inequality (Feldmann and Luna 2023). Democratic consolidation has proved challenging, while social unrest has resurfaced during the last decade, most prominently in Chile among our three cases.[1] Stated succinctly, the political economy of the transition out of conservative modernization has been contentious, and perhaps an unfinished task. This book problematizes empowered inclusion and cooperation in the political arena between elite and subordinate groups in Chile, Portugal, and Uruguay. The analysis provides a framework for understanding the linkages between long-term strategies toward the empowered inclusion of labor, the unity of the Left, the political challenges of a perceived tradeoff between employment and wages, and the use of wage policy as a pre-distributive instrument in leftist governments' distributive strategies.

The book explores the linkages between long-term factors – elite attitudes toward labor – and short-term ones – (dis)unity among the Left and wage policy – to improve our understanding of how leftist governments' distributive strategies unfolded and consolidated. Long-term elite attitudes toward labor and unity (or division) among the Left became deciding factors for the inclusion of wage policy as an instrument in these strategies. The importance of macroeconomic equilibriums and the prospect of empowering organized labor have been the two main obstacles to pursuing wage policy that goes beyond setting minimum wages to promote wage egalitarianism. As shown for north European countries (Mudge 2018; Bremer 2023), austerity pressures have conflicted the Left and posed new challenges to its' linkages with grassroots and intra-Left relationships. As shown in the analysis, these two issues proved highly sensitive to the relationship between a labor-mobilizing Left and non-mobilizing, usually more technocratic, leftist parties or factions.

---

[1] More broadly, in the two regions, social conflicts and political unrest have occurred in Brazil, Greece, Spain, and Argentina in recent decades.

LOOKING FORWARD

Important developments are unfolding regarding the unity of the Left. Some are still unfolding, and their relevance remains uncertain. Party systems grew volatile in the last decade in Europe and Latin America. Left parties linkages with grassroot movements and organized social actors has debilitated in many countries at both sides of the Atlantic. The combination of the two phenomena contributes to the relevance of analyzing left unity to understand the ability of center-left parties to maintain or strengthen their role as transmission belts between social actors and the political arena. It also contributes to the renewed relevance to analyze and understand long-term relationships between elites and labor for assessing the opportunity for strengthening ties between labor and the Left. The thesis of this book and the three stories portrayed strongly suggest pre-distributive policies and in particular wage policy options heavily depend on the robustness of such linkages. Recent developments in the three countries, briefly explained below, underline the relevance of social concertation and coalition politics as two prime vehicles for expanding wage policy options in different Left unity contexts. Chile appears to be the negative case for the near future, where the demise of the Concertación has triggered a new divide among left actors that is yet to settle. It is also unclear yet how these new Left parties and coalitions would direct their efforts to rebuild strong societal linkages.

In Portugal, the 2015 election witnessed the formation of an unprecedented, albeit brief, leftist coalition led by the PSP with the parliamentary support of the PCP and BE. The three parties joined forces in parliament to give the PSP a minority government after the Troika years. This coalition ended the exclusion of the Communist Party from the inner-party system. As explained in Chapters 4 and 5, the two parties – PSP and PCP – have been careful to make clear that this is purely a parliamentary understanding, not a governing coalition.

The Troika period has left its mark on the Left, distancing the old-time partners, PSP and PSD, at least in the short run, and making possible an all-Left coalition. Significantly, the sovereign debt also affected the center-right PSD, opening important internal discussions over its programmatic positioning regarding economic liberalism before the 2019 election. This election marked the party's worst electoral performance since 1983, which shows that the Troika period has weakened the party's electoral appeal in the short term.

The relationship between the PSP and PCP, provided the parliamentary understanding evolves into a less shy partnership, may even help the relationship between the CGTP and UGT, longtime rivals who distrust one another. Looking forward, an improvement in unity among the Left may promote a more productive dialogue between the two unions, which may, in turn, help labor lobby government and advocate its interests within the CPCS. While this imagined future may not come to pass, the speculative exercise is useful for understanding the opportunities that exist for a horizontally divided but vertically integrated Left and labor. Labor mobilization is not the problem in Portugal.

This strengthening of unity among the Left occurs in a context of highly restrictive macroeconomic conditions given Portugal's overall level of debt – 112 percent of GDP by 2019 (IMF 2020) – and chronic fiscal deficits. Moreover, under the leftist parliamentary agreement, the first since the Carnation Revolution in 1974, the PSP government of Antonio Costa has managed to deliver a budgetary surplus also for the first time since democratic restoration. This understanding between leftist parties in such a context is remarkable for two reasons: first, because the overall room for (social) expenditure is minimal. Second, the steep drop in unemployment during the period has been matched by the continuation of an upward trend in wage egalitarianism (see Figure 1.3 in Chapter 1) in the context of average wage stagnation and employment creation.

State-led concertation appears to be useful for governments pressed by austerity and redistributive mandates. Highly institutionalized concertation through the CPCS and the availability of critical administrative tools such as the extension of collective contracts allows governments to foster dialogue without ceding policy control.

In Chile, while the Concertación is defunct, center-left and labor-mobilizing parties have been unable to form a cohesive political front. The realignment of left parties and groups in the post-Concertación period has not been a linear process. Moreover, the fragility of the Chilean party system during the last decade suggests realignments are far from settled. The last decade brought a gradual increase in collaboration between the Communist Party and the center-left parties. Beginning with the 2009 electoral understanding that brought Communists to the Congress for the first time since democratic restoration, the relationship improved gradually. By 2013, the post-Concertación electoral coalition "Nueva Mayoría," which put Bachelet in office for the second time a year later, included the

Communist Party. However, the coalition did not survive the Bachelet administration, and did not even compete in the next election.

In 2021, the national referendum for forming a Constitutional Assembly to replace the 1980 Constitution inherited from the military period allocated a stunning 40 percent of the seats to independents, who came from highly inchoate groups. The coalition of leftist parties obtained a third of the seats, while another 20 percent went to the Right. This illustrates the inability of traditional parties and coalitions to connect with voters. Perhaps, leftist parties' lack of societal roots has proven too costly during the last decades.

After the election, which had a meager turnout of about 40 percent, ex-President Ricardo Lagos made a statement that speaks directly to the issues discussed in this book about elite strategies toward subordinate groups, particularly strategies regarding voting practices. Lagos stated that "there are still sectors that think it is unnecessary to express themselves. That is why I believe that in this Constitution, we must correct something fundamental. Make the right to vote an obligation" (Reyes 2021).

As the new proposed Constitution failed to be ratified by popular vote in 2022, a new vote for a second Constitutional Assembly took place on May 2023. Besides these late developments, which are yet too recent to ponder, the question remains whether the Left will continue to accommodate the needs of the conservative sectors to sustain the political order or turn toward empowering the inclusion of subordinate groups and developing stronger ties with its grassroots members. The lack of healthy linkages between the Left and the grassroots, and the progressive atomization of the Chilean Left in the last decade, support the hypothesis of the Chilean Left being unable – if not unwilling – to move out of the Left-liberal equilibrium.

In Uruguay, leftist unity under the Frente Amplio remains strong, with the FA even being a source of inspiration for other leftist parties and coalitions in Latin America, beginning with the Chilean Frente Amplio, which formed in 2017. The relationship between the FA and the PIT-CNT also remains strong, with the labor union able to mediate ever-growing tensions between the government and sectoral unions. The economic situation deteriorated between 2015 and 2019. During that period, the third FA administration (2015–2019) had to negotiate with unions over wage moderation or even policy reforms, such as during the 2015 conflict around education (Anria and Bogliaccini 2022; Bogliaccini and Queirolo 2017).

After the 2019 election of a conservative coalition led by the PN and the outbreak of the COVID-19 pandemic, the PIT-CNT strategically adopted a collaborative stance toward the government. Labor agreed to suspend the wage coordination rounds of 2020 for a year, a decision that illustrates the political maturity of labor and the importance of their political interests' centralization under the PIT-CNT during a period of crisis, a public health crisis in this case. This is an example of how the mandatory character of wage coordination operates as a guarantee for the labor movement, actor that may contribute with wage restraint in the short term in exchange for the certainty of future bargaining rounds as mandated by law.

The PIT-CNT willingness to exercise wage restraint, in agreement with a conservative government, defy Calmfors's and Drifill's proposed inverted-U-shaped distribution of conflict. With its semi-centralized wage-setting institutionalism, Uruguay should be at the maximum of the U-shaped distribution but is not. Neocorporatist policymaking and labor's experience with liberalization during the 1990s may help explain this deviation from theoretical expectations.

Finally, as this volume goes to press, the PN government of Lacalle Pou voted legislation modifying some aspects of collective wage bargaining for accommodating observations made by ILO to national legislation.[2] The voted project is highly similar to a previous one submitted on the last day of the previous legislature under the Frente Amplio administration but Congress did not consider in the plenary session.[3] In a nutshell, the new legislation eliminates a series of provisions, among which is important to note the following two: (i) the ultra-activity provision, under which old collective accords would continue indefinitely until a new accord was signed –as occurred in Portugal before; (ii) the provision under which an employer of a firm without unionized workers is obliged to negotiate with representatives of its' sector-wide union. These changes, not fought by the FA –albeit did not vote them in Congress– and PIT-CNT, show how collective bargaining provisions are subject to dynamic revisions in Uruguay as it has been the case in Portugal, as the country finetune its' regulatory environment. It also shows how the right has, in the present context, accepted the status quo but taking advantage of ILO observations to satisfy a long-lasting demand from employers.

[2] In 2010, the ILO Committee on Freedom of Association issued a report, in which it objected to various articles of Law No. 18,566 on the Collective Bargaining System in the private sector.

[3] See project at: https://medios.presidencia.gub.uy/legal/2019/proyectos/10/mtss_487.pdf (last accessed on May 18th, 2022)

FINDINGS AND CONTRIBUTIONS

The book brings together two elements theorized as central to the use of wage policy as a pre-distributive instrument by leftist governments: a long-standing strategy toward the empowered inclusion of labor and the cohesion of the political Left. It unpacks social-democratic leftist (or center-left) types and contributes to the left turn literature by (1) building on works that analyze the political economy of economic reforms (Etchemendy 2011; Flores-Macías 2012; Weyland, Madrid, and Hunter 2010); and (2) by showing significant variation within countries that followed macroeconomic orthodoxy that is not apparent from analyses solely of redistribution. More generally, the book shows, contra the influential work of Schneider (2013), that there is meaningful variation in how capitalist structures are organized in Latin America. It also underlines that such variation is directly related to the problem of empowered inclusion, a central problem for democracy pointed out by O'Donnell (1988) at the dawn of the third wave of democratization and further theorized by Warren (2017) and Fishman (2019) more recently.

The book argues and shows that empowering subordinate groups may provoke a crisis of social domination if established elites perceive threats to their interests. Finally, the book advances the idea that the study of pre-distributive instruments, particularly wage policy, is important for our understanding of variation in political and social inclusion in Latin America and across regions. The book stresses how wage policy is crucial for the empowerment of organized subordinate groups and, thus, for helping leftist parties maintain vibrant ties with social actors. As the cases of Portugal and Uruguay show, it is also important to refresh communication channels between center-right governments and social actors other than organized business. I unpack these contributions below.

The analysis anchors leftist governments' decisions about wage policy to their perception that a tradeoff between employment and wage-egalitarianism constrains them politically. Thus, it contributes to the literature on the long-term causes of cooperation (or lack thereof) between elites and subordinate groups in the political arena by underlining the role of wage policy as a pre-distributive instrument closely related to the empowerment of subordinate groups.

Distributive strategies vary meaningfully in Chile, Portugal, and Uruguay in their use of wage policy. This book exploits this variation to improve our understanding of cooperative versus dominative dynamics between elite and subordinate groups. Large-scale historical processes ground the proposed functional historicist explanation. These processes entail long-term strategies toward the empowered inclusion of labor and shape how emerging tensions challenge those strategies and force them to adapt during the dual transition. These processes are structured around strategic principles, such as the use of institutions and rules – for either excluding or including subordinate groups – or informal dialogue among political elites and leaders of organized groups such as labor. This large-scale process accounts for structural power-sharing mechanisms and equilibriums between elites and subordinate groups in the political arena. In this sense, the proposed framework also helps to account for the influence of other organized civil society groups in other historical periods, such as the currently pressing challenge of incorporating ethnic minority groups, women, or the LGBTQ community.

However, the emerging tensions during the dual transition did not prevent these large-scale elite strategies from adapting and sustaining the equilibrium between cooperation and domination. In theoretical terms, the main finding then is one of path dependence. While strategies toward the political inclusion of subordinate groups are not static over time, they show impressive stability and inertia in the face of tensions. Institutional patterns can be revived and used to favor different parties, depending on the distribution of power in society.

The cleavage within the Left offers an important, albeit sometimes overshadowed, structural cause for understanding differences between countries in how leftist parties and governments develop stable societal linkages. This perspective complements and improves upon the party-centered approach. This book contributes to this line of inquiry an analysis of how structural characteristics of the leftist political bloc affect policymaking in areas that are sensitive to labor movement empowerment and, therefore, to the future electoral opportunities of leftist parties in government. It also foregrounds, for the analysis of the empowerment of subordinate groups, how institutions in the case of Portuguese consociationalism or coalitional politics in the case of Uruguayan neocorporatist policymaking are two viable political paths by which unequal democracies can pursue political inclusion.

Contrary to previous work, the analysis presented here finds support for the argument that the strength of organized labor does not suffice to explain the characteristics – mandatory or voluntary, centralized or decentralized – of wage coordination. The inclusion in the analysis of long-term elite attitudes toward labor, the unity of the Left, and the ideational foundations of a perceived wage egalitarianism-employment tradeoff offers a more robust and complete picture of how and when wage policy is or could be advanced for pre-distributive purposes. The book contributes to the critical question regarding what kind of efforts governments are willing to make to alter the market allocation of wealth. It also constitutes a plea for the revitalization of the study of pre-distributive instruments for achieving higher levels of empowered inclusion and equality. Social cohesion, or the lack of it, remains a prime challenge for Latin American democracies to survive. Gradual advancements in the empowerment of subordinated groups is a prerequisite for the advancement of social cohesion.

The book also reintroduces wage policy to the analysis of the politics of distributive strategies through the idea of pre-distribution. The analysis notes the political consequences of the transition from Keynesian to neoliberal economics and beyond, particularly in terms of leftist reinventions. The book shows that, in the aftermath of the liberalization period, and contrary to the convergence hypothesis, leftist governments have varied significantly in their approach to wage policy. Some leftist parties follow some sort of convergence towards economic leftism, as found by Mudge (2018) for European social democracies. This is the case of Chile in the analysis, where the perceived room for political change was minimal during the Concertación period because of the hardships imposed by the employment-wages tradeoff. In other cases, parties with strong commitments toward macroeconomic stability still find, anchored in their long-term and short-term histories, that the perceived hardships leave ample space for using wage policy as a pre-distributive instrument. This is consistent with Bremer's (2018) evidence against the convergence hypothesis, also in Europe. The use of wage policy as a pre-distributive instrument, therefore, is shaped by long-standing political processes that extend far back to before the dual transition.

This long-term view of political processes affords a better understanding of large-scale continuities in the analyzed political processes, despite the emerging tensions of the 1929 crisis or the dual transition. Identifying such continuities in terms of elite strategies toward labor through specific political practices on different fronts, as explained in Chapters 2 and 3, affords a better understanding of political opportunities and limitations in the short term. Political developments are grounded in power-sharing processes, which are structural and show continuity over time alongside an impressive ability for adaptation to the emerging tensions posed during the historical ruptures discussed above.

The book contributes to the literature on the left turn by analyzing the politics and variation behind the curtain of the moderated left and ordered macroeconomics. The analysis is a contribution to the understanding of the politics behind moderate left parties' macroeconomic management in the region, and in comparison, with other regions – Southern Europe in this case. In this sense, it contributes to the growing literature on how parties relate to democratic representation and solve distributive problems connected to collective choices.[4] It also partners with the initial efforts to study wage policy in the region and neocorporatism in Uruguay and Argentina.[5] A particular contribution of this volume on the matter is the reintroduction of the idea of social concertation from the European literature as an alternative to the much-studied coalitional politics in the region.

Finally, by emphasizing the role of political conflict as a force shaping capitalist institutions, the book identifies meaningful differences between the models of capitalism in Chile and Uruguay. The analysis elucidates essential differences between the two countries in the use of coordination versus competition. The analysis of wage policy reveals how, after a period in which wage systems converged toward the neoliberal equilibrium, Uruguay departed from such a path and returned to its historical trajectory of tripartite wage setting. The countries also differ in terms of the political legitimacy afforded the labor movement. These differences seem to override the similarities previously described in the literature on Latin America (Schneider 2013). While there are indeed similarities among the countries analyzed here at the base of the hierarchical model of capitalism, the events and developments during the last two decades suggest the neoliberal equilibrium has broken in Uruguay as well as among other countries in the region. This opens the door to new accounts that can connect extant theoretical propositions to the new evidence. It also allows students of the region to examine the relative importance of economic coordination and political conflict over distribution as factors shaping the evolution of capitalist models.

The characterization of the distributive conflict and its politics may also shed light on the analysis of Latin American growth models. This new literature, which emphasizes the opportunities for rethinking the

---

[4] As mentioned in Chapter 2, see the recent additions to the literature of Luna et al. in discussing parties and their relation to democratic representation with a focus on Latin America (2021).

[5] As mentioned in previous chapters, see the recent work of Etchemendy (2019) and Schipani (2019).

perceived tradeoff between employment and wages through the lens of post-Keynesian economics (see Baccaro, Benassi, and Meardi 2019; Baccaro and Lim 2007; Baccaro and Pontusson 2016; Stockhammer 2022), distinguishes between different growth models, among which wage-led growth is a driving force for some of the most egalitarian advanced democracies. How do growth models and distributive strategies relate in peripheral economies? The analysis of wage policy use as a pre-distributive strategy is a starting point to answer this and other important questions.

LESSONS

What lessons can be learned from the different paths taken by countries in regions with a common past and shared root? Long-term and large-scale processes matter. Path dependencies regarding dominant elite strategies toward the empowered inclusion of labor are strong. These strategies have survived strong emerging tensions by adapting to the new contexts. This continuity of strategy is matched by a continuity of the institutions and rules Chile, Portugal and Uruguay have nurtured over time, as weak as these may be during specific periods. A recent book by Ondetti (2021) argues and puts forward important evidence for the relevance of path dependency and long-term processes in analyzing variation in tax structures and reforms in Latin America. Looking back to the dual transition period from a distance, it is self-evident that long-term large-scale processes, predating the dual transition and related to the distributive conflict and the role the state plays in it, continue to operate and influence democracy, distribution and market capitalism in the two regions.

Institutions and rules matter, even in a context that does not particularly value adherence to procedures and even in a context of institutional weakness. We observe meaningful variation along with solid path dependencies. Corporatist institutions for binding the action of social partners (Portugal), centralized collective bargaining settings under coalitional politics (Uruguay), and even the use of regulatory limitations for impeding or obstructing the empowered inclusion of subordinate groups (Chile) tend to help maintain the equilibrium in a country –as a system. This book points to the importance of understanding the political processes behind the formation of institutions and their change, of understanding when such changes provide opportunities for higher levels of cooperation and reciprocity. In line with the seminal works of Warren

(2017) and Fishman (2019), this book calls for a deeper understanding of how large-scale political practices shape subordinate actors' access to the political arena through the formation and maintenance of formal or informal – and even weak – institutions.

Emerging tensions matter. As suggested by Moore's seminal work on the social bases of obedience and revolt (1978), these tensions may foster the emergence of rules and institutions for increased reciprocity and cooperation between elites and subordinate groups. Such was the case, the book argued, of the CPCS in Portugal. As we already know, countries in both regions are experiencing periods of growing instability in which new actors can obtain political leverage. The political Left emerged or strengthened decisively in electoral terms as a viable contender during the dual transition. Some of these parties collapsed or had to overcome severe challenges during the sovereign debt crisis in Southern Europe or, more astonishingly, in the aftermath of the commodity boom in the Southern Cone. More importantly, unrooted leftist parties seem to be highly vulnerable during these periods, much more so than parties with intact linkages to their grassroots base. Such seems to be the case in Chile after the 2019 mobilizations, where the Left remains mostly directionless. During the decades after the dual transition, labor mobilization may not have paid off electorally in the short term, but it may have for the long term.

In line with Watson's (2015) contribution, this book offers another lesson: the unity of the Left matters for distributive purposes. Our two regions are laggards in terms of wellbeing and inequality. Poverty and informality remain challenges the political system must address. Distributive strategies incorporating wage policy as a pre-distributive instrument in Portugal and Uruguay defied the wage-employment trade-off in different forms, even during economic austerity. These experiences have challenged the common trend toward a "neoliberalization" of the Left that authors such as Mudge (2018) and others have argued about for advanced democracies. A fragmented Left, however, may have fewer incentives to push for wage egalitarianism. Also, arguably, leftist governments in contexts of united leftist blocs or with consolidated institutionalized concertation mechanisms arguably may be more vulnerable to budgetary constraints and to segmentation in access to welfare.

There are strategies and principles, passions and interests, but ultimately, every distributive strategy confronts its own perils and opportunities. However, Left liberalism did not seem to provide a sustainable equilibrium between political order and empowered inclusion after four decades in Chile. Political unrest has grown in recent years to levels not seen since the return to democracy. Over the long run, unrooted liberal-Left parties stepped into the vacuum. While excluding certain groups may be a source of political conflict in the long run, opening the door to the empowered inclusion of subordinate groups may be a source of political conflict in the short run. While it seems inevitable that empowered elites will attempt to maintain their grasp on power for as long as possible, political conflict is also inevitable. After all, Uruguay and Portugal, both countries with relatively good records of egalitarianism in the wage policy arena, both began to build their political practices in the aftermath of revolutions (in 1904 and 1974, respectively), after which liberal and left-wing elites obtained immense leverage in favor of the empowered inclusion of subordinate groups.

Will labor continue to be a relevant political actor? At the beginning of this chapter, I cited Nobel Prize laureate Angus Deaton's statement that "If the erosion of the minimum wage since the 1970s has been partially responsible for the total decline in real wages among low-wage workers, why didn't politics prevent this from happening? One reason is the decline of unions, especially in the private sector" (Deaton 2013, 224). There are already several literatures pointing to the important changes a service economy, in which knowledge and technology are increasingly important, is producing in employment and, thus, in the incentives that employees and independent workers have for centralizing their political interest. There are also important contributions pointing to the changing environmental conditions favoring or disfavoring the organization of subordinate groups in the labor market. However, subordinated groups are still key in peripheral economies' labor markets and the question of their political and social inclusion remains relevant.

The political salience of subordinate groups has proven to be a continuing issue of prime importance for political systems. This is the case when such groups are traditionally organized under labor unions as in Portugal, Argentina, or Uruguay, when organized under different sui generis organizations such as in Bolivia, or when they heavily disrupt the political order under spontaneous upheavals, as in Chile, Peru or even France. Without organized groups, the political system seems doomed to failure in its' task of representing and stably channeling demands. Parties have mostly failed to survive in the long-term when failing to maintain vibrant societal linkages.

Is pre-distribution a relevant topic for the next decades? I think that it will remain a key aspect of distributive strategies for peripheral economies for the foreseeable future. The middle-income trap and the complex characteristics of the low-skilled service sector in these countries, especially Latin American countries, call for the political system to seriously consider these kinds of policies. Pre-distribution is a key feature in terms of productivity gains, which is a key policy area for Latin America and Southern Europe in the decades to come. The inefficiencies of raising revenues from high-earning workers and then transferring them to low-wage earners may escalate in unequal peripheral economies when it is the only policy instrument for maintaining social cohesion. In the long-term, as even advanced democracies have recently begun to show, without social cohesion, political stability and even democracy itself may be at risk.

Envoi

In presenting the book manuscript at several venues, a question about the merits of the distributive strategies crafted in each case often emerges. The book argues that path dependencies limit opportunities for change in distributive strategies in the short term. Elites adapt political practices toward subordinate groups to new environments amid emerging tensions. These adaptations fail only when power constellations suffer qualitative changes, but such cataclysms are rarer than usually envisioned.

Success or failure is seldom definite, and every distributive strategy confronts tradeoffs. Is emulating a Uruguayan, Portuguese, or Chilean-like distributive strategy preferable? A more interesting question should be whether, or under what conditions, Chile can follow the Uruguayan or Portuguese paths in crafting its' distributive strategy or viceversa. Following the book's argument, the answer would be that those path changes -durable detours- are rather tricky in the short term. However, the comparative exercise helps convey to social and political actors at one place and time an understanding of the experience that made it possible for the neighbor to craft its' distributive strategy under the trying circumstances. The comparison is a valuable exercise for inspiration and for pondering the limits of the possibilities considering large-scale, long-term social and political dynamics in a given society.

The question, therefore, should only be answered by carefully pondering the historical trajectory of each country. That is the case because, as Cohen posits, "the justice of a society is not exclusively a function of its legislative structure, of its legally imperative rules, but is also a function of the choices people make within those rules." Therefore, in the short term, social and political actors may work for the long term. Questions such as the following are relevant in understanding the opportunity for change in each society: Are political and social actors pushing their political economies to strengthen social dialogue in their contexts? Are they reflecting on how their political practices improve political inclusion and how to embrace the reduction of relevant social distances in the contexts they confront?

Unfortunately, reliable blueprints are seldom available, and it is usually hard to ponder the limits of the possibilities of a given society. It is hard to unveil a perceived tradeoff's actual opportunities and limits. Political and social actors build the future based on apprehended experiences from past relations and successes and failures. Perhaps, through comparative exercises like this book, local actors may attempt to experiment with embracing distributive tensions and the new challenges and tradeoffs their society confronts. As Deaton invites us with his statement on the effect of the decline of unions -opening the concluding chapter, political cadres may reflect on the challenges and opportunities of dialoguing with organized social actors for the collective crafting of sustainable prosperity for all.

Appendix

Documentary Sources and Interviews

CHILE

Law 19753, Chilean Congress National Library www.bcn.cl/

Law 19753, History of the Law. Chilean Congress National Library www.bcn.cl/

Law 19759, Chilean Congress National Library www.bcn.cl/

Law 19759, History of the Law. Chilean Congress National Library www.bcn.cl/

Mining Council A.G., "Mining Council presentation to the Honorably Senate Labor Commission's. Comments to the Labor reform Initiative". Document stored at the Chilean Congress Archives.

CPC, "CPC position in relation to the law initiative on labor reform", Document stored at the Chilean Congress Archives

Sofofa, "Sofofa's position in relation to the law initiative that modifies the Labor Code", Document stored at the Chilean Congress Archives

Chilean Mining Confederation, "On the labor reform initiative that modifies the Labor Code", Document stored at the Chilean Congress Archives

SNA, "SNA observations to the initiative that modifies the Labor Code", Document stored at the Chilean Congress Archives

CChC, "CChC's position on the initiative that reforms labor legislation", Document stored at the Chilean Congress Archives

Sonami, "Sonami's comments to the labor reform initiative", Document stored at the Chilean Congress Archives

CAT, "Observations on the indications done by the Executive and the Honorable Senate on the norms that regulates the working day", Document stored at the Chilean Congress Archives

CAT, "Proposal to the initiative on labor reforms", Document stored at the Chilean Congress Archives

CAT, "Proposal on the working day: articles 22 to 40 on the actual code", Document stored at the Chilean Congress Archives

Economy of Labor Program, "Brief on the indications that substitute the Labor Code", Document stored at the Chilean Congress Archives

CONFESCOVE, "CONFESCOVE's opinion on the labor reform initiative sent by the Executive to the Parliament", Document stored at the Chilean Congress Archives

CNCS, "Initiative that modifies the Labor Code. Comments", Document stored at the Chilean Congress Archives

COTIACH, "Chilean workers: history and labor reform", Document stored at the Chilean Congress Archives

CUT, "CUT's position on the labor reform initiative", Document stored at the Chilean Congress Archives

CUT, "CUT's presentation on the initiative on new hiring forms to the Senate's Labor Commission", Document stored at the Chilean Congress Archives

CONUPIA, "CONUPIA's comments on the labor reform incidence on the actual distribution of working days and holidays", Document stored at the Chilean Congress Archives

URUGUAY

Law 18083, Uruguayan Parliament, www.parlamento.gub.uy/inicio1024sup.html

Law 18566, Uruguayan Parliament, www.parlamento.gub.uy/inicio1024sup.html

House, Hacienda Commission, Act 44. Integral modification of the tributary system, Law 18083, www.parlamento.gub.uy/inicio1024sup.html

House, Hacienda Commission, Act 46. Integral modification of the tributary system, Law 18083, www.parlamento.gub.uy/inicio1024sup.html

House, Hacienda Commission, Act 47. Integral modification of the tributary system, Law 18083, www.parlamento.gub.uy/inicio1024sup.html

House, Hacienda Commission, Act 48. Integral modification of the tributary system, Law 18083, www.parlamento.gub.uy/inicio1024sup.html

House, Hacienda Commission, Act 52. Integral modification of the tributary system, Law 18083, www.parlamento.gub.uy/inicio1024sup.html

House, Hacienda Commission, Act 53. Integral modification of the tributary system, Law 18083, www.parlamento.gub.uy/inicio1024sup.html

House, Hacienda Commission, Act 55. Integral modification of the tributary system, Law 18083, www.parlamento.gub.uy/inicio1024sup.html

House, Hacienda Commission, Act 57. Integral modification of the tributary system, Law 18083, www.parlamento.gub.uy/inicio1024sup.html

House, Hacienda Commission, Act 58. Integral modification of the tributary system, Law 18083, www.parlamento.gub.uy/inicio1024sup.html

House, Hacienda Commission, Act 60. Integral modification of the tributary system, Law 18083, www.parlamento.gub.uy/inicio1024sup.html

House, Hacienda Commission, Act 62. Integral modification of the tributary system, Law 18083, www.parlamento.gub.uy/inicio1024sup.html

House, Hacienda Commission, Act 69. Integral modification of the tributary system, Law 18083, www.parlamento.gub.uy/inicio1024sup.html

House, Hacienda Commission, Act 70. Integral modification of the tributary system, Law 18083, www.parlamento.gub.uy/inicio1024sup.html

House, Hacienda Commission, Act 72. Integral modification of the tributary system, Law 18083, www.parlamento.gub.uy/inicio1024sup.html

House, Hacienda Commission, Act 73. Integral modification of the tributary system, Law 18083, www.parlamento.gub.uy/inicio1024sup.html

House, Hacienda Commission, Act 74. Integral modification of the tributary system, Law 18083, www.parlamento.gub.uy/inicio1024sup.html

House, Hacienda Commission, Act 75. Integral modification of the tributary system, Law 18083, www.parlamento.gub.uy/inicio1024sup.html

House, Hacienda Commission, Act 76. Integral modification of the tributary system, Law 18083, www.parlamento.gub.uy/inicio1024sup.html

Senate, Hacienda Commission, Distributed document 1363, Integral modification of the tributary system, Law 18083, www.parlamento.gub.uy/inicio1024sup.html

Senate, Hacienda Commission, Distributed document 1364, Integral modification of the tributary system, Law 18083, www.parlamento .gub.uy/inicio1024sup.html

Senate, Hacienda Commission, Distributed document 1365, Integral modification of the tributary system, Law 18083, www.parlamento .gub.uy/inicio1024sup.html

Senate, Hacienda Commission, Distributed document 1366, Integral modification of the tributary system, Law 18083, www.parlamento .gub.uy/inicio1024sup.html

Senate, Hacienda Commission, Distributed document 1367, Integral modification of the tributary system, Law 18083, www.parlamento .gub.uy/inicio1024sup.html

Senate, Hacienda Commission, Distributed document 1376, Integral modification of the tributary system, Law 18083, www.parlamento .gub.uy/inicio1024sup.html

Senate, Hacienda Commission, Distributed document 1377, Integral modification of the tributary system, Law 18083, www.parlamento .gub.uy/inicio1024sup.html

Senate, Hacienda Commission, Distributed document 1378, Integral modification of the tributary system, Law 18083, www.parlamento .gub.uy/inicio1024sup.html

Senate, Hacienda Commission, Distributed document 1379, Integral modification of the tributary system, Law 18083, www.parlamento .gub.uy/inicio1024sup.html

Senate, Hacienda Commission, Distributed document 1385, Integral modification of the tributary system, Law 18083, www.parlamento .gub.uy/inicio1024sup.html

Senate, Hacienda Commission, Distributed document 1390, Integral modification of the tributary system, Law 18083, www.parlamento .gub.uy/inicio1024sup.html

Senate, Hacienda Commission, Distributed document 1391, Integral modification of the tributary system, Law 18083, www.parlamento .gub.uy/inicio1024sup.html

Senate, Hacienda Commission, Distributed document 1392, Integral modification of the tributary system, Law 18083, www.parlamento .gub.uy/inicio1024sup.html

Senate, Hacienda Commission, Distributed document 1393, Integral modification of the tributary system, Law 18083, www.parlamento .gub.uy/inicio1024sup.html

Senate, Hacienda Commission, Distributed document 1394, Integral modification of the tributary system, Law 18083, www.parlamento .gub.uy/inicio1024sup.html

Senate, Hacienda Commission, Distributed document 1396, Integral modification of the tributary system, Law 18083, www.parlamento.gub.uy/inicio1024sup.html

Senate, Hacienda Commission, Distributed document 1404, Integral modification of the tributary system, Law 18083, www.parlamento.gub.uy/inicio1024sup.html

Senate, Hacienda Commission, Distributed document 1405, Integral modification of the tributary system, Law 18083, www.parlamento.gub.uy/inicio1024sup.html

Senate, Hacienda Commission, Distributed document 1406, Integral modification of the tributary system, Law 18083, www.parlamento.gub.uy/inicio1024sup.html

House, Labor Commission, Act 231. Collective Bargaining System, Law 18566, www.parlamento.gub.uy/inicio1024sup.html

House, Labor Commission, Act 232. Collective Bargaining System, Law 18566, www.parlamento.gub.uy/inicio1024sup.html

House, Labor Commission, Act 233. Collective Bargaining System, Law 18566, www.parlamento.gub.uy/inicio1024sup.html

House, Labor Commission, Act 234. Collective Bargaining System, Law 18566, www.parlamento.gub.uy/inicio1024sup.html

House, Labor Commission, Act 235. Collective Bargaining System, Law 18566, www.parlamento.gub.uy/inicio1024sup.html

House, Labor Commission, Act 236. Collective Bargaining System, Law 18566, www.parlamento.gub.uy/inicio1024sup.html

Senate, Labor Commission, Distributed document 3330, Collective Bargaining System, Law 18566, www.parlamento.gub.uy/inicio1024sup.html

Senate, Labor Commission, Distributed document 3331, Collective Bargaining System, Law 18566, www.parlamento.gub.uy/inicio1024sup.html

Senate, Labor Commission, Distributed document 3332, Collective Bargaining System, Law 18566, www.parlamento.gub.uy/inicio1024sup.html

PORTUGAL

Assembleia da República. Decreto-Lei n.o 45–77., (1977).
Assembleia da República. Código Do Trabalho., (2003).
Assembleia da República. Lei n.o 7/2009., (2009).
Assembleia da República. Lei n.o 53/2011., (2011).
Assembleia da República. Lei n.o 64/2012., (2012).
Assembleia da República. lei 55/2014., (2014).

CGTP. (2003a). Parecer da CGTP-IN sobre anteprojecto do código de trabalho. 1–4.

CGTP. (2003b). Resolução Político Sindical da CGTP aprovada em 11 de Janeiro de 2003. 1–3.

Conselho Económico E Social. Acordo Económico E Social., (1990).

Conselho Económico E Social. Acordo De Concertação Estratégica 1996/1999., (1996).

Conselho Económico E Social. Acordo De Concertação Social De Curto Prazo., (1996).

Conselho Económico E Social. Acordo Sobre Política De Emprego, Mercado De Trabalho, Educação E Formação., (2001).

Conselho Económico E Social. Modernização da Protecção Social., (2001).

Grupo Parlamentar do Bloco de Esquerda. Propostas de alteração à proposta de lei 29/ix., (2003).

Lareau, A. (2002). Invisible Inequality: Social Class and Childrearing in Black Families and White Families. American Sociological Review, Vol. 67, p. 747. https://doi.org/10.2307/3088916

Ministério da Economia e do Emprego. Decreto-Lei n.o 189/2012., (2012).

Ministério do Emprego e da Segurança Social. Decreto-Lei n.o 210–92., (1982).

Ministério do Emprego e da Segurança Social. Decreto-lei 79-A/89., (1989).

Ministério do Trabalho. Decreto lei 372A/75., (1975).

Ministérios do Plano e Coordenação Económica, das F. e do T. Decreto-Lei n.o 353-H-77., (1977).

UGT. Parecer da ugt relativo ao anteprojecto de código de trabalho., (2003).

UGT. Parecer da UGT sobre a proposta de lei no 109/ix regulamenta a lei n.o 99/2003, de 27 de agosto que aprovou o Código do Trabalho., (2003).

UGT. Proposta de lei do código de trabalho continua inaceitável negociação deve prosseguir., (2003)

PERSONAL INTERVIEWS

Uruguay (2008–2010)

Academic; Academic at various institutions with strong knowledge of the labor movement

Academic; Associate Professor at Education Department at the Catholic University in Uruguay

Academic; Associate Professor at the Political Science Institute at the Republic University

Academic; Former Director at the Management and Evaluation of the State Division (AGEV) at the Budget and Planning Office (OPP)

Academic; Professor at the Education Department at the Catholic University and former division director at the Public Education Public Administration (ANEP)

Academic; Professor at the Political Science Institute at the Republic University

Business leader; President at the Construction Chamber (CCU)

Business leader; President at the Industry Chamber (CIU)

Business leader; President at the Merchants Chamber (CMPP)

Business leader; Transport firm (CITA) delegated negotiator in Wage Councils, transport sector

Economist at the Monetary Policy Division at the Uruguayan Central Bank (BCU)

Executive / labor leader; former Labor Minister and Director at the National Labor Direction (Dinatra); former private sector labor leader

Executive; Academic and National Institute for Employment and Professional Training Director (INEFOP)

Executive; Former Budget and Planning Office (OPP) Director

Government representative; Former Government's negotiator at the Wage Councils

Labor leader / Politican, Frente Amplio; Former labor leader in the beverage sector; Frente Amplio MP

Labor leader; Collective Bargaining Secretary at PIT CNT

Lawyer; Former Labor Minister

Lawyer; Lawyer specialized in Labor law and labor rights

Policy maker liked to Frente Amplio; advisor to the Director in the Technological University in Uruguay (UTU)

Politician, Frente Amplio; Frente Amplio MP; and former labor leader at the State owned Oil Company (ANCAP)

Politican, Partido Colorado, Former Economy Minister

Politician Partido Colorado; Partido Colorado MP, former Economy Minister; former member of the Senate's Labor Commission during the discussion of the Labor reform and the Hacienda Commission during the Tax reform

Politician, Partido Nacional; former National senator, former member of the Senate's Labor Commission during the discussion of the Labor reform; responsible for the draft of the "peace clause" included in the final initiative

Politician, Partido Nacional; youth movement leader at the Nacional Party

Chile (2008–2010)

Academic; Associate Professor at the Central University in Chile and labor expert and advisor to the Labor Ministry during Lagos term

Academic; Associate Professor at the Economic Department, Catholic University in Chile

Academic; Associate Professor at the Economic Department; Catholic University in Chile

Academic; Associate Professor at the Economic Department; Catholic University in Chile

Academic; Associate Professor at the Education Department; Alberto Hurtado University

Academic; Associate Professor at the Education Department; Chilean University; Education Ministry Undersecretary during Lagos and Bachelet governments

Academic; Associate Professor at the Political Science Institute; Catholic University in Chile

Academic; Associate Professor at the Political Science Institute; Catholic University in Chile

Academic; Associate Professor at the Political Science School; Diego Portales University

Academic; Professor at FLACSO; expert in AUGE program and health sector

Business leader; Businessman in the Financial Sector; Director at Security Financial Services

Business leader; President at Confedech

Business leader; Ex-President at CPC

Business leader; Ex-President at SOFOFA

Business leader; Ex-Vicepresident AG Mining Group

Economist; Advisor to the Communist Party and expert at the Centro de Estudios Nacionales de Desarrollo Alternativo-CENDA Think Tank

Executive; Political Secretary to the Renovación Nacional (RN) MP Andres Allamand

Labor leader (retired); Education sector leader during Allende's government

Labor leader; Advisor to the CUT President on Parliamentary issues

Labor leader; Ex-CGT Confederation President

Labor leader; Labor leader in the mining sector; CONFEMIN President

Lawyer; Labor expert at the Foreign Relations Ministry

Policy advisor; Advisor to President Lagos; Member of the so called "Lagos' second floor"

Policy advisor; Advisor to President Lagos; Member of the so called "Lagos' second floor"

Policy advisor; Economic advisor to the President of Chile during Lagos and Bachelet periods

Policy advisor; Former labor issues expert at Libertad & Desarrollo Think Tank

Policy advisor; Health sector expert at the Libertad & Desarrollo Think Tank

Policy maker; Policy maker in the education sector. School director

Policy maker; Policy maker in the education sector. School director

Politician, Partido por la Democracia; PPD MP and former member of Senate's Hacienda Commission during the Tax reform debate

Politician, Socialist Party; Former Labor Minister

Politician, Socialist Party; Former Labor Ministry

Politician, Socialist Party; Socialist Party MP

Politician, Socialist Party; Socialist Party MP and member of Labor Commission during the Labor reform

Politician, Socialist Party; Socialist Party MP and member of Labor Commission during the Labor reform

Chile (2019)

Academic; Lawyer, policy advisor in labor reforms

Business leader; Businessman former president of CONAPYME, business representative at Consejo Superior Laboral

Business leader; Businessman, president of SONAMI and CPCP, business representative at Consejo Superior Laboral

Economist; Former minister of Finance

Executive and Policy advisor; Lawyer, former advisor of Labor Minister and government representative at Consejo Superior Laboral

Executive; Government representative at Consejo Superior Laboral

Executive; Government representative at Consejo Superior Laboral
Labor leader; Former president of UNT
Politician, Partido Demócrata Cristiano; Former labor Minister
Politician, Partido Demócrata Cristiano; Former minister of Planifica-
tion and Cooperation (2000–2002) and former labor minister
Politician, ex-President of Chile
Politician, Socialist Party; Former Labor Minister and National Deputy

Portugal (2019)

Academic; Adjunct Assistant Professor at Nova School of Business
and Economics, specialized in Portuguese economic growth.
Academic; Aggregate Professor of Economic History at Facultade de
Economía at Universidad Nova de Lisboa.
Academic; Assistant Professor at Instituto de Política e Relações Inter-
nacionais – IPRI – UNL.
Academic; Assistant Professor of Sociology at University of Coimbra,
FEUC. Specialized in the Portuguese labor movement.
Academic; Associate Professor at the Sociology Department at IUL
Academic; Investigador FCT at Nova Information Management
School (Nova IMS), Universidade Nova de Lisboa
Academic; Invited Professor at the Insttituto de Estudos Politicos.
Academic; Professor at ISCTE-IUL and policy advisor on labor law
regulations.
Academic; Professor of labor sociology, industrial relations and vol-
untary associations at ICS-UL.
Acedemic; Research Professor at Lisbon University's Social Science
Institute and Professor of Modern European History and Politics at
ISCTE, Lisbon.
Business leader; General Secretary of Confederação do Comércio e
Serviços de Portugal (CCP).
Business leader; Ex-Member of CSCS board
Business leader; Member of the Executive Board of Confederation of
Portuguese Business
Business leader; Member of the Executive Commission at Portuguese
Confederation of Tourism
Business leader; President of the Executive Committee of the CIP.
Economist; Director of the Studies Office of the Ministry of Economy
Executive linked to Partido Socialista; Former Minister of Finance.
Executive, State Secretary for Employment.

Executive: Secretary of State of Employment.

Executive; Director at DGERT; Director of the Commission of Collective Regulation and Labor Organizations at the Direcção Geral do Emprego e das Relações do Trabalho (DGERT)

Labor leader; Ex-General Secretary of CGTP and CGTP's representative at CES

Labor leader; Ex-General Secretary of CGTP.

Labor leader; Ex-General Secretary of Corriente Sindical Socialista at CGTP.

Labor leader; Ex-General Secretary of UGT.

Policy advisor and member of CDS-PP. Lawyer and member of the CDS-PP party. President of the 2013 IRC Reform Commission

Policy advisor; Full Professor at the Faculty of Law and Pro-Rector of the NOVA University of Lisbon and Portuguese National Expert of the ELLN – European Labour Law Network and Legal advisor of the Ministry of Employment.

Policy advisor; Lawyer member of the Portuguese-British Chamber of Commerce Directory and policy advisor in 2003 labor code reform.

Policy advisor; Professor at ISG-UL and former chief economist to two ex-Prime Ministers.

Politician, Bloço de Esquerda; Deputy to the Assembly of the Portuguese Republic.

Politician, Bloço de Esquerda; Deputy to the Assembly of the Portuguese Republic.

Politician, Bloço de Esquerda; Founder and former leader of BE and Deputy to the Assembly of the Portuguese Republic.

Politician, Centro Democrático e Social/Partido Popular; Lawyer and deputy to the Assembly of the Republic.

Politician, Communist Party; Deputy in Assembleia da República for the Communist Party.

Politician, Partido Social Democrata; Deputy to the Assembly of the Portuguese Republic.

Politician, Partido Social Democrata; Deputy to the Assembly of the Portuguese Republic.

Politician, Partido Socialista; Secretary of State to a Prime Minister

Politician, Socialist Party; Deputy of the Assembly of the Portuguese Republic

Politician, Socialist Party; Member of Socialist Party and Secretary of State for Parliamentary Affairs.

References

Afonso, Alexandre. 2013. *Social Concertation in Times of Austerity: European Integration and the Politics of Labour Market Governance in Austria and Switzerland*. Amsterdam, Netherlands: Amsterdam University Press.

Alegre, Pablo, and Fernando Filgueira. 2009. "Assessment of a Hybrid Reform Path: Social and Labour Policies in Uruguay, 1985–2005." *International Labour Review* 148(3): 317–34.

Alexander, Robert Jackson, and Eldon M. Parker. 2005. *A History of Organized Labor in Uruguay and Paraguay*. London: Greenwood Publishing Group.

Alonso Eloy, Rosa, and Carlos Demasi. 1986. *Uruguay 1958–1968: Crisis y Estancamiento*. Montevideo: Ediciones de la Banda Oriental.

Alvez, Guillermo, Verónica Amarante, Gonzalo Salas, and Andrea Vigorito. 2012. *La Desigualdad Del Ingreso En Uruguay Entre 1986 y 2009*. Montevideo, Uruguay: Universidad de la República (UdelaR).

Amable, Bruno. 2005. *The Diversity of Modern Capitalism*. New York: Oxford University Press.

2016. "The Political Economy of the Neoliberal Transformation of French Industrial Relations." *Industrial and Labor Relations Review* 69(3): 523–50.

Angell, Alan. 1974. *Partidos Políticos y Movimiento Obrero En Chile*. Mexico DF: Ediciones Era.

Anria, Santiago. 2016. "Democratizing Democracy? Civil Society and Party Organization in Bolivia." *Comparative Politics* 48(4): 459–78.

2018. *When Movements Become Parties: The Bolivian MAS in Comparative Perspective*. Boston: Cambridge University Press.

Anria, Santiago, and Juan Bogliaccini. 2022. "Empowering Inclusion? The Two Sides of Party-Society Linkages in Latin America." *Studies in Comparative International Development* 57: 410–32.

Anria, Santiago, and Jennifer Cyr. 2017. "Inside Revolutionary Parties: Coalition-Building and Maintenance in Reformist Bolivia." *Comparative Political Studies* 50(9): 1255–87.

Anria, Santiago, and Sara Niedzwiecki. 2016. "Social Movements and Social Policy: The Bolivian Renta Dignidad." *Studies in Comparative International Development* 51: 308–27.

Ansolabehere, Stephen, and David M. Konisky. 2006. "The Introduction of Voter Registration and Its Effect on Turnout." *Political Analysis* 14(1): 83–100.

Arriagada, Genaro. 2004. *Los Empresarios y La Política*. Santiago de Chile: Editorial LOM.

Arriagada, Irma. 2004. "Estructuras Familiares, Trabajo y Bienestar En América Latina." In *Cambio de Las Familias En El Marco de Las Transformaciones Globales: Necesidad de Políticas Públicas Eficaces*, eds. Irma Arriagada, and Verónica Aranda. Santiago de Chile: CEPAL – SERIE Seminarios y conferencias N42, 43–74.

Assembleia da República. 2003. "Presentation of Social Partners to the General Assembly." [Video Transcript] 15th January 2003.

Avdagic, Sabina. 2010. "When Are Concerted Reforms Feasible? Explaining the Emergence of Social Pacts in Western Europe." *Comparative Political Studies* 43(5): 628–57.

Avdagic, Sabina, Martin Rhodes, and Jelle Visser. 2011. *Social Pacts in Europe: Emergence, Evolution, and Institutionalization*. New York: Oxford University Press.

Baccaro, Lucio, Chiara Benassi, and Guglielmo Meardi. 2019. "Theoretical and Empirical Links between Trade Unions and Democracy." *Economic and Industrial Democracy* 40(1): 3–19.

Baccaro, Lucio, and Sang Hoon Lim. 2007. "Social Pacts as Coalitions of the Weak and Moderate: Ireland, Italy and South Korea in Comparative Perspective." *European Journal of Industrial Relations* 13(1): 27–46.

Baccaro, Lucio, and Chris Howell. 2017. *Trajectories of Neoliberal Transformation: European Industrial Relations since the 1970s*. New York: Cambridge University Press.

Baccaro, Lucio, and Jonas Pontusson. 2016. "Rethinking Comparative Political Economy: The Growth Model Perspective." *Politics and Society* 44(2): 175–207.

Baccaro, Lucio, and Marco Simoni. 2008. "Policy Concertation in Europe: Understanding Government Choice." *Comparative Political Studies* 41(10): 1323–48.

Baer, Werner, and António P. N. Leite. 1992. "The Peripheral Economy, Its Performance in Isolation and with Integration: The Case of Portugal." *Luso-Brazilian Review* 29(2): 1–43.

Baiôa, Manuel Pimenta Morgado, Paulo Jorge Fernandes, and Filipe Ribeiro de Meneses. 2003. "The Political History of Twentieth-Century Portugal." *Historia y Política: Ideas, procesos y movimientos sociales* 7: 11–54.

Baklanoff, Eric N. 1992. "The Political Economy of Portugal's Later 'Estado Novo': A Critique of the Stagnation Thesis." *Luso-Brazilian Review* 29(1): 1–17.

Baland, Jean Marie, and James A. Robinson. 2008. "Land and Power: Theory and Evidence from Chile." *American Economic Review* 98(5): 1737–65.

Barran, Jose P., and Benjamin Nahum. 1984. *Batlle, Los Estancieros y El Imperio Britanico*. Montevideo: Banda Oriental.

Barrán, José Pedro. 2004. *Los Conservadores Uruguayos, 1870–1933.* Montevideo: Ediciones de la Banda Oriental.

Barreto, José. 1990. "Os Primórdios Da Intersindical Sob Marcelo Caetano." *Análise Social* 25(105/106): 57–117.

2000. "Os Sindicatos Nacionais Do Estado Novo." In *Dicionário de História de Portugal – Suplemento*, eds. António Barreto, and Filomena Mónica. Porto, Figueirinhas: Suplemento, Vol. IX, 436–45.

Barreto, Matt A., Stephen A. Nuo, and Gabriel R. Sanchez. 2009. "The Disproportionate Impact of Voter-ID Requirements on the Electorate New Evidence from Indiana." *PS – Political Science and Politics* 42(1) 111–16.

Beach, Derek, and Rasmus Brun Pederson. 2016. *Causal Case Study Methods: Foundations and Guidelines for Comparing, Matching, and Tracing.* Michigan: University of Michigan Press.

Bentancur, Verónica Pérez, Rafael Piñeiro Rodríguez, and Fernando Rosenblatt. 2019. *How Party Activism Survives: Uruguay's Frente Amplio.* Padstow, UK: Cambridge University Press.

Benza, Gabriela, and Gabriel Kessler. 2020. *La ¿nueva? Estructura Social de América Latina: Cambios y Persistencias Después de La Ola de Gobiernos Progresistas.* Buenos Aires: Siglo, XX.

Beramendi, Pablo, and Thomas R. Cusack. 2009. "Diverse Disparities: The Politics and Economics of Wage, Market, and Disposable Income Inequalities." *Political Research Quarterly* 62(2): 257–75.

Beramendi, Pablo, and David Rueda. 2014. "Inequality and Institutions: The Case of Economic Coordination." *Annual Review of Political Science* 17: 251–71.

Bermeo, Nancy. 1987. "Redemocratization and Transition Elections: A Comparison of Spain and Portugal." *Comparative Politics* 19(2): 213–31.

1993. "A Comment on Economic Liberalization in Portugal and Spain." In *The Political Economy of Policy Reform*, ed. John Williamson. Washington, DC: Institute for International Economics, 197–206.

1999. "What's Working in Southern Europe?" *South European Society and Politics* 4(3): 263–87.

Bitar, Sergio. 1995. *Chile 1970–1973: Asumir La Historia Para Construir El Futuro.* Santiago de Chile: Pehuén.

Blanchard, Olivier, and Pedro Portugal. 2001. "What Hides behind an Unemployment Rate: Comparing Portuguese and U.S. Labor Markets." *American Economic Review* 91(1): 187–207.

Blatter, Joachim, and Markus Haverland. 2012. "Two or Three Approaches to Explanatory Case Study Research?" APSA 2012 Annual Meeting Paper.

Bogliaccini, Juan A. 2012. "Small Latecomers into the Global Market Power Conflict and Institutional Change in Chile and Uruguay." ProQuest Dissertations and Theses.

2013. "Trade Liberalization, Deindustrialization, and Inequality: Evidence from Middle-Income Latin American Countries." *Latin American Research Review* 48(2): 79–105.

2019. "The Reconstruction of Business Interests after the ISI Collapse: Unpacking the Effect of Institutional Change in Chile and Uruguay." *Third World Quarterly* 40(7): 1378–93.

2020. "The Technocratic Barrier to Wage Policy: Theoretical Insights from the Chilean Concertación." *Third World Quarterly* 42(4): 831–54.

Bogliaccini, Juan A., and Fernando Filgueira. 2011. "Capitalism in the Southern Cone of Latin America after the End of the Washington Consensus: Notes without Score?" *Revista del CLAD Reforma y Democracia* 51: 45+.

Bogliaccini, Juan A., Juan Geymonat, and Martin Opertti. 2020. "Big Business and Bureaucratic Authoritarianism in Uruguay: A Network-Based Story of Policy Infiltration for Self-Preservation." In *Big Business and Dictatorships in Latin America: A Transnational History of Profits and Repression*, eds. Victoria Basualdo, Hartmut Berghoff, Marcelo Bucheli, and Manfred Grieger. London: Palgrave Macmillan, 127–56.

Bogliaccini, Juan A., and Aldo Madariaga. 2020. "Varieties of Skills Profiles in Latin America: A Reassessment of the Hierarchical Model of Capitalism." *Journal of Latin American Studies* 52(3): 601–31.

Bogliaccini, Juan A., Felipe Monestier, and Cecilia Rossel. 2021. "The Origins of Wage Councils in Uruguay: A Process-Tracing Analysis." SASE Conference: Río de Janeiro, Brasil. In REPAL Annual Meeting, Ithaca, NY.

Bogliaccini, Juan A., and Rosario Queirolo. 2017. "Uruguay 2016: Parliamentary Majority under Risk and Challenges to Sustain the Model." *Revista de Ciencia Politica* 37(2): 589–612.

Bosco, Anna. 2001. "Four Actors in Search of a Role: The Southern European Communist Parties." In *Parties, Politics, and Democracy in the New Southern Europe*, eds. Richard Gunther, and Nikiforos P. Diamandouros. Maryland: Johns Hopkins University Press, 329–87.

Boylan, Delia M. 1996. "Taxation and Transition: The Politics of the 1990 Chilean Tax Reform." *Latin American Research Review* 31(1): 7–31.

Bozio, A. et al. 2020. *Predistribution vs. Redistribution: Evidence from France and the U.S.* Working Papers 2020–24. London: Center for Research in Economics and Statistics.

Bradley, David et al. 2003. "Distribution and Redistribution in Postindustrial Democracies." *World Politics* 55(2): 193–228.

Brancaccio, Emiliano, Nadia Garbellini, and Raffaele Giammetti. 2018. "Structural Labour Market Reforms, GDP Growth and the Functional Distribution of Income." *Structural Change and Economic Dynamics*, 44: 34–45.

Branco, Rui. 2017. "Review of Sara Watson, The Left Divided. The Development and Transformation of Advanced Welfare States." *Análise Social* 222(LII(1)): 204–14.

Branco, Rui, and Edna Costa. 2019. "The Golden Age of Tax Expenditures: Fiscal Welfare and Inequality in Portugal (1989–2011)." *New Political Economy* 24(6): 780–97.

Brandl, Bernd, and Franz Traxler. 2005. "Industrial Relations, Social Pacts and Welfare Expenditures: A Cross-National Comparison." *British Journal of Industrial Relations* 43(4): 635–58.

Bremer, Björn. 2018. "The Missing Left? Economic Crisis and the Programmatic Response of Social Democratic Parties in Europe." *Party Politics* 24(1): 23–38.

2023. *Austerity from the Left: Social Democratic Parties in the Shadow of the Great Recession.* Oxford: Oxford University Press.

Bremer, Björn, and Sean McDaniel. 2019. "The Ideational Foundations of Social Democratic Austerity in the Context of the Great Recession." *Socio-Economic Review* 18(2): 439–63.

Brinks, Daniel M., Steven Levitsky, and María Victoria Murillo. 2020. "The Political Origins of Institutional Weakness." In *The Politics of Institutional Weakness in Latin America*, eds. Daniel M. Brinks, Steven Levitsky, and María Victoria Murillo. Cambridge: Cambridge University Press, 1–40.

Brito, Mónica, and Filipe Carreira da Silva. 2010. *O Momento Constituinte: Os Idreitos Sociais Na Constituçao*. Coimbra: Almedina.

Brooks, Sarah. 2009. *Social Protection and the Market in Latin America*. Cambridge: Cambridge University Press.

Brooks, Sarah M. 2001. "What Was the Role of International Financial Institutions in the Diffusion of Social Security Reform in Latin America?" In *Learning from Foreign Models in Latin American Policy Reform*, ed. Kurt Weyland. Washington, DC: Woodrow Wilson Center Press and Johns Hopkins University Press, 53–80.

Bruneau, Thomas, and Alex Macleod. 1986. *Parties in Contemporary Portugal: Parties and the Consolidation of Democracy*. Boulder, CO: Lynne Rienner Publishers.

Von Bülow, Marisa, and Germán Bidegain Ponte. 2015. "It Takes Two to Tango: Students, Political Parties, and Protest in Chile (2005–2013)." In *Handbook of Social Movements across Latin America*, eds. Paul Almeida, and Allen Cordero Ulate. Dordrecht, Netherlands: Springer, 179–94.

Burgess, Katrina. 2010. "Global Pressures, National Policies, and Labor Rights in Latin America." *Studies in Comparative International Development* 45(2): 198–224.

Busemeyer, Marius R. 2014. *Skills and Inequality: Partisan Politics and the Political Economy of Education Reforms in Western Welfare States*. Cambridge, UK: Cambridge University Press.

Busemeyer, Marius R., and Torben Iversen. 2012. "Collective Skill Systems, Wage Bargaining, and Labor Market Stratification." In *The Political Economy of Collective Skill Formation*. New York: Oxford University Press, 205–33.

Busemeyer, Marius R., and Christine Trampusch. 2012. *The Political Economy of Collective Skill Formation*. New York: Oxford University Press.

Caetano, Gerardo. 1984. *El Asedio Conservador (1925–1929) Tomo I*. Montevideo: Centro Latinoamericano de Economía Humana (CLAEH).

Caetano, Gerardo, and Raul Jacob. 1987. *Economía y Política En El Uruguay Del Centenario (De Espaldas Al Precipicio)*. Montevideo: Universidad de la Republica.

Cahuc, Pierre, and Franck Malherbet. 2004. "Unemployment Compensation Finance and Labor Market Rigidity." *Journal of Public Economics* 88(3–4): 481–501.

Cahuc, Pierre, Francois Marque, and Etienne Wasmer. 2008. "A Theory of Wages and Labor Demand with Intra-Firm Bargaining and Matching Frictions." *International Economic Review* 49(3): 943–72.

Cahuc, Pierre, and Fabien Postel-Vinay. 2002. "Temporary Jobs, Employment Protection and Labor Market Performance." *Labour Economics* 9(1): 63–91.

Calmfors, Lars. 1987. "Efficiency and Equality in Swedish Labour Markets: Comment to Flanagan." In *The Swedish Economy*, eds. Barry Bosworth, and Alice Rivlin. Washington, DC: Brookings Institution, 174–80.

Calmfors, Lars, and John Driffill. 1988. "Bargaining Structure, Corporatism and Macroeconomic Performance." *Economic Policy* 3(6): 14–61. www.jstor .org/stable/1344503%5Cn www.jstor.org/stable/pdfplus/1344503.pdf?accept TC=true.

Cameron, Maxwell A. 2021. "Pathways to Inclusion in Latin America." In *The Inclusionary Turn in Latin American Democracies*, eds. Diana Kapiszewski, Steven Levitsky, and Deborah Yashar. London: Cambridge University Press, 401–33.

Campero, Guillermo. 2007. "N° 37 Serie Estudios Socio/Económicos La Economía Política de Las Relaciones Laborales 1990–2006." Santiago de Chile.

Campos Lima, Maria da Paz. 2019. "Portugal: Reforms and the Turn to Neoliberal Austerity." In *Collective Bargaining in Europe: Towards an Endgame*, eds. Torsten Müller, Kurt Vandaele, and Jeremy Waddington. Brussels: ETUI-REHS, 483–504.

Campos Lima, Maria da Paz, and Reinhard Naumann. 2000. "Social Pacts in Portugal: From Comprehensive Policy Programmes to the Negotiation of Concrete Industrial Relations Reforms?" In *Social Pacts in Europe New Dynamics*, eds. Giuseppe Fajertag, and Philippe Pochet. Brussels: European Trade Union Institute, 321–42.

2011. "Portugal: From Broad Strategic Pacts to Policy-Specific Agreements." In *Social Pacts in Europe Emergence, Evolution, and Institutionalization*, eds. Sabina Avdagic, Martin Rhodes, and Jelle Visser. Oxford: Oxford Academic, 147–73.

Candia, Julio César González, and Miguel Portugal Campillay. 2018. "Reforma Laboral Chilena,¿ Un Avance Concreto Para El Sindicalismo o Una Continuación Renovada Del Plan Laboral Impuesto Por La Dictadura Militar?" *Revista Pilquen. Sección Ciencias Sociales* 21(4): 32–42.

Card, David, and Ana Rute Cardoso. 2022. "Wage Flexibility under Sectoral Bargaining." *Journal of the European Economic Association* 20(5): 2013–61.

Cardoso, Daniel, and Rui Branco. 2017. "Labour Market Reforms and the Crisis in Portugal: No Change, U-Turn or New Departure?" IPRI Working Paper N.56/2017.

2018. "Liberalised Dualisation. Labour Market Reforms and the Crisis in Portugal: A New Departure." *European Journal of Social Security*, 20(1): 31–48.

Carnes, Matthew E. 2015. "Conclusion: Politics and Labor Regulation in Latin America." In *Continuity Despite Change: The Politics of Labor Regulation in Latin America*. Stanford, CA: Stanford University Press, 191–200.

Carriére, Jean, Nigel Haworth, and Jacqueline Roddick. 1989. *The State, Industrial Relations and the Labour Movement in Latin America (Vol.1)*. London: The Macmillan Press LTD.

Castañeda, Jorge G. 2006. "Latin America's Left Turn." *Foreign Affairs* 85(3): 28–43.

Castedo, Leopoldo. 2001. *Chile, Vida y Muerte de La República Parlamentaria: De Balmaceda a Alessandri*. Buenos Aires: Editorial Sudamericana.

Castiglioni, Rossana. 2005. *The Politics of Social Policy Change in Chile and Uruguay: Retrenchment versus Maintenance 1973–1998*. New York and London: Routledge.

Cavarozzi, Marcelo. 1975. "*The Government and the Industrial Bourgeoisie in Chile 1938–1964.*" Berkeley: University of California.

Centeno, Miguel Angel. 1993. "The New Leviathan: The Dynamics and Limits of Technocracy." *Theory and Society* 22(3): 307–35.

Clifton, Judith, Francisco Comín, and Daniel Díaz Fuentes. 2005. "'Empowering Europe's Citizen': Towards a Charter for Services General Interest." *Public Management Review* 7(3): 417–43.

Código do Trabalho. 2003. "Lei N.º 99/2003." https://dre.pt/web/guest/pesquisa/-/search/632906/details/normal?p_p_auth=bVotgyeX.

Cohen, Gerald Alan. 2000. *If You Are an Egalitarian, How Come You're So Rich?* Cambridge: Harvard University Press.

Collier, Ruth, and David Collier. 1991. *Shaping the Political Arena.* Berkeley, CA: Princeton University Press.

Conselho Económico e Social. 1996. "Acordo De Concertação Estratégica 1996/1999."

Cook, Maria Lorena. 2007. *Politics of Labor Reform in Latin America: Between Flexibility and Rights.* Pennsylvania: Penn State Press.

Cook, Maria Lorena, and Joseph C Bazler. 2013. "Bringing Unions Back in: Labour and Left Governments in Latin America."

Correio da Manhã. 2002. "É Preciso Acabar Com a Concertação Social."

Costa Pinto, António. 2000. "Portugal: Crisis and Early Authoritarian Takeover." In *Conditions of Democracy in Europe, 1919–39,* eds. Dirk Berg-Schlosser, and Jereremy Mitchell. London: Palgrave Macmillan, 354–80.

  2003. "Twentieth-Century Portugal: An Introduction." In *Contemporary Portugal: Politics, Society and Culture,* ed. António Costa Pinto. New York: Columbia University Press, 1–46.

  2008. "Political Purges and State Crisis in Portugal's Transition to Democracy, 1975–76." *Journal of Contemporary History* 43(2): 305–32.

Crouch, Colin. 1993. *Industrial Relations and European State Traditions.* Oxford: Oxford University Press.

Cusack, Thomas R., and Pablo Beramendi. 2006. "Taxing Work." *European Journal of Political Research* 45(1): 47–73.

Dahl, Robert A. 1971. *Polyarchy: Participation and Opposition.* New Haven: Yale University Press.

Dargent, Eduardo. 2014. *Technocracy and Democracy in Latin America: The Experts Running Government.* New York: Cambridge University Press.

Deaton, Angus. 2013. *The Great Escape.* New Jersey: Princeton University Press.

Decreto-Lei 79-A/89. 1989. "Decreto-Lei 79-A/89. Diário Da República n.º 60/1989, 1º Suplemento, Série I de 1989-03-13." https://dre.tretas.org/dre/23127/decreto-lei-79-A-89-de-13-de-marco.

Decreto-Lei n.º 353-H/77. 1977. "Decreto-Lei n.º 353-H/77. Diário Da República n.º 199/1977, 2º Suplemento, Série I de 1977-08-29." https://dre.pt/pesquisa/-/search/240853/details/normal?jp=true/en.

Decreto-Lei n.º 398/83. 1983. "Decreto-Lei n.º 398/83. Diário Da República n.º 252/1983, Série I de 1983-11-02." https://dre.pt/web/guest/pesquisa-avancada/-/asearch/443683/details/normal?types=SERIEI&search=Pesquisar&numero=398%2F83&tipo=Decreto-Lei.

Decreto-Lei n.º 781/76. 1976. "Decreto-Lei n.º 781/76. Diário Da República n.º 253/ 1976, Série I de 1976-10-28." https://dre.pt/web/guest/pesquisa/-/search/409341/ details/maximized?filterEnd=1976-12-31&filterStart=1976-01-01&q=1976&per Page=100&fqs=1976.

Decreto-Lei n.º 841-C/76. 1976. "Decreto-Lei n.º 841-C/76. Diário Da República n.º 285/1976, 1º Suplemento, Série I de 1976-12-07." https://dre.pt/web/ guest/pesquisa/-/search/558991/details/maximized?perPage=50&sort=when Searchable&q=Constituição+da+República+Portuguesa&sortOrder=ASC.

Decreto-Lei n.º 90/2012. 2012. "Decreto-Lei n.º 90/2012. Diário Da República n.º 72/2012, Série I de 2012-04-11." https://dre.pt/pesquisa/-/search/552548/ details/maximized.

Demasi, Carlos. 2016. "El Apoyo de Las Cámaras Empresariales." In *El Negocio Del Terrorismo de Estado: Los Cómplices Económicos de La Dictadura Uruguaya*, ed. Juan Pablo Bohoslavsky. Montevideo: Penguin Random House Grupo Editorial.

DeShazo, Peter. 1983. *Urban Workers and Labor Unions in Chile, 1902–1927*. Wisconsin: University of Wisconsin Press.

DGERT. 2020. "Direção-Geral Do Emprego e Das Relações de Trabalho." *Data on Collective Relations*. www.dgert.gov.pt (September 20, 2012).

Doglio, Natalia, Luis Senatore, and Jaime Yaffé. 2004. "Izquierda Política y Sindicatos En Uruguay (1971–2003)." In *La Izquierda Uruguaya: En La Oposición y El Gobierno*, ed. Jorge Lanzaro. Montevideo: Editorial Fin de Siglo, 251–96.

Doner, Richard F., and Ben Ross Schneider. 2016. "The Middle-Income Trap: More Politics than Economics." *World Politics* 68(4): 608–44.

Dornelas, Antonio. 2003. "Industrial Relations in Portugal: Continuity or Controlled Change?" In *Portugal: Strategic Options in a European Context*, eds. Fátima Monteiro, José Tavares, Miguel Glatzer, and Ángelo Cardoso. Maryland: Lexington Books, 129–51.

——— 2010. "Social Pacts in Portugal: Still Uneven?" In *After the Euro and Enlargement: Social Pacts in the EU*, eds. Philippe Pochet, Maarten Keune, and David Natali. Brussels: European Trade Union Institute, 109–36.

Drezner, Daniel W. 2001. "Globalization and Policy Convergence." *International Studies Review* 3(1): 53–78.

Dube, Arindrajit. 2019a. *Impacts of Minimum Wages: Review of the International Evidence*. London: UK Government.

——— 2019b. "Minimum Wages and the Distribution of Family Incomes." *American Economic Journal: Applied Economics* 11(4): 268–304.

ECLAC (Economic Commission for Latin America and the Caribbean). 2012. *Social Panorama of Latin America*. Santiago de Chile.

Edwards, Alberto. 1928. *La Fronda Aristocrática En Chile*. Santiago de Chile: Imprenta Nacional.

Edwards, Pearce. 2022. "Political Competition and Authoritarian Repression." *World Politics* 74(4): 479–522.

Emmenegger, Patrick, Silja Hausermann, Bruno Palier, and Martin Seeleib-Kaiser. 2012. *The Age of Dualization: The Changing Face of Inequality in Deindustrializing Societies*. New York: Oxford University Press.

Erixon, Lennart. 2010. "The Rehn-Meidner Model in Sweden: Its Rise, Challenges and Survival." *Journal of Economic Issues* 44(3): 677–715.

Esping-Andersen, Gosta. 1990. *The Three Worlds of Welfare Capitalism*. Great Britain: Princeton University Press.

Esping-Andersen, Gosta, and Walter Korpi. 1985. *Social Policy as Class Politics in Post-War Capitalism: Scandinavia, Austria, and Germany*. Stockholm: Swedish Institute for Social Research.

1986. "From Poor Relief to Institutional Welfare States: The Development of Scandinavian Social Policy." *International Journal of Sociology* 16(3/4): 39–74.

Etchemendy, Sebastián. 2001. "Constructing Reform Coalitions: The Politics of Compensations in Argentina's Economic Liberalization." *Latin American Politics and Society* 43(3): 1–35.

2008. "Repression, Exclusion, and Inclusion: Government-Union Relations and Patterns of Labor Reform in Liberalizing Economies." *Comparative Politics* 36: 273–90.

2011. *Models of Economic Liberalization: Business, Workers, and Compensation in Latin America, Spain and Portugal*. New York: Cambridge University Press.

2019. "The Rise of Segmented Neo-Corporatism in South America: Wage Coordination in Argentina and Uruguay (2005–2015)." *Comparative Political Studies* 52(10): 1427–2465.

Etchemendy, Sebastián, and Ruth Berins Collier. 2007. "Down but Not out: Union Resurgence and Segmented Neocorporatism in Argentina (2003–2007)." *Politics and Society* 35(3): 363–401.

Fábrega, Jorge, Jorge González, and Jaime Lindh. 2018. "Polarization and Electoral Incentives: The End of the Chilean Consensus Democracy, 1990–2014." *Latin American Politics and Society* 60(4): 49–68.

Fairfield, Tasha. 2015. *Private Wealth and Public Revenue in Latin America: Business Power and Tax Politics*. Boston: Cambridge University Press.

Feldmann, Andreas, and Juan Luna. 2023. *Criminal Politics and Botched Development in Contemporary Latin America*. Cambridge: Cambridge University Press.

Fernandes, Tiago, and Rui Branco. 2017. "Long-Term Effects: Social Revolution and Civil Society in Portugal, 1974–2010." *Comparative politics* 49(3): 411–31.

Ferrera, Maurizio. 2005. *Welfare State Reform in Southern Europe: Fighting Poverty and Social Exclusion in Italy, Spain, Portugal and Greece*. London and New York: Routledge.

Filgueira, Carlos. 1988. "Concertación Salarial y Gremios Empresariales En Uruguay." In *Política Económica y Actores Sociales*, ed. Patricio Silva. Buenos Aires: PREALC, 473–509.

Filgueira, Carlos, and Fernando Filgueira. 2002. "Models of Welfare and Models of Capitalism: The Limits of Transferability." In *Models of Capitalism: Lessons for Latin America*, ed. Evelyne Huber. Santiago, Chile: Penn State Press, 127–58.

Filgueira, Fernando, Luis Reygadas, Juan Pablo Luna, and Pablo Alegre. 2012. "Crisis de Incorporación En América Latina: Límites de La Modernización Conservadora." *Perfiles Latinoamericanos* 20(40): 7–34.

Fishman, Robert M. 1990a. "Rethinking State and Regime: Southern Europe's Transition to Democracy." *World Politics* 42(3): 422–40.

Fishman, Robert M. 1990b. *Working-Class Organization and the Return to Democracy in Spain*. New York: Cornell University Press.

2011. "Democratic Practice after the Revolution: The Case of Portugal and Beyond." *Politics and Society* 39(2): 233–67.

2019. *Democratic Practice: Origins of the Iberian Divide in Political Inclusion*. New York: Oxford University Press.

2017. "How Civil Society Matters in Democratization: Setting the Boundaries of Post-Transition Political Inclusion." *Comparative Politics* 49(3): 391–409.

Fleckenstein, Timo, and Soohyun Christine Lee. 2017. "Democratization, Post-Industrialization, and East Asian Welfare Capitalism: The Politics of Welfare State Reform in Japan, South Korea, and Taiwan." *Journal of International and Comparative Social Policy* 33(1): 36–54.

Fligstein, Neil, Gerhard Lehmbruch, and Philippe C. Schmitter. 1982. *Patterns of Corporatist Policy-Making*. London: Sage Publications.

Flores-Macías, Gustavo A. 2010. "Statist vs. Pro-Market: Explaining Leftist Governments' Economic Policies in Latin America." *Comparative Politics* 42(4): 413–33.

2012. *After Neoliberalism?: The Left and Economic Reforms in Latin America*. New York: Oxford University Press.

Frank, Volker. 2002. "The Elusive Goal in Democratic Chile: Reforming the Pinochet Labor Legislation." *Latin American Politics and Society* 44(1): 35–68.

2004. "Politics without Policy: The Failure of Social Concertation in Democratic Chile, 1990–2000." In *Victims of the Chilean Miracle: Workers and Neoliberalism in the Pinochet Era, 1973–2002*, ed. Peter Winn. Durham, NC: Duke University Press, 71–124.

Fuentes, Claudio. 1999. "Partidos y Coaliciones En El Chile de Los 90. Entre Pactos y Proyectos." In *El Modelo Chileno*, ed. Paul Drake, and Ivan Jaksic. Santiago: LOM Ediciones, 191–222.

Gamboa, Ricardo, and Mauricio Morales. 2015. "Deciding on the Electoral System: Chile's Adoption of Proportional Representation in 1925." *Latin American Politics and Society* 57(2): 41–66.

Gamboa Valenzuela, Ricardo. 2011. "Changing Electoral Rules: The Australian Ballot and Electoral Pacts in Chile (1958–1962)." *Revista de Ciencia Política* 31(2): 159–86.

Garay, Candelaria. 2016. *Social Policy Expansion in Latin America*. Boston: Cambridge University Press.

Garrett, Geoffrey. 1998. *Partisan Politics in the Global Economy*. New York: Cambridge University Press.

Garrett, Geoffrey, and Peter Lange. 1995. "Internationalization, Institutions, and Political Change." *International Organization* 49(4): 627–65.

Gilardi, Fabrizio, Jacint Jordana, and David Levi-Faur. 2006. "Regulation in the Age of Globalization: The Diffusion of Regulatory Agencies across Europe and Latin America." In *Privatization and Market Development: Global Movements in Public Policy Ideas*, ed. Graeme Hodge. Cornwall: Edward Elgar Publishing, 127–47.

Goertz, Gary, and James Mahoney. 2012. *A Tale of Two Cultures: Qualitative and Quantitative Research in the Social Sciences.* New Jersey: Princeton University Press.

Goldthorpe, John H. 1984. *Order and Conflict in Contemporary Capitalism.* Oxford: Clarendon Press.

González, Luis E. 1993. *Estructuras Políticas y Democracia En Uruguay.* Montevideo: Fundación de Cultura Universitaria. Instituto de Ciencia Política.

    1999. "Los Partidos Establecidos y Sus Desafiantes." In *Los Partidos Políticos Uruguayos En Tiempo de Cambio,* eds. Luis E. González, Felipe Monestier, Rosario Queirolo, and Mariana Sotelo Rico. Montevideo: Fundación de Cultura Universitaria, 19–30.

González, Luis E. 1991. *Political Structures and Democracy in Uruguay.* Indiana: University of Notre Dame Press.

Grau, Nicolas, and Oscar Landerretche. 2011. *The Labor Impact of Minimum Wages: A Method for Estimating the Effect in Emerging Economies Using Chilean Panel Data.* Santiago de Chile: University of Chile.

Griffin, Larry J, Michael E Wallace, and Beth A Rubin. 1986. "Capitalist Resistance to the Organization of Labor before the New Deal: Why? How? Success?" *American Sociological Review* 51(2): 147–67.

Hacker, Jacob. 2011. "The Institutional Foundations of Middle-Class Democracy." *Policy Network* 6: 33–7.

Hacker, Jacob, and Paul Pierson. 2010. "Winner-Take-All Politics: Public Policy, Political Organization, and the Precipitous Rise of Top Incomes in the United States." *Politics and Society* 38(2): 152–204.

Haindl, Erik. 2007. *Chile y Su Desarrollo Económico En El Siglo XX.* Editorial Andrés Bello. Santiago de Chile: Independently published.

Hall, Peter A. 2002. "The Comparative Political Economy of the 'Third Way'." In *The Third Way Transformation of Social Democracy: Normative Claims and Policy Initiatives in the 21st Century,* ed. Oliver Schmidtke. Hampshire, UK: Ashgate, 31–58.

Hall, Peter A., and David Soskice. 2001. "An Introduction to Varieties of Capitalism." In *Varieties of Capitalism: The Institutional Foundations of Comparative Advantage,* eds. Peter A. Hall, and David Soskice. Oxford University Press, 1–70.

Hallerberg, Mark, and Joachim Wehner. 2018. "When Do You Get Economists as Policy Makers?" *British Journal of Political Science* 50(3): 1193–205.

Hancké, Bob, Martin Rhodes, and Mark Thatcher. 2007. *Beyond Varieties of Capitalism: Conflict, Contradictions, and Complementarities in the European Economy.* New York: Oxford University Press.

Harvey, Robert. 1978. *Portugal: Birth of a Democracy.* London: Palgrave Macmillan.

Hassel, Anke. 2014. "Adjustments in the Eurozone: Varieties of Capitalism and the Crisis in Southern Europe." *LEQS Paper* (76).

Hayman, Richard. 1975. *Industrial Relations. A Marxist Introduction.* London: Palgrave Macmillan.

Hijzen, Alexander, and Pedro S. Martins. 2016. *No Extension without Representation? Evidence from a Natural Experiment in Collective Bargaining.* Washington, DC: International Monetary Fund.

Hijzen, Alexander, Pedro S. Martins, and Jante Parlevliet. 2017. *Collective Bargaining through the Magnifying Glass: A Comparison between the Netherlands and Portugal.* Washington, DC: International Monetary Fund.

Hirschman, Albert. 1970. *Exit, Voice and Loyalty.* Cambridge, MA: Harvard University Press.

Huber, Evelyne. 2003. *Models of Capitalism: Lessons for Latin America.* Pennsylvania: Penn State Press.

Huber, Evelyne, and John D. Stephens. 2001. *Development and Crisis of the Welfare State: Parties and Policies in Global Markets.* Chicago: University of Chicago Press.

    2002. "Globalisation, Competitiveness, and the Social Democratic Model." *Social Policy and Society* 1(1): 47–57.

    2012. *Democracy and the Left: Social Policy and Inequality in Latin America.* Chicago, IL: University of Chicago Press.

Huntington, Samuel. 1968. *Political Order in Changing Societies.* New Haven, CT: Yale University Press.

    1991. *The Third Wave: Democratization in the Late 20th Century (Vol. 4).* Oklahoma: University of Oklahoma Press.

IMF. 2020. "Fiscal Monitor."

INE. 2020. "Instituto Nacional de Estadística." *Data on Salaries and Prices.* www.ine.gub.uy/precios-y-salarios.

Iversen, Torben. 1999. *Contested Economic Institutions: The Politics of Macroeconomics and Wage Bargaining in Advanced Democracies.* Cambridge: Cambridge University Press.

Iversen, Torben, and David Soskice. 2006. "New Macroeconomics and Political Science." *Annual Review of Political Science* 9(1): 425–53. www.annualreviews.org/doi/10.1146/annurev.polisci.9.072004.085858.

Iversen, Torben, and Anne Wren. 1998. "Equality, Employment, and Budgetary Restraint: The Trilemma of the Service Economy." *World Politics* 50(4): 507–46.

Joignant, Alfredo. 2011. "The Politics of Technopols: Resources, Political Competence and Collective Leadership in Chile, 1990–2010." *Journal of Latin American Studies* 43(3): 517–46.

Kahneman, Daniel. 1992. "Reference Points, Anchors, Norms, and Mixed Feelings." *Organizational Behavior and Human Decision Processes* 51(2): 296–312.

    2003. "A Perspective on Judgment and Choice: Mapping Bounded Rationality." *American Psychologist* 58(9): 679–720.

Kaiser, Vanessa. 2011. *En Vez de Una Sola Mirada.* Santiago de Chile: RIL Editores.

Kapiszewski, Diana, Steven Levitsky, and Deborah J. Yashar. 2021. "Inequality, Democracy, and the Inclusionary Turn in Latin America." In *The Inclusionary Turn in Latin American Democracies*, eds. Diana Kapiszewski, Steven Levitsky, and Deborah J. Yashar. Cambridge: Cambridge University Press, 1–56.

Katrougalos, George, and Gabriella Lazaridis. 2003. "Southern European Welfare States: Problems, Challenges and Prospects." *Challenges.*

Katzenstein, Peter J. 1985. *Small States in World Markets: Industrial Policy in Europe.* New York: Cornell University Press.

Keele, Luke, William Cubbison, and Ismail White. 2021. "Suppressing Black Votes: A Historical Case Study of Voting Restrictions in Louisiana." *American Political Science Review* 115(2): 694–700.

Keohane, Robert. 1984. *After Hegemony: Cooperation and Discord in the World Political Economy.* Princeton, NJ: Princeton University Press.

Kerr, Clark. 1983. *The Future of Industrial Societies: Covergence or Continuing Diversity?* Cambridge, MA: Harvard University Press.

Kharas, Homi, and Harinder Kohli. 2011. "What Is the Middle Income Trap, Why Do Countries Fall into It, and How Can It Be Avoided?" *Global Journal of Emerging Market Economies* 3(3): 281–89.

Kitschelt, Herbert. 1994. *The Transformation of European Social Democracy.* New York: Cambridge University Press.

2000. "Linkages between Citizens and Politicians in Democratic Polities." *Comparative Political Studies* 33(6): 845–79.

Kitschelt, Herbert, Kirk A. Hawkins, Juan Pablo Luna, Guillermo Rosas, Elizabeth J. Zechmeister. 2010. *Latin American Party Systems.* New York: Cambridge University Press.

Kitschelt, Herbert, Peter Lange, Gary Marks, and John D. Stephens. 1999. *Continuity and Change in Contemporary Capitalism.* Cambridge, MA: Cambridge University Press.

Korpi, Walter. 1978. *The Working Class in Welfare Capitalism: Work, Unions and Politics in Sweden.* London: Routledge & Kegan Paul.

Korpi, Walter, and Joakim Palme. 2003. "New Politics and Class Politics in the Context of Austerity and Globalization: Welfare State Regress in 18 Countries, 1975–95." *American Political Science Review* 97(3): 425–46.

Kuznets, Simon. 1960. "Economic Growth of Small Nations." In *Economic Consequences of the Size of Nations*, ed. Edward Robinson. London: Springer, 14–32.

Lanza, Federico. 2013. "Factores Endógenos y Exógenos En La Crisis Del PCU (1989–1992)."

Lanzaro, Jorge. 1986. *Sindicatos y Sistema Político: Relaciones Corporativas En El Uruguay, 1940–1985.* Montevideo: Fundación de Cultura Universitaria.

1993. "La 'Doble Transición' En El Uruguay. Gobierno de Partidos y Neo-Presidencialismo." *Nueva Sociedad* 128: 132–47.

2004. "Fundamentos de La Democracia Pluralista y Estructura Política Del Estado En El Uruguay." *Revista Uruguaya de Ciencia Política* 14: 103–35.

2011. "Izquierdas y Derechas Gobernantes En América Latina." https://forum.lasaweb.org/files/vol42-issue3/Debates1.pdf.

2013. "Continuidad y Cambios En Una Vieja Democracia de Partidos: Uruguay (1910–2010)." *Opiniao pública* 19 (2): 235–69.

Law 19759 History of the Law. 2001. "Law 19759, History of the Law." www
.bcn.cl/.

Lei n.º 99/2003. 2003. "Lei n.º 99/2003." https://dre.pt/pesquisa/-/search/632906/
details/normal?q=Lei+n.099%2F2003%2C de+27+de+agosto.

Leonardi, Marco, and Giovanni Pica. 2007. "Employment Protection Legislation
and Wages." Working Paper Series 778. European Central Bank.

2013. "Who Pays for It? The Heterogeneous Wage Effects of Employment
Protection Legislation." *Economic Journal* 123: 1236–73.

Levitsky, Steven. 2003. *Transforming Labor-Based Parties in Latin America:
Argentine Peronism in Comparative Perspective*. Cambridge: Cambridge
University Press.

Levitsky, Steven, and Kenneth M. Roberts. 2011. "Latin America's 'Left Turn':
A Framework for Analysis." In *The Resurgence of the Latin American Left*,
eds. Steven Levitsky, and Kenneth M. Roberts. Maryland: Johns Hopkins
University Press, 1–28.

Lijphart, Arend. 1969. "Consociational Democracy." *World Politics* 21(2): 207–25.

Linz, Juan J. 1978. *The Breakdown of Democratic Regimes: Crisis, Breakdown
and Reequilibration*. Baltimore, MD: Johns Hopkins University Press.

1996. *Problems of Democratic Transition and Consolidation: Southern
Europe, South America, and Post-Communist Europe*. Baltimore, MD:
Johns Hopkins University Press.

2017. "Toward Consolidated Democracies." In *The Politics of the
Postcommunist World*, eds. Stephen White, and Daniel N. Nelson. Maryland:
Johns Hopkins University Press, 503–22.

Lipset, Seymour Martin. 1959. "Some Social Requisites of Democracy: Economic
Development and Political Legitimacy." *American Political Science Review*
53(1): 69–105.

Lipset, Seymour Martin, and Stein Rokkan. 1967. "Cleavage Structures, Party
Systems, and Voter Alignments: An Introduction." In *Party Systems and
Voter Alignments: Cross-National Perspectives*, eds. Seymour Martin Lipset,
and Stein Rokkan. New York: The Free Press, 1–64.

Lloyd-Jones, Stewart. 2001. "Portugal's History since 1974." *ISCTE–Instituto
Superior de Ciências do Trabalho e da Empresa (Lisbon)*. www1.ci.uc.pt/
cd25a/media/Textos/portugal-since-1974.pdf (accessed December 15, 2010).

2002. "The 1999 Parliamentary Elections and 2001 Presidential Elections in
Portugal." *Electoral Studies* 21(1): 114–22.

Louçã, Francisco, João Teixeira Lopes, and Jorge Costa. 2014. *Os Burgueses*.
Lisbon: Bertrand Editora.

Lucena, Manuel de. 1976. *A Evolução Do Sistema Corporativo Português: O
Salazarismo*. Lisbon: Perspectivas e Realidades.

Luebbert, Gregory M. 1987. "Social Foundations of Political Order in Interwar
Europe." *World Politics* 39(4): 449–78.

1991. *Liberalism, Fascism, or Social Democracy: Social Classes and the
Political Origins of Regimes in Interwar Europe*. New York: Oxford
University Press.

Luna, Juan Pablo. 2014. *Segmented Representation: Political Party Strategies in
Unequal Democracies*. Oxford: Oxford University Press.

Luna, Juan Pablo, and David Altman. 2011. "Uprooted but Stable: Chilean Parties and the Concept of Party System Institutionalization." *Latin American Politics and Society* 53(2): 1–28.

Luna, Juan Pablo, Felipe Monestier, and Fernando Rosenblatt. 2014. "Religious Parties in Chile: The Christian Democratic Party and the Independent Democratic Union." In *Religiously Oriented Parties and Democratization*, eds. Luca Ozzano, and Francesco Cavatorta. New York: Routledge, 119–40.

Luna, Juan Pablo, Rafael Piñeiro Rodríguez, Fernando Rosenblatt, and Gabriel Vommaro, eds. 2021. *Diminished Parties*. Cambridge: Cambridge University Press, 294–307. www.cambridge.org/core/product/identifier/9781009072045/type/book (May 29, 2023).

Luna, Juan Pablo, Rafael Piñeiro Rodríguez, Fernando Rosenblatt, and Gabriel Vommaro. 2021. "Political Parties, Diminished Subtypes, and Democracy." *Party Politics* 27(2).

Macedo, Jorge Braga. 2003. "Portugal's European Integration: The Limits of External Pressure." In *Portugal: Strategic Options in a European Context*, eds. Fatima Monteiro, Jose Tavares, Miguel Glatzer, and Ângelo Cardoso. Maryland: Lexington Books, 61–97.

Madariaga, Aldo. 2020. *NEOLIBERAL RESILIENCE: Lessons in Democracy and Development from Latin America and Eastern Europe*. Princeton, NJ: Princeton University Press.

Madureira, Nuno Luís. 2007. "Cartelization and Corporatism: Bureaucratic Rule in Authoritarian Portugal, 1926–45." *Journal of Contemporary History* 42(1): 79–96.

Mahoney, James. 2000. "Strategies of Causal Inference in Small-N Analysis." *Sociological Methods and Research*. 28(4).

2004. "Comparative-Historical Methodology." *Annual Review of Sociology* 30: 81–101.

Mahoney, James, and Dietrich Rueschemeyer. 2012. *Comparative Historical Analysis in the Social Sciences*. New York: Cambridge University Press.

Mahoney, James, and Kathleen Thelen. 2009. *Explaining Institutional Change: Ambiguity, Agency, and Power*. New York: Cambridge University Press.

Makler, Harry M. 1976. "The Portuguese Industrial Elite and Its Corporative Relations: A Study of Compartmentalization in an Authoritarian Regime." *Economic Development and Cultural Change* 24(3): 495–526.

Malamud, Andrés, and Philippe C. Schmitter. 2011. "The Experience of European Integration and the Potential for Integration in South America." In *New Regionalism and the European Union: Dialogues, Comparisons and New Research Directions*, eds. Alex Warleigh-Lack, Nick Robinson, and Ben Rosamund. Perth, UK: Routledge, 135–57.

Marambio, Alexis, Patricio Navia, Cristian Figueras, and Ariel Madera. 2017. "La Cohesión Legislativa Entre La Concertación y El Partido Comunista En Chile, 2010–2013." *Perfiles Latinoamericanos* 25(50): 179–202.

Mares, Isabela. 2005. "Social Protection around the World External Insecurity, State Capacity, and Domestic Political Cleavages." *Comparative Political Studies* 38(6): 623–51.

Markoff, John, and Verónica Montecinos. 1993. "The Ubiquitous Rise of Economists." *Journal of Public Policy* 13(1): 37–68.

Marks, Gary. 1986a. "Neocorporatism and Incomes Policy in Western Europe and North America." *Comparative Politics* 18(3): 253–77.

1986b. *Unions in Politics*. Princeton, NJ: Princeton University Press.

2014. "Negative and Positive Integration in the Political Economy of European Welfare States." In *Governance in the European Union*, eds. Gary Marks, Fritz W. Scharpf, Philippe C. Schmitter, and Wolfgang Streeck. London: SAGE Publications, 15–39.

Martins, Pedro S. 2020. "30,000 Minimum Wages: The Economic Effects of Collective Bargaining Extensions." *British Journal of Industrial Relations* 59(2): 335–69.

Martins, Pedro S., and Joana Saraiva. 2019. "Assessing the Legal Value Added of Collective Bargaining Agreements." GLO Discussion Paper.

McIlroy, John. 1998. "The Enduring Alliance? Trade Unions and the Making of New Labour, 1994–1997." *British Journal of Industrial Relations* 36(4): 537–64.

Meidner, Rudolf. 1974. *Coordination and Solidarity: An Approach to Wages Policy*. Stockholm: Bokforlaget Prisma.

El Mercurio. 2000. "Government Will Enforce Their Majority for Labor Reform." December 14th.

2001a. "DC Asks to Use Frei's Labor Initiative." April 3rd.

2001b. "Longueiras Shows Disposition to Talk with Lagos." November 11th.

2001c. "Presidential Offensive for Aligning the Concertacion." April 3rd.

Mill, John Stuart. 1872. *System of Logic*. 8th Edition. London: Longman, Green.

Monestier, Felipe. 2007. *Movimientos Sociales, Partidos Políticos y Democracia Directa Desde Abajo En Uruguay: 1985–2004*. Buenos Aires: CLACSO. http://biblioteca.clacso.org/clacso/becas/20190809055042/mone.pdf.

Montecinos, Veronica. 1998. *Economists, Politics and the State*. Amsterdam: CELDA.

Moore, Barrington. 1978. *Injustice: The Social Bases of Obedience and Revolt*. White Plains, New York: M.E. Sharpe Publisher.

Morlino, Leonardo. 1986. "Consolidamento Democratico: Definizione e Modelli." *Italian Political Science Review/Rivista Italiana di Scienza Politica* 16(2): 197–238.

Moulian, Tomás. 1986a. *El Gobierno de Ibáñez, 1952–1958*. Santiago de Chile: Programa FLACSO.

1986b. "288 La Democracia Cristiana En Su Fase Ascendente, 1957–1964." Programa FLACSO.

Moulián, Tomás. 2003. "El Sistema de Partidos En Chile." In *El asedio a la política: los partidos latinoamericanos en la era neoliberal*, eds. Marcelo Cavarozzi, and Juan Manuel Abal Medina. Rosario: Homo Sapiens/Fundación Konrad Adenauer, 241–57.

Moulián, Tomás. 1989. *El régimen de gobierno 1933–1973: Algunos problemas institucionales. Documento de Trabajo Programa*. Santiago de Chile: FLASCO, 406.

Moulian, Tomás, and Isabel Torres. 1989. "La Problemática de La Derecha Política En Chile, 1964–1983." In *Muerte y resurrección de los partidos políticos en el autoritarismo, en las transiciones en el Cono Sur*, eds. Marcelo Cavarozzi, and Manuel A. Garretón. Santiago de Chile: FLASCO, 335–94.

Mudge, Stephanie. 2018. *Leftism Reinvented: Western Parties from Socialism to Neoliberalism*. Cambridge: Harvard University Press.

Muñoz Gomá, Oscar. 2007. *El Modelo Económico de La Concertación 1990–2005: ¿Reformas o Cambio?* Chile: Flacso.

Muñoz Gomá, Oscar, and Ana María Arriagada. 1977. *Orígenes Políticos y Económicos Del Estado Empresarial En Chile*. Santiago de Chile: Corporación de Investigaciones Económicas para Latinoamérica.

Murillo, M. Victoria. 2001. *Labor Unions, Partisan Coalitions, and Market Reforms in Latin America*. Cambridge: Cambridge University Press.

Murillo, M. Victoria, and Andrew Schrank. 2005. "With a Little Help from My Friends: Partisan Politics, Transnational Alliances, and Labor Rights in Latin America." *Comparative Political Studies* 38(8): 971–99.

Navia, Patricio. 2006. "Three's Company: Old and New Alignments in Chile's Party System." In *The Chilean Road to Democracy and the Market*, eds. Silvia Oppenheim, and Lois Borzutzky. Florida: University Press of Florida, 42–63.

Navia, Patricio, and José Miguel Sandoval. 1998. *Binomial Electoral Law and Multi-Party System: The Chilean Contradiction*. Chicago, IL: Latin American Studies Association.

North, Douglass C. 1990. *Institutions, Institutional Change and Economic Performance*. Cambridge University Press.

2010. *Understanding the Process of Economic Change*. Princeton, NJ: Princeton University Press.

Notaro, Jorge. 2016. "La Estrategia y La Política Económica de La Dictadura 1973–1984." In *El Negocio Del Terrorismo de Estado: Los Cómplices Económicos de La Dictadura Uruguaya*, ed. Juan Pablo Bohoslavsky. Montevideo: Penguin Random House Grupo Editorial, 83–100.

O'Donnell, Guillermo A. 1988. *Bureaucratic Authoritarianism: Argentina, 1966–1973, in Comparative Perspective*. Berkeley, CA: University of California Press.

1996. *El Estado Burocrático Autoritario: Triunfos, Derrotas y Crisis*. Buenos Aires: Editorial de Belgrano Buenos Aires.

OECD. 2017. *Labour Market Reforms in Portugal 2011–15: A Preliminary Assessment*. Paris: OECD Publishing.

2020. "Income Distribution Database." https://stats.oecd.org/Index.aspx?DataSetCode=IDD.

Ominami, Carlos. 2009. *El Debate Silenciado*. Santiago de Chile: LOM Ediciones.

Ondetti, Gabriel. 2021. *Property Threats and the Politics of Anti-Statism. The Historical Roots of Contemporary Tax Systems in Latin America*. Cambridge: Cambridge University Press.

Oppenheim, Lois Hecht. 1993. Politics in Chile: Democracy, *Authoritarianism, and the Search for Development*. New York: Routledge, 118–20.

Palacios-Valladares, Indira, and Gabriel Ondetti. 2018. "Student Protest and the Nueva Mayoría Reforms in Chile." *Bulletin of Latin American Research* 38(5): 638–53.

Palma Ramalho, Maria do Rosário. 2013. "Portuguese Labour Law and Industrial Relations during the Crisis." In *The Governance of Policy Reforms in Southern Europe and Ireland*, eds. Konstantinos Papadakis, and Youcef Ghellab. Geneva: International Labour Office, 147–62.

Pérez Ahumada, Pablo. 2021. "Why Is It So Difficult to Reform Collective Labor Law? Associational Power and Policy Continuity in Chile in Comparative Perspective." *Journal of Latin American Studies* 53(1): 81–105.

Pérez, Verónica, Rafael Piñeiro, and Fernando Rosenblatt. 2019. *How Party Activism Survives: Uruguay's Frente Amplio*. Cambridge: Cambridge University Press.

Pierson, Paul. 1994. *Dismantling the Welfare State? Reagan, Thatcher, and the Politics of Retrenchment*. New York: Cambridge University Press.

2012. "Big, Slow-Moving, and … Invisible: Macrosocial Processes in the Study of Comparative Politics." In *Comparative Historical Analysis in the Social Sciences*, eds. James Mahoney, and Dietrich Rueshemeyer. New York: Cambridge University Press.

Piketty, Thomas. 2017. *Capital in the Twenty-First Century*. Cambridge: Harvard University Press.

Piñeiro Rodríguez, Rafael, and Fernando Rosenblatt. 2018. "Stability and Incorporation." *Party Politics* 26(2): 249–60.

Pochet, Philippe, and Giuseppe Fajertag. 2000. "A New Era for Social Pacts in Europe." In *Social Pacts in Europe – New Dynamics*, eds. Giuseppe Fajertag, and Philippe Pochet. Brussels: European Trade Union Institute/Observatoire Social Européen, 9–40.

Polanyi, Karl. 1944. *The Great Transformation*. Boston: Beacon Press.

Polga-Hecimovich, John, and Peter M. Siavelis. 2015. "Here's the Bias! A (Re-) Reassessment of the Chilean Electoral System." *Electoral Studies* 40: 268–79.

Pontusson, Jonas. 2005. *Inequality and Prosperity: Social Europe vs. Liberal America*. New York: Cornell University Press.

2018. "Comparative Political Economy and Varieties of Macroeconomics." (August).

Pontusson, Jonas, and Peter a Swenson. 1996. "Labor Markets, Production Strategies, and Wage Bargaining Institutions." *Comparative Political Studies* 29(2): 223. http://cps.sagepub.com/content/29/2/223.short.

Porrini, Rodolfo. 2003. "Clase Obrera, Sindicatos y Estado En El Uruguay de La Expansion Industrial (1936–1947): Algunas Conclusiones y Nuevos Problemas Para Su Investigación." *Estudos Ibero-Americanos*.

Pribble, Jennifer. 2013. *Welfare and Party Politics in Latin America*. Cambridge: Cambridge University Press.

Pribble, Jennifer, Evelyne Huber, and John D. Stephens. 2010. "The Chilean Left in Power: Achievements, Failures, and Omissions." In *Leftist Governments in Latin America: Successes and Shortcomings*, eds. Kurt Weyland, Raúl L. Madrid, and Wendy Hunter. New York: Cambridge University Press, 77–97.

Przeworski, Adam, and John Sprague. 1988. *Paper Stones: A History of Electoral Socialism*. Chicago: University of Chicago Press.

Przeworski, Adam, and Michael Wallerstein. 1982. "The Structure of Class Conflict in Democratic Society." *American Political Science Review* 76(2): 215–38.

Pucci, Francisco, Soledad Nión, and Fioretta Ciapessoni. 2014. "La Negociación Colectiva En El Primer Gobierno de Izquierda Del Uruguay." *Latin American Research Review* 49(2): 3–23.

Putnam, Robert. 1994. *Making Democracy Work*. Princeton: Princeton University Press.

Ragin, Charles C. 1992. "'Casing' and the Process of Social Inquiry." In *What Is a Case? Exploring the Foundations of Social Inquiry*, eds. Charles C. Ragin, and Howard S. Becker. New York: Cambridge University Press, 217–26.

Raitzin, Keila. 2017. "Nueva Mayoría. Condiciones Políticas Para Un Nuevo Acercamiento Entre El PS y El PC En Chile En 2013." *Revista Política Latinoamericana* 4.

Rama, Carlos. 1976. *Historia Del Movimiento Obrero y Social Latinoamericano Contemporáneo*. Barcelona: Editorial Laia.

Rasmussen, Magnus B., and Carl Henrik Knutsen. 2023. *Reforming to Survive*. New York: Cambridge University Press.

Raymond, Christopher, and Brian M. Barros Feltch. 2014. "Parties, Cleavages and Issue Evolution: The Case of the Religious-Secular Cleavage in Chile." *Party Politics*.

Real de Azua, Carlos. 1984. *Uruguay, ¿una Sociedad Amortiguadora?* Montevideo: Banda Oriental.

Rehn, Gosta. 1985. "Swedish Active Labour Market Policy: Retrospect and Prospect." *Industrial Relations* 24(1): 62–89.

Remmer, Karen. 1984. *Party Competition and Public Policy: Argentina and Chile, 1890–1930*. Lincoln: University of Nebraska Press.

La República. 2009. "Alternative Project: Chambers Limit Participation of the State Only for the Wage Councils." *La República*.

Reyes, Carlos. 2021. "Expresidente Lagos: 'Esta No Es La Madre de Todas Las Batallas, Ésta Debiera Ser La Madre de Todos Los Acuerdos Que Queremos Alcanzar En Una Constitucion'." *La Tercera*, 1. www.latercera.com/politica/noticia/expresidente-lagos-esta-no-es-la-madre-de-todas-las-batallas-esta-debiera-ser-la-madre-de-todos-los-acuerdos-que-queremos-alcanzar-en-una-constitucion/A6572WOREJEERNZGQRDTXFO2SM/.

Rhodes, Martin John. 2011. "Coordination, Concertation and Conflict in Labour Market Reform: Spain and Italy in the Crisis." APSA 2011 Annual Meeting Paper.

Roberts, Kenneth M. 1995. "From the Barricades to the Ballot Box: Redemocratization and Political Realignment in the Chilean Left." *Politics & Society* 23(4): 495–519.

2002. "Social Inequalities without Class Cleavages in Latin America's Neoliberal Era." *Studies in Comparative International Development* 36(4): 3–33.

2007. "The Crisis of Labor Politics in Latin America: Parties and Labor Movements during the Transition to Neoliberalism." *International Labor and Working-Class History* 72: 116–33.

2013. "Market Reform, Programmatic (De)Alignment, and Party System Stability in Latin America." *Comparative Political Studies* 46(11): 1422–52.

Rodríguez, Héctor. 1966. *Nuestros Sindicatos*. Montevideo: Centro de Estudiantes de Derecho.

Rodriguez, Juan Manuel, Beatriz Cozzano, and Graciela Mazzuchi. 2001. *La Transformacion de Las Relaciones Laborales. Uruguay 1985–2001*. Montevideo: Universidad Catolica del Uruguay.

2006. "Las Relaciones Laborales En El Año 2005."

Rodríguez, Juan Manuel, Beatriz Cozzano, Graciela Mazzuchi, and María Eloísa González. 2015. *Las Relaciones Laborales En 2015 y Perspectivas Para El 2016*. Montevideo: Universidad Católica del Uruguay.

Rodrik, Dani. 2016. "Premature Deindustrialization." *Journal of Economic Growth*. 21: 1–33.

Rosenblatt, Fernando. 2018. *Party Vibrancy and Democracy in Latin America*. Oxford: Oxford University Press.

Royo, Sebastián. 2002. "'A New Century of Corporatism?' Corporatism in Spain and Portugal." *West European Politics* 25(3): 77–104.

2010. "Portugal and Spain in the EU: Paths of Economic Divergence (2000–2007)." *Analise Social* 45(195): 209–54.

Rueda, David. 2007. *Social Democracy Inside Out: Partisanship and Labor Market Policy in Advanced Industrialized Democracies*. New York: Oxford University Press.

2008. "Political Agency and Institutions: Explaining the Influence of Left Government and Corporatism on Inequality." In *Democracy, Inequality, and Representation: A Comparative Perspective*, eds. Pablo Beramendi, and Christopher J. Anderson. New York: Russell Sage Foundation, 169–200.

Rueda, David, and Jonas Pontusson. 2000. "Wage Inequality and Varieties of Capitalism." *World Politics* 52(3): 350–383.

Rueschemeyer, Dietrich, Evelyne Huber Stephens, and John Stephens. 1992. *Capitalist Development and Democracy*. Chicago: University of Chicago Press.

Salinas, Maximiliano. 1980. *Clotario Blest: Vida de Un Dirigente*. Santiago de Chile: Vicaría de la Solidaridad, Arzobispado de Santiago.

Sandbrook, Richard, Marc Edelman, Patrick Heller, and Judith Teichman. 2007. *Social Democracy in the Global Periphery: Origins, Challenges, Prospects*. New York: Cambridge University Press.

Schipani, Andres. 2019. *Strategies of Redistribution: The Left and the Popular Sectors in Latin America*. Berkeley: University of California.

Schmitter, Philippe C. 1974. "Still the Century of Corporatism?" *The Review of Politics* 36(1): 85–131.

1999. *Portugal: Do Autoritarismo à Democracia*. Lisbon: Instituto de Ciências Sociais da Universidade de Lisboa.

Schmitter, Philippe C., and Jurgen R. Grote. 1997. "The Corporatist Sisyphus: Past, Present and Future."

Schneider, Ben Ross. 2004. *Business Politics and the State in Twentieth-Century Latin America*. New York: Cambridge University Press.

2013. *Hierarchical Capitalism in Latin America*. New York: Cambridge University Press.

Schrank, Andrew. 2009. "Understanding Latin American Political Economy: Varieties of Capitalism or Fiscal Sociology?" *Economy and Society* 38(1): 53–61.

Schwartz, Ira M et al. 2003. *Portugal: Strategic Options in European Context.* Maryland: Lexington Books.

Seawright, Jason, and John Gerring. 2008. "Case Selection Techniques in Case Study Research." *Political Research Quarterly* 61(2): 294–308.

Sehnbruch, Karen. 2006. *The Chilean Labor Market: A Key to Understanding Latin American Labor Markets.* New York: Palgrave Macmillan.

Senatore, Luis, and Jaime Yaffé. 2005. "Los Sindicatos Uruguayos Ante El Primer Gobierno de Izquierda." *OSAL* 5(16): 91–99.

Siavelis, Peter. 1997. "Continuity and Change in the Chilean Party System: On the Transformational Effects of Electoral Reform." *Comparative Political Studies* 30(6): 651–74.

2000. *The President and Congress in Postauthoritarian Chile: Institutional Constraints to Democratic Consolidation.* University Park: Pennsylvania State University Press.

2001. "Fiscal Decentralization in Chile's Centralized Polity." In *Meeting of the Latin American Studies Association.* Washington, DC: Estados Unidos.

Silva, Eduardo. 1993. "Capitalist Coalitions, the State, and Neoliberal Economic Restructuring: Chile, 1973–88." *World Politics* 45(4): 526–59.

1996. "From Dictatorship to Democracy: The Business-State Nexus in Chile's Economic Transformation, 1975–1994." *Comparative Politics* 28(3): 299–320.

Simon, Herbert A. 1979. "Information Processing Models of Cognition." *Annual Review of Psychology* 30(1): 363–96.

Slater, Dan, and Erica Simmons. 2010. "Informative Regress: Critical Antecedents in Comparative Politics." *Comparative Political Studies* 43(7): 886–917.

Slater, Dan, and Daniel Ziblatt. 2013. "The Enduring Indispensability of the Controlled Comparison." *Comparative Political Studies* 46(10): 1301–27.

Smith, Rand. 2012. *Enemy Brothers: Socialists and Communists in France, Italy and Spain.* Lanham, MD: Rowman & Littlefield.

2014. *Enemy Brothers: Socialists and Communists in France, Italy and Spain.* Lanham, MD: Rowman & Littlefield.

Soskice, David. 1999. "Divergent Production Regimes: Coordinated and Uncoordinated Market Economies in the 1980s and 1990s." In *Continuity and Change in Contemporary Capitalism*, eds. Herbert Kitschelt, Peter Lange, Gary Marks, and John D. Stephens. Cambridge and New York: Cambridge University Press, 101–34.

2008. "Macroeconomics and Varieties of Capitalism." In *Beyond Varieties of Capitalism: Conflict, Contradictions, and Complementarities in the European Economy*, eds. Bob Hancké, Martin Rhodes, and Mark Thatcher. New York: Oxford University Press, 89–121.

Soskice, David, and Torben Iversen. 2000. "The Nonneutrality of Monetary Policy with Large Price or Wage Setters." *Quarterly Journal of Economics* 115(5): 265–484.

Steiner, Jurg, and Thomas Ertman. 2002. *The Fate of Consociationalism in Western Europe, 1969–1999.* Amsterdam: Boom.

Stepan, Alfred C. 1978. *The State and Society: Peru in Comparative Perspective.* Princeton, NJ: Princeton University Press.

Stephens, John D. 1979. *The Transition from Capitalism to Socialism.* London: Springer.

Stinchcombe, Arthur. 1968. *Constructing Social Theories.* Chicago, IL: Chicago University Press.

2005. *The Logic of Social Research.* Chicago, IL: University of Chicago Press.

Stockhammer, Engelbert. 2022. "Post-Keynesian Macroeconomic Foundations for Comparative Political Economy." *Politics and Society* 50(1): 156–87.

Stoleroff, Alan. 2013. "Employment Relations and Unions in Public Administration in Portugal and Spain: From Reform to Austerity." *European Journal of Industrial Relations* 19(4): 309–23.

Stolovich, Luis, Luis Bértola, and Juan Manuel Rodríguez. 1991. *El Poder Económico En El Uruguay Actual.*

Streeck, Wolfgang. 2012. "Markets and Peoples: Democratic Capitalism and European Integration New Left Review." *New Left Review* 73: 63–71.

Streek, Wolfgang, and Lane Kenworthy. 2005. "Theories and Practices of Neocorporatism." In *The Handbook of Political Sociology: States, Civil Society and Organizations*, eds. Thomas Janoski, Robert Alford, Alexander Hicks, and Mildred Schwartz. Cambridge: Cambridge University Press, 441–60.

Sugiyama, Natasha Borges. 2011. "The Diffusion of Conditional Cash Transfer Programs in the Americas." *Global Social Policy* 11(2–3): 250–78.

Taylor, Marcus. 2006. *From Pinochet to the "Third Way."* London: Pluto Press.

Teodoro, António. 2003. "Globalização e Educação: Políticas Educacionais e Novos Modos de Governação."

La Tercera. 2000a. "Chronology: The Vagaries of the Concertación to the Initiative." December 13th.

2000b. "Businessmen Call for a 'Change of Direction' to Lagos." December 9th.

2000c. "Government Gives in to Pressure and Modifies Again Labor Reform." December 12th.

2000d. "Lagos Defines His Position about Changes in Labor Reform." December 15th.

2000e. "Riesco's Confessions, Outgoing President of the CPC." December 11th.

2000f. "Tightening of Labor Reform Shakes the Ruling Party." December 13th.

2000g. "Alejandro Foxley Disagrees with the Government and Send Signals to the Right." December 18th.

2001. "Softening of the Labor Reform and Support for Lower Taxes Seeks to Clear Uncertainties That Threaten Reactivation." March 23rd.

Thelen, Kathleen. 2001. "Varieties of Labour Politics in Developed Democracies." In *Varieties of Capitalism: The Institutional Foundations of Comparative Advantage*, eds. Peter A. Hall, and David Soskice. Oxford: Oxford University Press, 71–103.

Traxler, Franz. 2003. "Bargaining (de) Centralization, Macroeconomic Performance and Control over the Employment Relationship." *British Journal of Industrial Relations* 41(1): 1–27.

2004. "Employer Associations, Institutions and Economic Change: A Crossnational Comparison." *Industrielle Beziehungen/The German Journal of Industrial Relations* 11(1/2): 42–60.

Traxler, Franz, Sabine Blaschke, and Bernhard Kittel. 2001. *National Labour Relations in Internationalized Markets.* Oxford: Oxford University Press.

Tversky, Amos, Daniel Kahneman, and Paul Slovic. 1982. *Judgment under Uncertainty: Heuristics and Biases.* New York: Cambridge University Press.

Valadas, Carla. 2017. "A Changing Labour Market under the Intensification of Dualization. The Experience of a Southern European Society." *Social Policy & Administration* 51(2): 328–47.

Valdez, Jimena. 2020. "What Capital Wants: Business Interests and Labor Market Reform in Portugal and Spain." *Comparative Politics* 53(4): 571–96.

Valdéz, Rodrigo. 2018. "Reflexiones Practicas Con 842 Días En Hacienda." *Estudios Públicos* 150(Otoño). www.cepchile.cl.

Valenzuela, Arturo. 1999. "Chile." In *Democracy in Developing Countries: Latin America*, eds. Larry Diamond, Jonathan Hartlyn, Juan J. Linz, and Seymour Martin Lipset. Boulder, CO: Lynne Rienner, 159–206.

Valenzuela, J. Samuel. 1985. *Democratización Vía Reforma: La Expansión Del Sufragio En Chile.* Santiago de Chile: Ediciones del IDES.

1995. "Orígenes y Transformaciones Del Sistema de Partidos En Chile." *Estudios Públicos* 58: 5–80.

Valenzuela, Samuel. 1976. "The Chilean Labor Movement: The Institutionalization of Conflict." In *Chile: Politics and Society*, eds. Arturo Valenzuela, and Samuel Valenzuela. New Brunswick, NJ: Transaction Books, 135–71.

Visser, Jelle. 2015. "ICTWSS Data Base. Version 5.0." *Amsterdam Institute for Advanced Labour Studies AIAS.*

Wallerstein, Michael. 1990. "Centralized Bargaining and Wage Restraint." *American Journal of Political Science* 34(4): 982–1004.

1999. "Wage-Setting Institutions and Pay Inequality in Advanced Industrial Societies." *American Journal of Political Science* 43(3).

Warren, Mark E. et al. 2016. "Deliberative Negotiation." In *Political Negotiation: A Handbook*, eds. Jane Mansbridge, and Cathie Jo Martin. Washington, DC: Brookings Institution Press, 141–98.

2017. "A Problem-Based Approach to Democratic Theory." *American Political Science Review* 111(1): 39–53.

Watson, Sara. 2015. *The Left Divided: The Development and Transformation of Advanced Welfare States.* New York: Oxford University Press.

Weyland, Kurt. 2009a. *Bounded Rationality and Policy Diffusion: Social Sector Reform in Latin America.* Princeton, NJ: Princeton University Press.

2009b. "The Rise of Latin America's Two Lefts: Insight from Rentier State Theory." *Comparative Politics* 41(2): 145–64.

2010. "The Performance of Leftist Governments in Latin America." In *Leftist Governments in Latin America: Successes and Shortcomings*, eds. Kurt Weyland, Raul Madrid, and Wendy Hunter. New York: Cambridge University Press, 1–27.

Weyland, Kurt, Raúl L. Madrid, and Wendy Hunter. 2010. "The Policies and Performance of the Contestatory and Moderate Left." In *Leftist Governments in Latin America: Successes and Shortcomings*, eds. Kurt Weyland, Raul Madrid, and Wendy Hunter. Cambridge: Cambridge University Press, 140–80.

Wiarda, Howard. 1973. "Toward a Framework for the Study of Political Change in the Iberic-Latin Tradition: The Corporative Model." *World Politics* 25(2): 206–35.

1974. "Corporatism and Development in the Iberic-Latin World: Persistent Strains and New Variations." *The Review of Politics* 36(1): 3–33.

Wiarda, Howard, and Margareth Mac Leish Mott. 2001. *Catholic Roots and Democratic Flowers: Political Systems in Spain and Portugal.* Connecticut: Praeger Publisher.

Williamson, John. 1994. "In Search of a Manual for Technopols." In *The Political Economy of Policy Reform*, ed. John Williamson. Washington, DC: Institute for International Economics, 11–28.

World Bank. 2020. "World Development Indicators Online Database." https://databank.worldbank.org/source/world-development-indicators.

Yaffé, Jaime. 2001. "El Intervencionismo Batllista: Estatismo y Regulación En Uruguay (1900–1913)."

2005. "Sindicatos e Partidos No Uruguai-Da Fundação Da CNT Ao Triunfo Da Esquerda (1964–2004)." *Esboços: histórias em contextos globais* 12: 63–74.

Zubillaga, Carlos, and Jorge Balbis. 1985. *Historia Del Movimiento Sindical Uruguayo.* Montevideo: Ediciones de la Banda Oriental.

Zurbriggen, Cristina. 2006. *Estado, Empresarios y Redes Rentistas Durante El Proceso Sustitutivo de Importaciones: Los Condicionantes Históricos de Las Reformas Actuales.* Montevideo: Editorial Banda Oriental.

Index

semi-centralized wage-setting process,
7–8, 35, 87, 91, 121, 126, 136, 155,
164
setting system, 18
voluntary coordination, 31
wage-led inflation, 17, 19, 156. *See also*
inflation
wage-setting decentralization, 22, 60
wage policy, 1–5, 7, 10–13, 16–17, 21,
24, 28, 31, 33, 36, 38, 49–50, 56–60,
64–65, 72, 101, 117, 119–120, 125,
137, 141–143, 145, 149, 151, 153,
158, 160, 165, 167–170
after dual transition, 10, 24. *See also*
dual transition
bargaining tables, 117, 151. *See also*
bargaining rounds
bilateral collective bargaining, 125
bipartite accords, 149, 158
bipartite centralized bargaining, 117
center-left parties and far-left
labor-mobilizing parties/factions
relationship, 50. *See also* labor; party
class conflict, 17
distributive conflicts, 1, 11, 21, 36,
58–59, 72, 101, 168–169
divergence, 4, 28, 59
domestic structural factors, 59
firm-level agreements, 145
governments' distributive strategy, 58,
158. *See also* distributive strategy
political economy of party-labor
relations, 57. *See also* labor; party

political factors, 17
political power of labor. *See* labor
as a pre-distributive instrument, 2, 4–5,
7, 13, 16–17, 31, 33, 38, 49–50,
56, 59–60, 64–65, 119–120, 137,
142–143, 149, 158, 160, 165, 167,
170. *See also* instrument
sectorial-level collective bargaining,
153
as setting minimum salaries. *See* wage
tripartite agreements, 143
welfare, 1–2, 10, 15–16, 19, 37, 47–48,
56, 82, 88, 105, 134, 170
arena, 82
conflicts related to welfare capitalism,
37
legislation, 88
state, 2, 10, 15–16, 19, 37, 47–48, 56,
105
state retrenchment, 1
worker, 1, 15, 33, 35, 42, 73–74, 77–79,
90, 101, 108, 114–115, 117, 127,
129–130, 134, 150, 153, 159,
171–172
anarchist, 77
domestic, 150
independent, 171
low-skilled, 1
low-wage, 159, 171–172
rural, 79, 153
striking, 129–130, 134
temporary, 108
working class, 73–74, 78, 90

Milton Keynes UK
Ingram Content Group UK Ltd.
UKHW010850140324
439422UK00010B/78